THE NEW DEMONS

THE NEW DEMONS

JACQUES ELLUL

MOWBRAYS
LONDON & OXFORD

Original edition: *Les Nouveaux Possédés*
© Librairie Arthème Fayard, 1973

English translation © 1975 by The Seabury Press, Inc.
This edition published by
A. R. Mowbray & Co., Ltd.
The Alden Press, Osney Mead, Oxford

ISBN 0 264 66409 4

Printed in Great Britain by
Lowe & Brydone Printers Limited, Thetford, Norfolk

CONTENTS

PREFACE

The modern world is secularized: everyone takes that for granted now. We are supposedly in the third (positivist or scientific) age of Saint-Simon and Auguste Comte. Religious society indeed existed once upon a time, but we have left those primitive forms behind. Religions are old, ruptured cocoons, fit only to be studied by antiquarians; they cannot support or manifest life, for the butterfly has left the chrysalis. Man and his world have developed into mature insects and have nothing left to do but reproduce themselves and die.

But is it really possible to reconstruct the social evolution of man by taking religious society or religion generally as the starting point? The conventional wisdom again says Yes: all early societies were religious!

Yet no thinking person will really regard "religion" (a rather grabbag word) and religious societies as simple curiosities and toss them aside as though there were only one way to explain the historical development of mankind.

If we really want to understand in any degree our present situation, we must try to understand better the situation out of which we emerged and which we reject. This approach means that we will not be dealing with the kind of religious society to be found in ancient Greece or the Egypt of the Old Kingdom or among the Polynesians or the Bantus (to take four different types of religion and of correlation between religion and society). We will be dealing, rather, with the specific kind of society that emerged from Christianity and was called Christendom. Modern society is not to be understood in relation to just any religious society whatever, nor is it to be taken simply as the opposite of religious society in the abstract. No, it emerged from a specific society that thought of itself as Christian, and is to be understood in relation to it.

There is no point, then, in talking about an abstract, general relationship between "religion" and "society." The important thing is to focus our attention on Christendom as a specific type of religious society that is not identical with any other. In other words, if we are accurately to understand our own situation, we must reflect on what Christendom was; only then can we interpret our own "areligious" condition.

I

CHRISTENDOM

Even before attempting to give a positive description of Christendom, we must emphasize one great difference between it and
almost all other religious societies. We think of religious societies as
a primitive phenomenon; that is, no matter how far back we go and
no matter how early the social forms and the religious expressions,
the two are always found united to each other. It seems to have
been that way from the very beginning: socio-economic structures
and religions developed together and in dependence on each other,
so much so that we cannot distinguish what is proper to each.
Christianity, on the other hand, is not as old as the society within
which it developed, and evidently that society did not develop out
of Christianity. Instead, the society had already reached its full
development in every area of culture when the new religion entered
into it and reshaped it.

I know of but one comparable case: Islam. Islam, however, was
brought to bear on much less developed peoples and on societies
that were still chiefly tribal. Nor was there the same rupture
between Islam and the bedouin tribes in which it arose as between
Christianity and the empire.

The great difference, therefore, between Christianity and almost
all religious societies has two causes. On the one hand, in the

religious societies there was a kind of connaturality between religion and the socio-political institution, whereas Christianity would be opposed, at the practical level, to everything that Romano-Hellenistic society stood for.

Second, there is the volitional character of the relationship between Christianity and society. In the religious societies the union of institutions, lifestyles, and religion was spontaneous. Religion was just as much a part of everyday life as table manners or the training of children (and indeed these were controlled by religion). The sacredness of the king's person was not maintained on doctrinal grounds; it was taken as self-evident, for it was a direct manifestation of the collective consciousness.

Christianity, on the contrary, consciously and deliberately produced Christendom as an embodiment of Christian thought. Christendom was to be an attempt to translate Christian doctrine into concrete, experiential, institutional forms. Just as the individual's behavior was to be a deliberate, controlled expression of his faith in Christ, so the reconstruction of the state, the economic order, and social relationships would be an embodiment of Christian thought and reflect an interpretation of the Bible.

Christendom was not a religious society in the sense that it was a translation into social forms of religious feeling that had always been present in man. On the contrary, Christendom was the result of a conscious, deliberate process. How was society to be made Christian? Or: how was Christian faith to permeate every area of life, public as well as private? After all, the God of Jesus Christ was the God of all reality; everything belonged to him, including the economic and social orders. This relationship should be rendered visible, especially since the life of man too is a single whole and should not be divided into unrelated parts.

We moderns have a very false idea of what Christians believed in the third or the eleventh centuries. We are used to reading that the Greeks separated body and soul and that the Christians followed suit; we find the theologians constantly repeating the same texts about contempt for the body and the need for asceticism; we know that since the eighteenth century the bourgeoisie have turned Christianity into a disembodied wraith. Therefore we are convinced that this is how the Christians of every period lived and thought, right down to our day. Then we lucky people came along and, after two thousand years of error, rediscovered authentic Christianity and early Jewish thought. Here is ignorance indeed! And what monstrous presumption it has tricked us into!

Some theologians may well have maintained the views described, but those views were neither widespread and generally accepted nor did they form an unbroken tradition. If all Christians had thought this way, Christendom would never have come into existence. The Cathars and Spirituals indeed professed such a theology and they drew the logical conclusions for their behavior: we must take seriously the separation of soul and body, we must reject the world in a fully real way, and we must look for the end of this world in the very near future. And the ending did not have to come simply from God; man could bring it about. The revolts of Thomas Münzer and John of Leiden were intended to lead to the kingdom of God which is no longer of this world. In like fashion, the Cathar prohibition against having children was to lead to the rapid elimination of the human race.

But such was not the general trend of Christian thought. On the contrary, Christians had to continue living in a society and a world which they were to bring to God and make conformable to his will. There was union, not opposition, between soul and body, church and society, but the body was to obey the soul and society was to be permeated and shaped by Christian thought, volition, and holiness.

What Christians were really trying to elaborate, as they gradually created Christendom, was a social morality. They were more serious about it than we are today, because they courageously set about applying their moral principles and effectively modifying structures in the light of what they considered to be the true and the good. And they succeeded. If we read the moral treatises of the third to the fifteenth centuries, we find that they raised all the questions, confronted all the difficulties, and tried almost all the solutions we today conceitedly believe we were the first to think of. Naturally, they did all this in the language of their time and in relation to the structures and cultures of their society. Our first task, therefore, is to try to grasp what Christendom was. Only then can we ask to what extent it was genuinely grounded in the Christian faith.

The intention, therefore, was to shape the whole of society in the light of "Christian truth." It would be childish, then, to focus our attention solely on the primacy given the church's authority or the subordination of the temporal power to the spiritual. These were indeed parts of the total picture, but they were secondary parts, even though they catch our attention. The first really important

4 · THE NEW DEMONS

fact to be considered is that, like it or not, Christianity found itself the heir to a whole infinitely complex and rich culture.

What was it to do with that culture? It had no plan ready to hand. Consequently, when the educated elites, the politicians, the administrators, the professors, the philosophers, and the business-men became converts and sought to take Christianity seriously, what was to be done with them? Were they to be told that faith in Christ meant the abandonment of politics, philosophy, and all these other things (the spiritualism we mentioned above)? Were they to be given a personal moral code to guide them in the exercise of these various activities? Or were they to tackle the problem head on and try to transform the culture in a radical way (and not simply at the level of moral motivation), so as to integrate it into Christianity? Christianity, after all, was an all-embracing creed and should transform reality as a whole!

Moreover, Christians found themselves members of the first society to be conscious that the "social system" was created by man himself. That is, it was the first society in which the social system and all its forces (the economy, etc.) were not considered to be simply the product of spontaneity, tradition, and metaphysical laws. They were considered, rather, to be the product of deliberate thought and organization and of the conviction that men could shape institutions according to reason so that these could express man's free decisions and choices and not be determined solely by inherited custom. We cannot overestimate the importance of the new force which the Greeks and Romans thus introduced into human affairs.

Not only was the social system conceived as a human product. It was also for the first time regarded as a system. In other words, it was not the product of individual wills and the lives of obscure men, but the result of a combination of mechanisms, organizations, and institutions. Consequently, if the God of Jesus Christ was indeed the God of all creation, his presence must be perceptible not only in the individual conscience but in social structures as well—all social structures without exception. This attitude was the basis for assimilation and integration. Since Christianity found itself heir to Greco-Roman culture, it was in a position to effect such an integration.

As a result—and this is a first essential aspect of Christendom—Christianity assimilated all the religiosity and magic that was part of the culture. We have often ridiculed the Christians of that period for "baptizing" pagan gods and pagan institutions and thinking that nothing more was needed, that such a step would easily win over the pagan peoples.

It is clear enough that the local presiding Genius (or spirit of a place) was converted, in many places, into a Saint Genis or Genesius, and the goddess Birgitta into a Saint Bridget. That is common knowledge. So too, when the emperor became a Christian, the rites of emperor worship were Christianized and prostration before him was given a new meaning on the basis of the idea that the emperor was God's representative on earth. Christian panegyrists of the fourth century took over the addresses of their pagan predecessors in the third century, changing only the theological vocabulary. At a later period, the Scandinavian and Germanic pagan brotherhoods were taken over, adapted, and transformed into the Christian brotherhoods. The ceremonies of knighthood came from two quite distinct sources: one part—the dubbing—was purely pagan and Germanic; the other vigil under arms, prayer, Holy Communion—was a Christian addition.

But, to begin with, we must not think that this process of "Christianizing," which seems to us so useless, simplistic, and superficial, was taken for granted. On the contrary, it often excited violent opposition. There was no quiet, smooth passage from the pagan form to the Christian form. Thus when the pagan brotherhoods were being transformed into Christian, the bishops sharply opposed the rites involving blood and beer. The result was an ongoing conflict between the brotherhoods whose communion rite took the form of the Eucharist, and the brotherhoods which claimed to be no less Christian but had kept the old pagan ceremonies while turning them into a simple feast. The latter were the "unofficial brotherhoods" of the day. And this conflict lasted for six centuries.

Furthermore, it is simplistic to say that the assimilation and Christianizing of the pagan religious past was just a mistake or that in doing it people were taking the easy way out. The real question in men's minds was: is Jesus Christ the Lord of history or is he not? We think the idea of Jesus as Lord of history is a modern discovery, but in fact the idea was a commonplace at the beginning of the Middle Ages. If he is Lord of all history, then he is Lord even of that history that unfolded before his coming. Moreover, all of human history had been moving toward him; all history had been a preparation for the Incarnation, just as all subsequent history was to be a manifestation of the Incarnation. All of history; not just the history of the Jews. History is not divided into sacred and profane, for it was the very history of the human race that contained the promise of Christ and manifested the action of God.

The men of the High Middle Ages were deeply convinced of all this. But they went a step further: the history of mankind had always been full of religious creations, for it represented mankind's immense striving toward a God. How then could *this* aspect of man's history be excluded from the great movement toward the Messiah? Christians were thus led to discover in the pagan religions authentic ancestors of and witnesses to Christ: Virgil's Fourth Eclogue and the Cumean Sibyl had clearly prophesied concerning Jesus. And how many forms, rites, and legends there were that seemed to fit in neatly with Christian piety and Christian thought. If philosophy could be deliberately used as a framework for expressing Christian thought, then the pagan religions too had their contribution to make. They were reinterpreted in the light of Christian universalism.

Here then is a first aspect of Christendom: when Christianity assimilated all the sacral, religious, and magical elements in the ancient societies within which it developed, this was not an act of weakness or imperialism but the logical consequence of a principle. It is easy enough to criticize the decision and the tendency as based on a deadly confusion, which everyone denounces today, between revelation or Christian faith and religion. But I am not at all sure that these virtuous condemnations are marked by intellectual honesty. I am waiting for someone to explain to me how Christianity could survive while excluding everything "religious." When the kingdom failed to appear at the end of the first generation, Christianity either had to break down into spontaneous, short-lived little groups and eventually disappear or it had to organize for survival, and once it did this, the "religious" had to come into the picture. Then the challenge had to be faced: the kingdom did not come and transform the world in "the twinkling of an eye"; was this whole immense world that God had created to be left therefore in paganism? No: it must be Christianized; the world must be freed from the power of darkness and made to serve the kingdom.

This enterprise soon proved to have certain consequences. To begin with, in such a vast undertaking it was impossible to rely on the individualized faith of Christians. Not every member of Christendom could be a convinced believer who had had an experience of the Lord Jesus Christ and undergone a conversion or passed through a long process of spiritual growth. A dedicated faith and a corresponding lifestyle could not be taken for granted.

As a result of this situation two things became characteristic of Christendom. First, a person became a member of it by means of outward symbols (for example, baptism) and because of the supposition that everyone who lived within the boundaries of Christendom should be a Christian. Because they served this purpose the sacraments were interpreted realistically, that is, as having an objective efficacy inherent in them (*opus operatum*). Second, as far as faith was concerned, the Christian became part of a huge mass in which the faith and works of all who made it up were pooled, thanks to the church. Thus any given individual did not have to have a genuinely personal faith, for he would in any event be nourished by and profit from the faith of others, that is, of the church as a whole. In this scheme the church was conceived of as a body in which each member had his place and in which each would have faith applied to him, as it were (the "implicit faith" of the theologians). The very idea of Christendom therefore implied that a great many of its members were not Christians in an individual, personal way. To say that medieval society was a Christendom is to say, not that all its members had a personal internalized faith in Jesus Christ, but simply that all profited from the faith common to the body as a whole.

This attitude necessarily tended to turn Christianity into an ideology; that is, Christianity became a set of presuppositions that determined the life of the collectivity. It was taken for granted that every individual was meant to be a Christian (how could he be anything else?) and that he became a Christian in a full and unqualified way through baptism. Christianity provided a scale of shared values, a store of patterns for behavior and attitudes, a set of ready-made ideas and of goals, norms of judgment, and reference points for evaluating words, feelings, thoughts, and actions. Here, then, was belief based on social fact; belief that was generally accepted yet no longer implied a total self-giving or a high degree of fervor. This did not mean, of course, that men did not sincerely accept the truths of the gospel, although the latter had to be transposed to a lower register, as it were, so as to be accessible to all.

A second consequence of the vast enterprise which Christendom represented was formalism. Everybody had become Christian, every citizen of Christendom was a Christian. Therefore there was no need to evaluate inner spiritual authenticity; the important thing was how a man acted. Morality was primary. The compiling of the sixth-century Irish penitential books was a critical factor in this development. Soon, moreover, concern for morality became concern for law.

The church of Christendom would soon be characterized by its concern for morality (a very legitimate concern in western society between the third and eleventh centuries when the moral corruption was so great that anyone not a professional theologian will have difficulty in imagining it) and by its striving for organization. Morality and organization were necessary if the vast totality called Christendom were not to fall apart but were to function properly. But a theological principle was also at work in this functioning. Faith was taken for granted; attention could therefore be turned to the works which had their origin in faith. But, at the same time, it was possible to influence the presumed "implicit faith" through these same works. In other words, rectify and Christianize men's behavior and you have indirect access to their faith itself. The aim, therefore, was not to arouse or control faith directly, but to stimulate it by controlling its outward expressions. Once this approach was adopted, all behavior had to be precisely and unambiguously described, measured, and circumscribed. Models of behavior had to be provided and aberrant behavior condemned; patterns of organization for the church and for everyday life had to be established and prohibited areas clearly marked off. The church was on the way to becoming a great ethico-juridical organism.

But Christendom showed another basic trait: it not only absorbed man's whole religious past, it also provided the framework in which the church could control culture (in the narrow sense of this word). We need not insist on this point, for it has been frequently made and fully documented. All the thought, knowledge, and intellectual life of Greco-Roman society were carefully preserved in and *thanks to* the church. We would know almost nothing of the Greeks and Romans, were it not for the patient scribes and manuscript collectors in the monasteries and episcopal palaces. Yet people talk so readily today about medieval obscurantism and fanaticism. Well, those "obscurantists" busied themselves wholeheartedly with the entire intellectual legacy of earlier societies, and those "fanatics" copied all the pagan manuscripts available to them, even those that were scandalous to faith and morals.

My interest, however, is not in these facts as such but in the larger problem: why did the church take on the role it did? It's silly to say: "Because the clergy were the only educated people," for then you merely push the question back a step: why were the clergy educated? After all, the destructive fury of the uncultured monks at Alexandria was also an expression of Christian faith!

What we really have here is an essential facet of Christendom. A certain number of services had to be provided if society were to survive and men were to live together in society. The church had to step in and provide any services that no one else was providing; she was a universal servant, intervening wherever there was no one else available. No one was interested anymore in intellectual culture and philosophy, in care of the poor and the ill, in the improvement of agriculture and the development of arable land. No one was interested anymore in alleviating the daily routine of men's lives with festivals and days of rest, or in planning styles of social life in which men would cease to be wolves preying on their fellow men. Well then, the church would do all these things, simply as services without which society could not survive. That was the very meaning of "Christendom."

Such an intervention implied that on behalf of society the church would lay down a certain number of pertinent "Christian principles," from which specific conclusions and applications could be drawn. The principles were derived from faith, revelation, and the Bible, and applied to every area of life, none excluded. Christianity was evidently meant to affect the whole of man's life (political and economic as well as moral) and the life of society too. Therefore it had things to say about man's political and economic activity, and it said them in the form of principles for action and organization.

The situation was ripe for Christianity to play this role, for, if no one else was interested, the church had to step in. Consequently, it was not a restless quest of power that led the church to formulate economic principles in comformity with Scripture, but rather, the conviction that everything should manifest the Lordship of Jesus Christ and that no area of human life is unrelated to him.

The medieval economy with its strengths and weaknesses was not the result simply of circumstances, as the contemporary historical dogma would have it, but of the conscious, deliberate, organized activity of the church. The prohibition of illicit trading and of usury (a prohibition that was far more widely enforced than people today like to admit), the refusal of primacy to economic factors, the effort to detach men from wealth and the desire for it, the search for stability and justice in the economic area, the concept of an organization made up of self-sufficient entities (this was not the result of an effort to make the best of a bad situation and lack of communications, but was the expression of a whole view of life)—all these were the deliberate application to the economic sphere of a set of "Christian principles" and were inspired by the concern to manifest the Lordship of Jesus Christ in that sphere no less than anywhere else.

In still another area the idea of Christendom had two kinds of consequences.[1] First of all, Christendom meant that every local society must be part of the all-embracing Christendom. Every feudal domain, every city, every kingdom, knew that it belonged, and wanted to belong, to the larger whole which was Christendom. ("Christendom," at this point, is a geographical term rather than a qualitative one, as above.) Every human, political, and social group was subordinate to the totality which was Christendom, so that in the last analysis civil society as a whole was (and had to be) identical with the universal church. The two entities were geographically coextensive and were organized with reference to each other.

As a result, no political organization within Christendom could be allowed sovereignty, nor could the boundaries between nations, kingdoms, and feudal domains be absolute and impenetrable. *Before* being a kingdom, a political unit was a *part* (not "member," for that would imply a certain precedence of the kingdom in its association with the other members) of the one unit which alone possessed authentic unity: Christendom. Christendom was not a sum of social groups, but a unity, and it put up with its own division into groups only for the sake of greater ease in acting.

In this politico-social whole (at one level, the Roman empire; at another, the one body of Christ) there was no confusion between the church and the political powers, but the two orders were nonetheless organized with reference to each other. The church claimed no right to control the political order, but at the same time it could not accept that the faith should be a matter of indifference in political life. For it was evident that if Christianity was significant for the whole of man's life, it must influence the political order too. In order, therefore, to show forth the unity of Christen-

---

[1] For a more extensive treatment of the subject, cf. Jacques Ellul, *Histoire des Institutions*, vol. 2.

dom, just as there was only one church, so there must be a single political authority, at least of a symbolic kind, set over all the local authorities. Moreover, while there was to be no confusing of the spiritual and the political power, neither could the latter be wholly autonomous and independent, since Christianity had the duty, in every sphere, of permeating, inspiring, initiating, and, after a very rapid development, certifying and, finally, controlling.

We are all aware of the countless problems raised by this distinction of authorities, authorities which existed for the sake of functions and not as separate and independent sources of power. What the church wanted was not control and direction, but simply the right to exercise a function in the form of innumerable services. This exercise implied of course a freedom, and this in turn implied an authority. This approach, it goes without saying, quickly led from authority to power, especially once the church (beginning with the papacy) became a directly political force, that is, once it acquired a territory and a political organization with the pope acting as head of state. This latter development further complicated the relation between the "two powers," which was already difficult enough. But we must not forget the original conception out of which the later situation finally emerged.

The second kind of consequences which the idea of Christendom produced may be expressed in the formula, identification of church and society. Church and society were coextensive geographically. Whenever missionaries brought the church into new pagan lands and established the faith there, the converted groups automatically became part of the totality called Christendom and were expected to adopt the political or economic patterns proper to Christendom. The converse was also true: for a man to become part of the (civil) society of Christendom, he had to be a Christian (in the sense defined earlier). Within the boundaries of the civil society only Christians were permitted to live, men who shared the same implicit faith, the same vision of man and the world.

Those outside the boundaries were pagans. With them there could hardly be any "normal" relations; only mutual instinctive hostility. From the viewpoint of Christendom pagans did not add up to a genuine society, for how could society be just and properly ordered if it was not Christian? By the same token the king, a subject of the church, was required to show justice and mercy only to the Christian people. In his coronation oath he accepted responsibilities toward this people, but to non-Christian peoples he had no duties. Consequently heretics (who were worse than pagans) were driven out not only from the church but from Christendom itself.

A pagan who entered within the domain of Christendom was obliged to become a convert if he was to survive. Here we have the explanation of why the Jewish problem was insoluble and a permanent irritant: Jews were the only ones to be tolerated within Christendom without being Christians. They lived in this society, however, as though they did not live there at all, having neither rights nor duties in it. Their physical presence and activity were tolerated and ignored. They lived in communities that had their own rules and statutes, but the latter were given no juridical recognition by the larger society. As a result, the Jews were an abiding problem in the eyes of this society: how could someone be a man yet not a Christian? To exist in such a state was to be a living challenge to the basic principle of Christendom.

We all of us today live with the materialistic persuasion that everything is done from economic motives and with the deeply rooted suspicion that beneath every surface lurk motives that cannot stand the light of day. As a result our vision of Christendom is evidently distorted. We attribute our contemporary experiences and assumptions about fact to the period from the eighth to the fourteenth centuries. Thus we are convinced, for example, that the crusades were mounted because of the papacy's capitalistic interests, that the cathedrals were built by an oppressed and terrorized proletariat, that slavery was eliminated by technological progress, and that the church's regulations for politics and economics were never enforced. Correspondingly, we think of the church of that time as a political and financial power, of the conflicts between emperors and popes as mere conflicts between power blocs, and so forth.

Now all that is not *entirely* inaccurate; we need only add an "also" to each of the explanations given. Thus the crusades were a great act of faith, an implementation of the conviction that God's kingdom would come on earth once Jerusalem became a Christian city again. The popes and other ecclesiastical authorities certainly believed this, but there was *also* a good deal of the financial corruption that inevitably accompanies such vast enterprises.

We today, in reaction to the positive evaluations offered in earlier centuries, have also got into the habit of seeing only the negative effects of Christendom: the intolerable political claims of the popes, the formalism and magical interpretation of the sacraments, the layers of theological error that accumulated over the centuries, the superstitions, the acceptance of exploitation of the poor and weak by the rich and powerful, the economic stagnation that resulted from turning men's attention away from serious matters to paradise, the consecration of the king as supreme Christian authority, etc. Once again, all these complaints are not unjustified, provided we add an "also." We must also bear in mind the positive and fruitful side of the church's activity and of the organization of Christendom (even though we need not exaggerate this positive side nor focus our attention on it to the exclusion of all else).

To begin with, there was the suppression of slavery. After a century of unchallenged claims that the suppression was due to Christianity it became the fashion from 1930 on to say that Christianity had nothing to do with it and that the suppression of slavery was the result of slave labor being no longer productive or of economic change or of technological progress. But no serious recent historian has ever proved any such thing. In fact, there is growing agreement among historians that material causes cannot explain the suppression of slavery. The decisive factor was the change of mentality due to Christianity. There was technological progress indeed, but it came about *as the result of* the suppression of slavery and the need to offset the consequent lack of manpower.[2] Historians who are not Christian but do face up to the documents are coming to that position today.

Christendom had other undeniable positive effects. The protection of the weak, for example, was a central preoccupation. The protection given was not merely verbal or of no practical value; it was real and well organized. The disadvantages of a society that contained both powerful and lowly, rich and poor, were reduced to a minimum. I am not at all sure that other documented societies, including our own, have got anywhere as far in this area as Christendom did. All economic and political means of protecting the poor were used, and most of the time successfully.

The measures taken by the church in the interests of peace were

---

[2] There is no more room for argument on this point since the studies of B. Gille and Lynn White, Jr., which, while not dealing with our specific question, do show the remarkable progress of technology during the Middle Ages in contrast to the stagnation that characterized antiquity. As long as slavery provided a solution to the manpower problem, there was no technological progress; once slavery was suppressed, other resources had to be tapped and so technology developed.

also very effective: the Peace Leagues, the Truce of God, and the Peace of God, for example, were institutions in which the church did not limit itself to pious exhortations to peace but took concrete means to achieve it. In a very unsettled and troubled situation, where often neither faith nor law were evident, the church produced almost a miraculous order and justice. She has been accused of juridicism, but in circumstances in which men had lost all sense of right and the common good, the restoration of law and order certainly represented important human progress and a force for good.

The church has also been blamed for her interference in the political sphere, but when disorder and rivalry between powers were the order of the day the church was able by her interference to create a context in which men could live. So too she established regulations and institutions for an economic order that had completely broken down. The doctrine on the just price (which was indeed applied, whatever people today may think) and the prohibition of usury were essential if exploitation was to be restrained and stability restored to the economy.[3] The principles which the church applied were admittedly principles leading to stagnation and not to progress, but we must bear in mind the real dilemma which the church faced. That dilemma was either to lay great stress on economic activity, production, and consumption, which would lead to increased power of the rich over the poor, or to protect the poor and strive for the greatest possible measure of economic stability (stability, or *ordo*, was equated with justice at that time, whereas we today see justice as meaning equality), which would cause stagnation. The church chose the second horn of the dilemma. But we cannot condemn the church for her choice unless we accept a progressivist ideology and a mythology in which growth in production is identified with the good.

The points I have been making (and I could offer many more examples of positive interventions by the church) do not represent simply my own opinion. They are backed up by countless precise and detailed historical studies that contrast sharply with the

---

[3] In regard to usury it is often pointed out that the church did in fact tolerate usury, since the Jews and Lombards were allowed to practice it. But the objection is simply another manifestation of the critics' bad faith: the church could not prevent the Jews and Lombards from practicing usury *because they were not Christians*. The prohibition applied only to Christians. The church did not extend it into a law applying to everyone because to do so would have been to arrogate to itself the function of the political authorities.

grandiose ideological pictures we have become accustomed to since Marxism came on the scene.[4] Such studies show that, given the widespread disorder, the church thought it her duty to take charge of society. That means that she had the courage to face a wide range of difficult problems in a concrete, practical way. She was not satisfied simply to hold forth on the need of incarnating the faith, as we do today, and to send out messages and proclamations, even those of a pope or a World Council of Churches. As a result of these practical interventions the church of course dirtied her hands. Christendom was an order in which men attempted to put the Christian faith into practice in a collective way. Any criticisms we can level against it are simply an acknowledgment that intervention in the political and economic worlds is always contaminating.

The final point I want to make is that when the church and Christians not only elaborated the teachings of Christendom but put them into practice as well, they did so in consequence not of eccentric ideas but of their faith and theology. The basic principles of Christianity contained Christendom as a logical conclusion. A fine French theologian recently reminded us that Christianity has been political since its very beginnings. This idea is now taken for granted and has become central in the thinking of many. Fine! But there is another truth of basic importance: the Incarnation; and the Incarnation requires that principles be put into practice. A Christian cannot stop at declarations of intention. Moreover, Jesus Christ is Lord of all history, and his Lordship must be manifested. Bring these three truths together and, if you take them seriously, you will inevitably move toward "Christendom."

The shape Christendom takes will depend on the energy of Christians, on the one hand, and on the extent of social disorder and the inadequacy of the political powers, on the other. But it is impossible to refuse to establish a Christian society. If we want each Christian to live out his faith in a concrete way in his personal life, how can we not want all Christians to do so in a collective way? And if Christianity is political, can we help but want a political order that is inspired by faith?

This point has been splendidly illustrated in one of the finest examples I know of modern (non-Christian) thinking: Erich

---

[4] But we must make an exception among contemporary historical studies for J. Le Goff, *Civilisation de l'Occident médiéval* (1965), which represents the most insipid kind of materialism.

Auerbach's *Mimesis*. With extraordinary subtlety he shows how the Incarnation gave rise to a certain kind of collective lifestyle and to a way of representing the real that implicitly led to Christendom. Not to proceed along this path is either to play down the Incarnation or to belie one's own principles, that is, to be a hypocrite.

We may, of course, claim that the men of the Middle Ages were mistaken or that their theology was bad. But at least they made an honest attempt, and this without any illusion that they were establishing God's kingdom on earth. (It is through the testimonies of Christians that we know of all the disasters, the mistakes, the injustices of the Middle Ages.) They wanted to build a Christendom, but they were well aware how far they still were from the kingdom of God.

The important, indeed the decisive, fact about their effort was that the passage from theology or faith to politics and action generally was mediated by an attitude to reality which Auerbach has analyzed for us. They took reality seriously and positively (not negating it, as people often claim) and were basically realists, but at the same time they refused to stop at this reality: for them reality was a "figure." The Middle Ages had a figural conception of reality; this means that "an occurrence on earth signifies not only itself but at the same time another, which it predicts or confirms, without prejudice to the power of its concrete reality here and now. The connection between occurrences is not regarded as primarily a chronological or causal development but as a oneness within the divine plan, of which all occurrences are parts and reflections." [5]

Such an attitude to reality makes one take reality very seriously, as did the men of the Middle Ages. They were deeply concerned with the political life of society and attributed great importance to it, but this was because they saw in the activities of peoples and kings and in the decisions taken by the masses an action of God: *Gesta Dei per Francos* [the deeds of God performed through the French]; *omnis potestas a Deo per populum* [all power is from God by way of the people]; etc.

Such an attitude represents, does it not, an interpretation of history that derives from the Incarnation and life of Jesus "with its ruthless mixture of everyday reality and the highest and most

---

[5] Erich Auerbach, *Mimesis: The Representation of Reality in Western Literature*, trans. Willard Trask (Princeton: Princeton University Press, 1953; Garden City, N.Y.: Doubleday Anchor Books, 1957), p. 490 (in the Anchor Books edition).

sublime tragedy." [6] The life of Jesus led to a transformation in the way men looked at reality. "A tragic figure from such a background, a hero of such weakness, such a to and fro of the pendulum" [7] was unintelligible to the Greco-Roman mind. It led to a new way of representing the real "which is ready to absorb the sensorily realistic, even the ugly, the undignified, the physically base," [8] while referring it to that which gives it its basic meaning: *this* reality, while being itself, also represents another *reality*. The whole complex of realities was situated in time (not one terminus of the *figura* in time, the other in eternity). Nonetheless the two events (the one foretelling, the other fulfilling) were not linked by a causal relation on the purely horizontal level. "The horizontal, that is the temporal and causal, connection of occurrences is dissolved; the here and now is no longer a mere link in an earthly chain of events, it is simultaneously something which has always been, and which will be fulfilled in the future." [9]

This conception of reality was never rejected in the Middle Ages, despite what is often too readily assumed. "They wanted heaven; therefore they scorned earth." No, some mystics may have thought that way, but not the Christian populace of the West. Christendom tried to embody this conception of reality, for it was the conception clearly at work in the person and life of Jesus Christ as Incarnation of the Word of God.

---

[6] *Ibid.*
[7] *Ibid.*, p. 37.
[8] *Ibid.*, p. 63.
[9] *Ibid.*, p. 64.

II

THE POST-CHRISTIAN ERA AND SECULARIZATION

A current commonplace, the truth of which is taken for granted, is that the modern world is secular, secularized, atheistic, laicized, desacralized, and demythologized. In most contemporary writing, moreover, these various terms are taken as synonyms, and there seems to be little awareness that there may be important differences between laicization and secularization or desacralization and demythologization. As a matter of fact, these writers intend to say only that the modern world has become adult or has reached maturity. This means, concretely, that the modern world no longer believes but wants proof; it obeys reason and rejects beliefs, especially religious beliefs; it has got rid of God the Father and all gods, and if you talk to it of religion, it won't understand you. It has adopted a new way of thinking, worlds apart from the traditional way of thinking that found expression in myths.[1] It cannot understand the language of transcendence and can live only at the level of concrete reality. The day of religion is over.

---

[1] There is a good deal of food for thought in Claude Lévi-Strauss's claim (in his *The Savage Mind*) that there is no real difference between the thinking of contemporary man and the thinking of the "primitive."

This is the kind of talk we constantly hear today in most Christian intellectual circles and especially in the World Council of Churches. It is often difficult, however, to decide whether a speaker is stating a fact, expressing a wish, making a sociological observation, or painting an imaginary picture of a hypothetical human type based on the speaker's conception of the scientifically oriented man.

If we analyze the way such statements are developed, we find that the writer or speaker is presenting us with an a posteriori explanation (arguing from effect to cause). He will usually start with the facts in evidence: "Contemporary man isn't interested in Christianity any more; he has lost his faith; the church has no influence on contemporary society; it has lost its audience; the Christian message evidently has nothing to say to the men of our day." Then he connects all that with the scientific criticism of the origins, history, and contents of Christianity and with the fact that modern man's training is pretty much along technological, if not scientific, lines. Therefore he concludes, at least implicitly: "Modern man is areligious because he is permeated by the scientific outlook," and thinks that the rejection of Christianity is the result of some new traits of modern man who has become areligious.

This assumption is the basis for the impressive effort at renewal that is now going on in the churches as they attempt to communicate with this contemporary man and to make the gospel acceptable to him. We have new theologies, new ecclesiastical structures, integration into the modern world, efforts to develop nonreligious forms of witnessing and preaching, and so on. The whole "crisis" of the church and all the movement going on within it rest on this assumption or conviction. For this reason I think the first order of business is to find out whether or not the analysis of the situation is accurate and whether or not we live in an age that has thrown religion aside. What if the analysis is wrong? What if the facts (assuming they are certain) are due to some other cause and should be interpreted differently? What if there is error both in the observation of facts and in their interpretation?

I cannot understand pushing this question aside, saying it is unimportant, or claiming that it is not the real issue. I can well understand someone saying: "Even if we concede that Bonhoeffer and Bultmann sin by oversimplification, their questions, which do not depend on their cultural appraisals, remain: what does faith become in the modern world?" That much is indeed certain, but I do not think we can blithely evade the question of fact by saying:

"[Bonhoeffer's] casualness toward past history seems to me to relieve us from the necessity of discussing the accuracy of Bonhoeffer's analyses" of the contemporary situation. Bonhoeffer is mistaken when it comes to history; are we therefore exempted from questioning our position when he also proves wrong in his analysis of our society? How can we say it is as useless to discuss the question, "whether man and the contemporary world have really come of age or not," as it is to challenge the non-mythological outlook of modern man? Isn't it statements about coming of age (and not any theological principles) that are the basis for everything else? Of course it is basic to determine whether modern man is religious or areligious.[2]

The first thing we must do, however, is gain clarity on the various words used to describe the contemporary situation, for the very heaping up of these words points to a good deal of intellectual confusion. To begin with, we have "post-Constantinian era" and "post-Christian era." The facts behind the first of these two descriptions are simple enough. From the time of Constantine there was an active alliance between the church and the political authorities. The latter supported the church, gave it preferential treatment, helped it in its undertakings and expansion, gave special and privileged status to its personnel, protected their persons and possessions, put the secular arm at its service, accepted its advice, gave it an important role in the state's deliberations and decisions, and supported the claim of Christianity to absolute truth. The church in return had to support the secular authorities. It had to give them a part in its undertakings, become their public relations officer, and put up with their interventions into its own sphere, even when they sought to settle the church's internal problems or theological questions.

The partners were never complete equals, for sometimes the church was subservient to the state, sometimes the state to the church. The association between the two did not arise simply out of the perverse desire of the political authorities to make the church a servant; it also arose out of good will on the part of these authorities and a desire to serve the church, for the heads of state had themselves become Christians (and who could object to that?). But the association nonetheless led the church into a position both

---

[2] The quotations in this paragraph are from André Dumas's otherwise profound and remarkable book, *Dietrich Bonhoeffer: Theologian of Reality*, trans. Robert McAfee Brown (New York: Macmillan, 1971), p. 185, n. 42.

of conformism and of power, and this was the basic error, the fundamental heresy, of Christendom. As long as the church had maintained the strict and intransigent attitude of an Ambrose of Milan to a Theodosius the Great, there was nothing to fear from the association of church and state. But Ambrose was an exception. For the most part the church sold out and was led astray by the exercise of power and by association with the political powers. This was the most sinister aspect of the entire period we know as Christendom.

Nowadays, however, it can be said that by and large the association of church and state is a thing of the past. Ever since the great break in France between church and state, first during the French Revolution and again in 1905, French life has been characterized by a strict separation between the two. The church today cannot be regarded as in any way a real power, certainly not a political power. This is not to say, of course, that development during the Constantinian era was all in one direction, for while Napoleon subjected the church completely to the state, the state in turn became completely subservient to the church under the Restoration.

The name "post-Constantinian era" refers chiefly, then, to the relations between church and state. The break between the two became final wherever socialist regimes were established; it is now taking place everywhere else, even if at a slower pace. On this point there can be no doubt. The fact is clear and all the easier to observe inasmuch as it is a limited kind of fact relating to a well-circumscribed situation. The term "post-Constantinian era," however, does not sum up the whole of the contemporary situation. Other terms, therefore—post-Christian era, laicization, secularization—are also used, but the reality they describe is less clearly defined.

1. The Post-Christian Era

The post-Christian era, or a-Christian society, is the end-result of a process of dechristianization. I shall not attempt to add another description of the process to the countless ones we already have, but shall simply recall some points we all know.

Christianity had lost some of its vitality and degenerated into a moral code, a philosophical system, an ecclesiastical organization, conformism, hypocrisy, etc. Meanwhile, non-Christian and anti-Christian forms of thought were gaining strength, and were reinforced by the discovery that morality and religion were relative things. Wasn't the world full of moral codes and religions that were quite different from Christianity and were regarded as true by their practitioners? Weren't there non-Christians who lived lives as good as any Christian's? The separation of church from state helped, of course, to speed up the process of dechristianization. Finally, the growth of science, and especially of the physical and historical sciences which dealt with different aspects of the real, came along to put the finishing touches on the whole process. All this is well known and I need not dwell on it.

The effects of dechristianization are quite evident. Individuals have no interest anymore in the questions put to them by Jesus Christ; the questions are regarded as irrelevant and the Christian faith and truth are considered to be completely ineffective for transforming men's situation. The chief preoccupations of men today are political, not spiritual. Modern man no longer understands the language of Christianity. Christian words have no weight, no content, and this shows that the Christian conception of life is so alien that the words used to express it awaken no echo in men's minds (piety, salvation, grace, redemption, lordship of Jesus Christ) or else evoke false ideas, since the same words now have a political meaning (justice, peace).

A further proof of dechristianization is a materialistic view of life. The materialism I refer to is not intellectual and philosophical but practical (concern for comfort, living standard, longer life) and is connected with a belief in progress that claims to be based on facts (man is constantly moving toward a better state and constantly making the good more of a reality; he will reach perfection as the result of a long-range movement of material progress that cannot be frustrated).

We could go on listing modern man's ideological and emotional convictions: that fate determines everything; that man is made for happiness; that man is naturally good; and so on. All these positions have fostered dechristianization and the establishment of frames of reference other than Christianity. We shall not attempt to answer the unanswerable question of the real cause of the present situation: has Christianity been pushed back because hostile movements have gained strength, or did Christianity become distorted and thus stimulate the growth of a new outlook, a new vision of the world and man? The only answer that can be given is that the two developments seem to have had an equal share in the end-result.

In any event, we see that individuals today find it much more difficult to "believe" in God's revelation and that far fewer people claim to be Christians. The movement of dechristianization has led to a "post-Christian era," which implies that we are now in a post-Constantinian era but also says a good deal more than that. I myself was one of the first to speak of a post-Christian era (in 1937), but my use of the term was not understood. Karl Barth issued a sharp reply to the effect that there could not be a post-Christian era because Jesus Christ has certainly come and is the always contemporary Lord of this world and its history. There can be no "after" in relation to that.

We must of course distinguish between a post-Christian world in Barth's sense (and I fully agree with him that there cannot be such a world) and the post-Christian era which is a historical and sociological concept. The term "post-Christian era," as I use it, says nothing about the truth of Jesus Christ but asserts only that Christendom, as I described it in the previous chapter, is a thing of the past. On the other hand, it is not enough simply to say: "Christendom used to exist; now it is over and done with." It is not enough, because the term "post-Christian era" says something very important. It says, first of all, that Christianity is no longer taken for granted; that Christianity no longer supplies a set of shared values, a norm of judgment, and a frame of reference to which men spontaneously relate all their thoughts and actions. Christianity is no longer the "taken-for-granted frame of reference"; in the collective awareness socialism now plays this indispensable role.

The church, then, is no longer coextensive with society; it is no longer a power to be reckoned with. In addition, it is strictly limited to a specific role, and this limitation is an important aspect of the post-Christian era. Spiritual and ethical judgments based on the Christian faith play no role in serious matters. Just as church has been separated from state, so two spheres are carefully distinguished: on the one side, the social, political, intellectual, scientific, and artistic areas in which the church and Christianity are allowed no voice, since each of these areas follows its own proper laws; and, on the other, the religious, spiritual, and moral areas in which Christianity is allowed a place, even though only as one of many competing ideologies.

The church is carefully limited to these areas. She is not asked to disappear or yield her place, but she is allowed only one seat in the vast amphitheater of society and she may not budge from it. She has her own special area of activity, just as the universities, the administrative bureaucracies, or the medical profession have theirs. Society at large assigns her her function, which is to take care of the spiritual and the religious, to provide ritual, and to help man achieve certain of his aspirations. It is taken for granted, however, that she will not attempt to interfere in the more serious business of politics and economics. She is expected to be at the service of the current powers that be, whether in the economic area, so as to foster social stability (as in France or the United States), or in the political area (as in the Soviet Union, Hungary, Poland, Czechoslovakia, etc.). She is tolerated provided she does what is expected of her and nothing more. She is there to promote morality (friends and foes alike expect this of her); if she does not raise her voice against crime, adultery, and drug abuse, she is not playing the game in post-Christian society, for in this society she has a definite, limited purpose, which everyone agrees in assigning to her.

The last and most important aspect of post-Christian society is the very fact that it has experienced Christianity and left it behind. Contemporary society cannot, therefore, be regarded as a simply pagan society. It does not have the innocence and simplicity that come from ignorance of Christianity and of all it entails. Post-Christian society is marked by its experience of Christianity and at the same time it thinks it knows what it is turning away from.

Post-Christian society has been deeply affected by Christianity, and bears the latter's mark: the mark of original sin, of the desire for salvation, hope, and a kingdom of God, of the conviction that a Saviour is needed, of the anxiety of those who are aware of radical guilt yet know that they cannot pardon themselves. We have not ceased to be products of the Christian era, but we have managed to reject what is specifically Christian in this product and retain only its psychic aspect. Thus, post-Christian society is a society of men who are at the point to which Christianity brought them but who no longer believe in the specific truth of the Christian revelation.

At the same time, post-Christian society is convinced that it knows all there is to be known about Christianity. Christianity has degenerated into religiosity, as Gabriel Vahanian puts it, not indeed in itself but in the eyes of all who live in post-Christian society. Revelation is identified with religiosity, and consequently faith no longer has any meaning or content. The very movement which inspired Christendom has betrayed it: Christianity absorbed mankind's whole religious past (and thus identified itself with religion), therefore Christianity is now seen simply as one of the great religions and must take its place among all the other religions in mankind's pantheon. From now on, people can be at peace, for they know just where they are: Religion? We know all about that!

All that is left of Christianity is morality, a bourgeois morality with which everyone is familiar, and a few conventional ideas (the clergy have a role to play in society; the cathedrals are an attractive element of the civic scene). Post-Christian society, therefore, is not simply a society which followed upon Christendom. It is a society which is no longer Christian, a society that has had the experience of Christianity, is the heir of the Christian past, and believes it has full knowledge of the Christian religion because it retains vague memories of it and sees remnants of it all around. Nothing new, surprising, or unexpected, above all nothing relevant to modern life can come from Christianity; the church and the faith are simply vestiges from the past.

That is the contemporary situation to which the name "post-Christian era" must be given; that, and nothing else, is the heart of the matter. Once we have seen that, we can add any number of other points that are purely secondary: the decadence of the churches, the lukewarm faith of believers, the fall-off in attendance at Sunday worship, and so forth.

This negative attitude to Christianity is accompanied, in the post-Christian era, by a positive attitude of atheistic humanism. We do not mean, of course, that men are explicitly promoting a doctrine or philosophy of atheistic humanism; relatively little importance is attributed to such a philosophy. We are speaking, rather, of a change in the basic convictions of contemporary man, a change in the very context in which all their thinking takes place. We are speaking of an ideology that is unquestioningly adopted, a spontaneously accepted frame of reference, something that is usually implicit and rarely is consciously adverted to. It is the basis for a vision of the world that all accept and for a common language and a norm by which behavior is judged. It shows through in the newspapers and advertising, in our approach to contemporary society, in the content of radio broadcasting, film, and political speeches, and in the platforms of all groups whether leftist or rightist.

The ideological content of this attitude can be summed up, I think, as follows. First of all, man is the measure of all things. Henceforth nothing is to be judged in relation to an absolute or a revelation or a transcendent reality. Everything is to be judged by its relation to man and is therefore as relative as man himself. He is both judge and criterion for judgment. In judging and making decisions he is thrown back on his own resources, and the only basis on which he can build is his own accomplishments. He knows of no higher court of appeals and no source of pardon, for he is alone on earth and is alone responsible for all that happens.

Whatever happens, happens within earthly time, for man's existence stretches only from his birth to his death. His life bears no relation to anything higher than himself, since there is neither transcendent reality nor other world. Consequently his life in this world becomes unconditionally important; to live is the supreme value, for at his death the game is over and lost. The adventures that make up the story of his life are the really serious matter, since in the short time he has he must accomplish whatever he is to accomplish. The greatest of crimes, therefore, is the attack on a man's physical life. A man has to be given time to make a success of his life; if he doesn't succeed in that he is a total failure and there is no way of making up for the loss.

At the same time, however, man's life must contain its own meaning. But man himself, being the measure of all things, cannot give meaning to his own life: that would be totally artificial. The only alternative, then, is for life to be lived to the full; in other words, happiness is what gives meaning to a man's life. There can be no other meaning, for happiness alone is something objective even though experienced subjectively.

A second principle follows from the first: man is autonomous. The law that is to govern him resides within himself, or rather, he determines that law for himself; he acknowledges no limitation, value, or law imposed from without. He is responsible only to himself and need not obey any objective, "eternal," or "natural" law or render an account of his life before any supreme tribunal. His decision is the only thing that counts. In the last analysis he decides what morality is to be, just as at an earlier time he determined the content of positive law.

Man himself, then, decides what is or is not to be allowed. Nothing obliges him to decide one way or another, and therefore what is not possible or permitted today may well be possible or permitted tomorrow. If that happens, we can only say that there has been an evolution in the manners and customs of men, but not that any absolute imperative has directed or inflected the development. All experiences and experiments will sooner or later be accepted as legitimate; morality could hardly take any other course in constantly changing technological society. Even when man tries to look outside himself for something to relate to, or when he looks for some overarching meaning for his life, anything he finds and any frame of reference will have its origins in man himself (history, for example). The choice of such a source of meaning is an explicit choice. It must be so, since man's life has no meaning in itself: it goes nowhere but is simply carried along by the river of history; it is a dimensionless point in a line, and nothing more.

Autonomy is a burdensome dignity, for it means that man is left entirely alone as he confronts reality. Wretchedness, suffering, anxiety, injustice, death: they are all around him and he must face them alone. He must take a position and act, without anything to fall back on, without any source of hope. In atheistic humanism, then, man adopts a very lofty conception of his own fate, but the price for it is high: his own existential anxiety. A high value is set on man. Man is the subject of all discourse, and this leads either to a lightheaded idealism that refuses to face facts, or to a bottomless anxiety and despair which those who experience it are constantly trying to escape. In short, the concern for man, the desire to emancipate him on all fronts, and the determination to make him the sole and final court of appeal—all these set him on a pinnacle, but they also put him in a very dangerous situation.

There is a third conviction in the ideology of atheistic humanism: man is a rational being. But here again people are caught between what ought to be and what really is. Everything should follow the dictates of reason. There is a tendency to reject what is not rationally proved: religion, morality, metaphysical laws, tradition, and even political convictions not based on rational principle (for example, monarchy). Men are therefore tempted to build a rational society and a rational political entity (democracy), and socialism is the usual result.

In this area, however, atheistic humanism has been undermined during the past half century by the recognition of the irrational within man and by the resurgence of "obscure forces." Examples of these forces would be developments within communism, the phenomenon of nazism, and the contemporary explosion of movements that exalt the irrational as such. All this has been a serious setback for atheistic humanism. The contradiction between his well-established and reassuring convictions and the actual behavior of twentieth-century men is a source of deep distress for contemporary Western man.

A final element in the ideology of atheistic humanism is that man is good or at least free to choose good or evil and that, barring error, ignorance, or passion (which resists rational analysis), he chooses the good. Man has to be regarded as good, since he is the measure of everything, is his own master, and takes it on himself to direct everything else (technology, for example). How could we live in a world in which man has such power, if he were himself evil? It would drive us to madness if he were the measure of all things and the measure were itself deceiving. Such a state of affairs is simply not possible. Even the theater of the absurd or existentialism or the focus on horror is but a dialectical counterpoint to this basic conviction. Tell Beckett or Genet that man is evil, and he will be horrified. It is precisely because man is presumed to be infallibly good that we can put up with all the grimness and all the shameful reality: all that is not man but the negation of man, and the negation does not have its source in man!

This deeply rooted conviction of our contemporaries leads to two further principles. The first is that if evil exists—and it obviously does—it is not the fault of man. Institutions, society, education, the economic system (capitalism), the division of society into classes, bureaucracy—any or all of these are to blame, but not man. Put man into a situation that is free and fosters liberty or is just and fosters equality, and everything will be fine, because man is good.

The second principle is that whatever is "normal" is also good and moral. "Normal" means whatever a majority of individuals do or whatever a group accepts as a self-evident opinion or attitude. This means that in the last analysis everything can be permitted.

We must add, of course, that atheistic humanism both rests on and legitimizes unlimited growth of power, technology, and the economy. The higher the living standard and the greater the productivity, the more intelligent, artistic, cultivated, just, and good man will become.

On the basis of these convictions concerning man which are spontaneously held and taken for granted today and which everyone shares, a further doctrine has been developed: the doctrine that modern man has come of age. Since we are not interested here in pure theory, I shall simply recall two facets of this doctrine. First of all, "come of age" means that modern man in his concrete reality and in *this* society in which we live is in fact able to take charge of his own life; he has no further need of a guardian, a fatherly hand, or indeed any external guidance. Second, it means that he is now free and must exercise choice and authority.

I shall not discuss these two points, but I do want to stress what has been happening, namely, that we are seeing today the transition from a widespread but vague and imprecise belief to a doctrine that claims to reflect the real state of affairs. There were thus two stages of development. After being simply a theory that expressed an ideal, atheistic humanism became a commonplace, a belief, something taken for granted but in a vague sort of way. At this stage it gave men a unified overall picture of life; thanks to this belief men could manage to live in a difficult world. In the second stage, a new set of theoreticians started with the belief and developed new concepts and a new doctrine which, they claimed, explains *reality*. Atheistic humanism offered an ideal of what man should be. "Man come of age" claims to be a sociological statement of fact.

But, while atheistic humanism could and did become a collective ideology, "man come of age" claims to reflect reality and, for that very reason, will always express a doctrinaire position that bears no relation to reality. This passage from atheistic humanism to man come of age must be understood if the limitations inherent in contemporary claims are to be grasped.

In any event, man come of age is presented to us as necessarily nonreligious. The disappearance of God and the Father is no longer a prerequisite if man is to exist (that was the traditional view in atheistic humanism), but the disappearance did occur and now man does exist. That statement represents something quite different from the collection of beliefs that make up atheistic humanism today.

We now turn to a new concept the meaning of which has likewise undergone an evolution: the concept of laicization. Initially the term referred simply to the lay state. It was a limited concept that served in the effort to break out of the Constantinian framework; it said only that the state should no longer be subject to the influence of the church. Gradually it was extended to mean: the state should not be subject to any religious influence or allow religion a dominant role.

At this point two new and divergent paths were followed. On the one hand, there is laicism or the doctrine that the state should take an "aggressive" stand against church and religion. Here laicity becomes a value in its own right and not simply a reasonable approach to the exercise of power. On the other hand, there is the doctrine which I have urged since 1944, that the state should not itself promote any kind of belief or religion but should simply be a political, administrative, and economic manager. The only ideas it should have are those needed for effective management, and these are not to be regarded as truths in their own right. The state does not have to know, much less decide on, the true or the good any more than the beautiful. This second position is evidently radically different from and opposed to laicism.

In any event, these various conceptions of the lay character of the state refer to a concrete situation. They express theories of the state that can be translated into institutions and produce a certain kind of organization. For the last twenty years we have been moving from the laicized state to a laicized society, the latter being the product of the former. Society is guided and dominated by the lay state, and consequently religion has no real place in this society. Society is also molded by the lay state, especially through education, instruction, and democracy.

Democracy, when linked to laicization, means for example that political discussion cannot have religion as its subject nor be inspired by religious motives. If it does, the whole discussion loses its serious character for those involved, and the situation becomes somewhat embarrassing. If the current laicity is liberal in outlook, it will put up with such freakish occurrences, but they are nonetheless freakish for being tolerated. Moreover, to the extent that all instruction is lay in character and trains men to think in a lay fashion, socio-political discussion is less and less likely to touch on religion. In such an atmosphere, anyone who uses religion as a criterion tends to be regarded as divisive and sectarian, a disturber of civic unity.

To the extent that the lay state came into being in reaction to the church, the laicized society which emerged from the lay state is also spontaneously thought of as set over against the Christian religion. In other words, "lay society" says the same thing to the non-Christian that "post-Christian society" or "dechristianized society" says to the Christian. Consequently there is no ambiguity about the term "laicization," nor any difficulty in using it, but it is important to emphasize this fact in order to prevent confusion at a later point. Moreover, everybody knows that the laicized society has also been the result of technological growth, the spread of information and science, and a humanistic movement first toward freedom, then toward socialism; to say this, then, is simply to state a fact and causes no difficulty. There is no doubt that we are called on to live in a post-Christian era and a laicized social order.

2. The Secularized Society

But the question is entirely different when we come to the idea of the secularized society.[3] These terms are often confused, whereas in the final analysis they have *nothing* in common. The term "secularized society" arose especially in philosophical and theological circles, and principally in the United States. On the other hand, beginning with Bonhoeffer's famous *Letters and Papers from Prison*, we find the concepts of man come of age, of the areligious society, and even of areligious Christianity, as characterizing the current situation. Then the cult of Bultmann established simply the idea that the advance of science has transformed modern man. Hence we have to start with a view of man for whom scientific conviction is basic, and who has abandoned the mythical thought patterns in favor of a new thought pattern. That harmonized very well with the studies of Niebuhr and Tillich in the United States.

Thus emerged the concept of a secularized society, which was adopted in its entirety by the World Council of Churches, and which, after 1950, became the foundation dogma for every affirmation, the underlying interpretation legitimizing all research. It goes without saying that society is secularized and that all the problems of contemporary Christianity stem from that fact. How is one to continue to be a Christian in a society of this kind? What possible place can the church have? How make the necessary adjustment to this society?

---

[3] For example, one can cite No. 16 of "La communauté des disséminés" (1963), and in particular the significant article by Colson ("Un monde sécularisé"), in which, by a glorification of science, one goes so far as to say that the profane is the form in which the sacred is considered as part of our era and of our world. Yet, while accepting the difference between Christianity and religion, the author doesn't hesitate an instant to treat our world as profane and secularized. Likewise in C. Combaluzier (*Dieu, demain,* 1971) we find a reissue of the "law of the three states": "Science has demonstrated that there are no gods anywhere. . . . Science makes it possible to say that we are going through the puberty crisis of humanity. . . . In discovering his place in the universe and his responsibility in evolution, adult man is free to accept or to reject God." This essay contains all the commonplaces on the subject. In contrast, attention needs to be called to the only weighty book (even though it adopts the outlook of secularization), S. Acquaviva, *L'Éclipse du Sacré dans la civilisation industrielle* (French trans., 1967). This book gives us an excellent picture of religion in practice, and a good study of contemporary paganism. It is a noteworthy work in religious sociology, but it simply goes to prove the decline of Christianity, which it assimilates with religion.

It took a little longer for the concept of a secularized society to penetrate France. Perhaps we were vaccinated by the laicized society. In the course of time, however, we adopted the secularized society, first of all because the belief reigned in France that good theology was to be found only in Germany and the United States. Then, second, French intellectuals were prepared for it to some extent by their acquaintance (accurate or confused) with Saint-Simon and Auguste Comte, and the "law of the three states." We had *obviously* entered upon the industrial, technological, and scientific state, which now replaces the earlier religious state.

At least this doctrine had the merit of clarity and of presenting itself as a prophecy. In contrast, what makes thinking about the secularized society seem terribly difficult is the fact that it is an appalling mixture. A common factor among the diverse authors dealing with this subject is a total confusion between the formulation of a moral doctrine, a presentation of what ought to be (secularization is desirable for man), and the observation of a set of facts (the situation is such-and-such). Then there is the interpretation of those facts, which becomes confused with the facts themselves, so that the facts as such are scarcely recognizable, drowned as they are in the interpretive flood. There emerges finally a derivative doctrine, a formulation which starts with these interpretations of fact (things being what they are, here is what we can say about man, about society, etc.). This derivative doctrine then is used as a justification of the situation, to the effect that things are going very well as they are.

Harvey Cox is a striking and popular example of this absence of method, of this mental confusion. The greater the confusion the more the theory enjoys an outstanding success. It's the same situation as the one we were examining above in connection with atheistic humanism and man come of age. The underlying mechanism works as follows: first we have a doctrine, which can reflect a certain reality, and which in fact brings concrete results. Then comes a restatement of those results, which one generalizes, absolutizes, interprets. Meanwhile, one claims to be giving an account of the factual situation, whereas one is really formulating a doctrine.

The latter has no chance of being applied because (in contrast with atheistic humanism and the lay state) it is no longer a presentation of a need, of an ought-to-be, of a program to be put into effect. It prefers not to present itself as a doctrine. Instead, it pretends to be an account of the factual situation. It proclaims that these are the facts. However, since the whole rests on true facts falsely interpreted, on ideological generalizations and on dogmatic finalities, it bears no relation at all to reality. These would-be factual reports are in truth illustrative of basic beliefs which one is trying to prove! A radical rupture between what is and the discourse about what is is characteristic of statements about the secularized society.

In this society religion has no place. One bases this position on two principal factors. The first is that modern society is secularized because it is modern, which means that we have broken with the past. Modern man, thrown as he is into the midst of a constantly accelerated progress, into indescribable change, has no roots in the past. Now, not only were the societies of the past religious, but there can be no religion except by reason of a past. All religion refers to a past and embodies it. Such is the very mechanism of religion. That is now over and done with. Science and technology are projecting us inescapably toward a future. Hence the debate is no longer between science and religion, with their differing explanations of the world. The debate now is between that which breaks all connection with the past in order to project us endlessly toward an ever accelerated future, and that which cannot be anything other than a reference to the past, a repeat or a continuation of the past.

The second of these two factors is that modern man has come of age. This statement exhibits perfectly the confusion between fact (dechristianized man) and the interpretive doctrine (man come of age). We shall try to straighten out the tangle.

First of all,[4] there is a preliminary doctrinal explanation, an "ought-to-be."[5] Secularization is "the affirmation of the self-con-sistency and autonomy of the sphere of the profane in relation to the sphere of the religious. . . . Formally it does not characterize the objective order, but the attitude of man in confrontation with it. . . . Secularization is defined by its positive content. . . . It is a movement of conscious intent. . . . The thing aimed at includes culture, reality, values. The aim itself is either intellectual or existential. In brief, secularization is a development in man's

---

[4] This "first of all" has no reference to antecedence in time, but to the first aspect to be grasped in our effort to bring order out of chaos.

[5] For a summary of this portion of the doctrine see G. Girardi, "Sécularisation et sens du problème de Dieu," in L'Analyse du Langage théologique (1969).

attitude which causes him to seize upon the profane aspects of the culture, of the natural and human reality, of values in their consistency and autonomy, and to react accordingly. . . ." We need to bear in mind the secularization of science, then of philosophy and the arts, all of which imply a certain image of the world. Everything takes place as though God did not exist. We are here in the presence of the celebrated formula: "The God hypothesis is no longer useful."

At a second level of the ought-to-be, secularization which is an expression of atheistic humanism is presented as a formulation of moral values in the domain of the profane: justice, solidarity, equality, dignity of the person, and on the global scale the project of a new earth, a humanity of the future. "The awareness of man's powers doubles for an awareness of his rights, duties and responsibilities." This attitude is treated as good, as much for scientific research as for the formulation of values. That is how science can advance (and has in fact advanced). That is how man can become fully himself.

In this first doctrinal approach, secularization is, according to C. A. van Peursen, the means whereby man delivers himself "first from religious and then from metaphysical control over his reason and his language." [6] This has now been translated into action. Modern man has put the doctrine to work.

That granted, however, a confusion of theory with facts enters the picture. One notes a certain desacralization of the world. The sacred in this society is identified as a set of social or of neurotic conventions. Until now, there has been a sort of sickness of humanity, but the latter is now achieving its health by ridding itself of the sacred, for it is a fact that modern man no longer believes in the sacred. There no longer is a sphere of the sacred. Man has tangibly profaned everything which previous generations had held sacred, and he is even consumed with a desire to desacralize all sacred objects. "The world is abandoning the religious idea that it had of itself." Thus secularization is the historic fact in accordance with which society is no longer religious. The world is indeed giving up "sacred symbols." Man is no longer interested in the sacred.

Right away the confusions begin to appear. "Religion has been privatized," says Cox, which is strictly laicization. "The gods of traditional religions live on as private fetishes or the patrons of

---

[6] Quoted in Harvey Cox, *The Secular City* (rev. ed.; New York: Macmillan, 1966), p. 1.

congenial groups, but they play no significant role in the public life of the secular metropolis," which, for the West, is strictly post-Christendom.[7] Thus we have entered upon a new era, that of unbelief, which is in fact characterized by a certain state of mind, an attitude of man toward society, toward the world, etc., which Cox designates as pragmatism and as preliminary to the profane. This is all very simple. Modern man is athirst for action, for efficiency. He judges everything in terms of results and of possibilities for action. On the other hand, he can only understand the world as profane. There is no longer a religious glory. He naturally adheres to any religious explanation for economic or incidental reasons. He is filled with suspicion, etc., though he has never read Marx, Nietzsche, and Freud. I shall not get into a new description of this man and of this desacralized society. Hundreds of others have done that and it would be a futile waste of time.

What is most interesting is the transition to the third stage, in which Christian writers put up a bold front by reasoning that, since this is the way things are, it is just as well that they should be like this and Christians should go the way of secularization. But I stress the fact that Christianity and Christians have no choice. They live in a (western) society which has no further interest in Christianity. They are confronted with people who are naturally unbelieving and who do not seek God. It is a factual situation. Consequently, when they say they are going to enter into this secularized society, they are deluding themselves. They cannot do otherwise, and are simply obeying necessity, not their religion.

When, like Cox, they conclude that this secularized society corresponds exactly to what took place in the Bible, they are, as usual and in the wake of numerous Christian writers, proceeding to a justification, a posteriori, of the factual situation. Harvey Cox, with a touching ingenuousness, is the most obvious example of these attempts at Christian recovery through theological justifications ex post facto.

Various lines of argument are attempted. There are those who joyously proclaim that Christians should pursue desacralization. "Desacralization is in progress in the Catholic Church. The Church is about to desacralize herself. The saints are being challenged, and so is the Virgin. God himself does not escape. God is dead. Celibacy is being questioned, and one asks oneself whether we should continue to build churches." Just as Christianity was a

---

[7] *Ibid.*, p. 2.

desacralization of nature, so now desacralization is an action on the part of society addressing itself to Christianity, and the latter should submit to being desacralized! [8]

For others (e.g., Paul Ricoeur), the challenge of desacralization has left the Christian conscience two choices. "One is to agree that man's growth and his mastery over the world inevitably involve the death of religion. According to this approach, faith is not extinguished by the disappearance of the sacred. It has its own contribution to make to the desacralizing of the universe and of society. The other is to make of religion—that is, the attestation of the sacred—an irreducible dimension of the human conscience." This second choice, however, is becoming untenable. Hence we must adopt the first. One gives up religion, acknowledging that the world is on the right road and that man is come of age. One saves faith (or thinks to save it) by opposing it to religion and by assigning it its place in the process of desacralization.

How wonderful! According to Cox, "Man is giving up wearing blinders. That is, he is smashing the sacred symbols." Thanks to secularization, we are making giant strides toward the good. "Pluralism and tolerance are the children of secularization. They represent a society's unwillingness to enforce any particular world view on its citizens. . . . The world looks less and less to religious rules and rituals for its morality or its meanings." [9] We are familiar with his efforts to show that secularization has a biblical foundation and that what is happening is in complete conformity with what the Bible tells us.[10]

One is left a bit agog over these discoveries. Poor Christians, who have been deceived continually for two thousand years, and have never discovered that the truth of Christianity is secularization. It's annoying to think we had to be put in the present fix through circumstance in order to find out what the content of revelation really is.

Immediately after presenting his excellent exposé on the biblical

---

[8] I had, in 1943, in *Actualité de la Réforme*, taken up this line of reasoning, but in a different sense: "Just as Christianity has desacralized nature, so it should desacralize our culture and our society," which is quite another thing from simply accepting the movement currently afoot!

[9] *The Secular City*, p. 3.

[10] Granted I am entirely in agreement with him on the three following themes: the creation, the disenchantment of nature—the exodus, the desacralization of politics —the covenant, the desacralization of values; but I wrote all that long ago. What a shame that he fails to apply it.

roots of desacralization, Cox goes off the track, precisely because his own theology is not primarily biblical but is, rather, a justification of the situation. He goes off the track when he tries to explain how God's plan for man, as revealed in Jesus Christ, is entirely compatible with urban anonymity, mobility (despatialization), pragmatism (is it working?)—all of which are characteristics of secularization.

Why does Cox never get around to questioning the validity of this secular society as a society turned in on itself? It seeks no external reference. Secular man has no horizon further than the earthly. All superterrestrial reality which could determine his life has disappeared (at least that is Cox's assessment). How treat that as something favorable when, in the last analysis, it signifies a society with nowhere to go and with efficiency as its sole criterion? To behave like that is precisely characteristic of the secular mentality. It acts on the assumption that "What is, is—and there's no reason to pass judgment," in disregard of the fact that such an attitude calls for at least two correctives. The first is that one should be certain that the statement of fact is correct, and that a whole set of value judgments and generalizations is not mixed in with "what is." Second, not to pass judgment is in fact to join up, that is, to render a positive judgment.

Such is indeed the attitude in this whole Christian trend. One avoids any evaluation of the factual situation and allows the facts to judge faith, revelation, the Bible, etc. In other words, the very attitude of these Christians is a noteworthy instance of secularization. When all is said and done, they accept the ultimate criteria adopted by this society, to wit, fact and efficiency. With that as a beginning, they employ crude devices like the following: Secular pragmatism corresponds to what the Bible shows us about God's activity. God is primarily the one who acts, and man is made by God to act, to seek fecundity, hence efficiency, in everything. Score one.

The profanity of the secular world is nothing other than the fact that the God of the Bible gives man an entire share in the creation of the world. Man is made to rule the world without having to bother about anything else. It was through a perversion that the church and Christianity placed man and society under tutelage. They should be free to develop themselves. Man is made to have a share in the creation and to open it out, that is, to exploit it and to bring it up to snuff. Therefore the technological effort is in perfect conformity with the will of God, and the secularized society devolving from that technology is, in a roundabout way, the expression of God. Score two.

Those explanations are quite characteristic of the overall phenomenon known as secularization. Secularization does not consist solely in the *fact* that man is turning away from God (the Christian God) and from traditional religious forms. It consists as well (and perhaps more importantly) in the reworking of these "facts" by Christians, who pin on them the label of "secularization," and who give them a justification and an extreme interpretation.

We have just dealt with the justification. Now it is necessary to stress the extremism, which is indeed characteristic of our times, and which is precisely the significant ingredient in secularization. Every time a Christian today takes note of a cultural fact, he not only joins in with it but builds it up. He carries the tendency to extremes and absolutizes it. Perhaps he does this in token of his propensity to see everything from the point of view of God, but, more prosaically and with this particular society in mind, it would seem to me more likely that he does it because he feels relegated to the sidelines.

Surely, if the society is really secularized, neither the Christian nor the church can have any place in it, or rather, they can have only that restricted, minimal place which we noted in connection with the post-Christian society. Isn't that what drives the Christian to enter this society talking very loudly and clearly, making himself visible to all, attracting attention through the extremism of his statements and thus making a place in it for himself? The non-Christian listener will be slightly surprised and amused in the presence of this self-destructive outburst. So, by claiming to be more laicized and more secularized than anybody else, the Christian assures himself of something more than the obscurity of the back seat.

We need to bear in mind that the secularized society is an invention of Christians. By that I mean that maybe the non-Christians are secularized, maybe they have gone down the road toward the rejection of Almighty God, maybe they are totally pragmatic, but that scarcely concerns them at all. That's the way they are, and it doesn't matter to them in today's world. Non-Christians do not characterize their society as a secularized society precisely inasmuch as the "problem of God" is not their problem and they have turned to positivism.

It is the Christians who are worried by the situation. They would like to play their role, and they desperately want to hold onto it.

Yet they cannot avoid looking back and assessing the difference between the times when people believed and the times when they no longer believe. Those are the conditions under which the Christians set up this concept, but in so doing they push it to extremes. Not content to record the facts, they have to build them into a system. Not content to examine the real, they have to draw absolute conclusions.

All of this means that their doctrine of the secularized society is something entirely different from the laicized society and from post-Christendom. It is a society in which there is no religion at all, in which man is not touched by the language of myth. He has gone beyond that, having advanced toward a total transformation of his thinking, in the process of which the sacred has disappeared.

What is more, the Christian in his ardor formulates all this as a new ought-to-be. On the one hand are facts, circumstances, science and technology, the primacy of production, etc., together with, as we have seen, a certain philosophic attitude. On the other hand is a doctrine which puts all the consequences together, which presents the scattered facts as an ordered whole and links them with a belief in imperatives. Not only is the God-hypothesis abandoned, but the Christian, in his longing for martyrdom and glory at the same time, tells modern man that he should definitely abandon God if he would be a man and fulfill his vocation. For the Christian to speak of God means to speak of the Non-God, and to speak of him as a political and sociological problem. At that stage all is accomplished, for in talking on the level with, and in terms of, the ideological context of the man of these times, the Christian is not talking about anything other than what the non-Christian is talking about, that is, he is no longer talking about God.

It does no good to call this "positive secularization," in contrast to negative secularization which consists simply in ignoring the situation. The non-Christian can see in it only a confirmation of his own position. We are offered (Fuchs) the theology of the death of God as the dawn of a new awareness of man. I would like very much to agree, but I fail to understand how the abandonment of the God-hypothesis would imply in the slightest a Christianity to be lived in the world come of age. That there should be a desire to bring Christianity into harmony with this society—well and good. That, therefore, there should be a desire to formulate an areligious Christianity for this world which has been described as areligious— that is clear enough on the assumption that the world and Christianity should be on the same wavelength and embrace the same things in the name of an all-powerful culture. Finally, since the sciences imply the abandonment of the God-hypothesis, that Christians should also abandon it as a religious concept—that too I can understand.

But I am less certain that all this is a way of recovering Christianity. In any event, the result is surely to enclose man in his own system. William Hamilton notes, at first with regret, that God has disappeared from the conscience of modern man. Then, since he cannot resign himself to that, he joins in with it joyfully and proclaims that it represents the liberation of man (after Proudhon, Marx and Bakunin). Van Buren affirms the decisive absence of sense in the word "God," which restricts us to a secularized interpretation of the gospel. Thus, since there are those who reject the meaning of God, witnesses for God must sanction and record this development and follow that trend.

This is indeed the absolutizing to which I referred above, and the formulation of an ought-to-be. It is no longer an observation, but an affirmation by the "experts" that, if man would be man, he should stop believing in this Father, this Guardian, etc. The theologians having joined forces with Bakunin (occasionally using his very words without knowing it), the circle is complete.

Nothing is less certain than that society is the way these theologians say it is. Nothing is less certain than that modern man has abandoned God, and that the word no longer has any meaning for him. I shall call attention only to a passage in Granel (which can hardly be suspect of Christian self-satisfaction) and to which I shall return later. In it he clearly shows that one side of the *problem* of God has disappeared as a problem (and, I would add, the God-hypothesis has in fact disappeared *as a hypothesis* for intellectual and scientific work), but the presence of God is still, for the most modern man, just as disquieting and certain, just as vitalizing and challenging as ever. It is a presence which is indeed qualified as God by innumerable people today. Nothing is happening to confirm the absolutizing indulged in by the theologians, according to which modern man is totally and radically atheistic. I shall go no further with that for the moment.

My question is the following: it is easy to see that we are in a post-Christendom and that society is laicized—well and good. But how does it happen that, in a single stroke, we should be whisked from there to this famous secularized society? It seems to me that an initial fact, perhaps unimportant and circumstantial, ought not to be overlooked. The idea of the secular society arose with the Americans. Now, nothing more retained the aspect of Christendom than the United States in 1930. The president was always calling upon the Lord. The Bible was in all the hotels. Advertising was based on Christian maxims, when it wasn't Christianity itself which was engaged in competitive advertising. There was an identification made between the American way of life and Christianity. The businessman was successful because blessed by God, etc. Everyone was struck by the Christianization of institutions, morals, and habits of thought, as well as by the sociological, outward, and rigorous character of it all.

Then suddenly the whole thing toppled and fell apart, in spite of heroic efforts by religious conservatives. Christianity was no longer the court of final appeal invoked to regulate every situation. The Americans were simply panicked, as though what was happening to them were something terrific, unique, and total. In their magnificent ignorance of what was happening elsewhere, they never considered, for example, the astonishing resurrection of Christianity in the U.S.S.R., after a half century of anti-Christian dictatorship, or the fact that the church found it possible to live in France, which has been laicized for three quarters of a century. The French have a cooler head for the alleged phenomenon of secularization because they are used to it by this time. The American statements have to be treated as a spell of fever on the part of the threatened, and not as something of great importance.

Yet, while this explains the effusive talk by the World Council on the subject, it does not explain the process of generalization. In reality, one passes from the statement that "modern man no longer believes in Jesus Christ" to "modern man is atheistic," from "modern man is no longer Christian" to "modern man is no longer religious," from "modern man no longer reads the Bible and no longer listens to sermons" to "modern man is rational and takes no part in mythical discourse." Finally, modern man scoffs at church ceremonies. He no longer considers as mysteries the things so considered by the people of the Middle Ages. Therefore he no longer believes in the sacred.

I stress the fact that this necessarily presupposes the prior assimilation of Christianity with religion, the mystery of revelation with the sacred, and the recitation of the Bible with myth. To be specific: first of all, we can readily admit that, from a sociological point of view, Christianity is a religion. In any history of religion it is properly classified as one of the monotheistic religions. Second, it is a certainty that the biblical accounts fall into the category of myth, that the Bible contains myths which are explicitly presented as such, and that mythical thinking underlies the whole. Finally, it is certain that the rites, ceremonies, and expressions of the Christian faith can be viewed in the category of the sacred. That is all quite simple and obvious, but it in no way implies as a consequence the transition from dechristianization to the secular society. To arrive at that result, one would have to turn those propositions around, and then proceed to a formalizing principle.

The turning around consists in saying: Christianity is the most evolved religion. It represents the peak of religious evolution (which is what Christians were saying with great satisfaction a century ago), so that, when Christianity falls, religion itself, all religion and every religion, vanishes. Therefore, if man has become non-Christian, he is also areligious.

Yet how can one fail to see that this generalization rests, from the outset, on a great self-conceit and on a reduction of the religious phenomenon? The same is true of the other statements: the God of Jesus Christ is the only God, the true God, a proposition set forth with pride by preceding generations (and, in fact, carefully nurtured by this one), so, if man no longer believes in the God of Jesus Christ, he doesn't believe in any God and is atheistic. Again, the mysteries revealed by this God are the most profound of all mysteries. Nothing equals the *mysterium tremendum* surrounding his presence. Everything connected with him is sacred in the most comprehensive possible way. Since he is the only God, no other sacred counts in comparison with him. Now we have seen[11] his consecrated hosts trampled under foot, his ceremonies ridiculed, his edifices profaned, in fact all kinds of attempts, intellectual and material, made against *this* sacred, and yet nothing happened after all. Hence modern man has desacralized everything (everything, because this was the highest sacred of all). He is living in a nonsacral universe.

Finally, but this is more recent, the Bible is the myth of all myths, the most elaborated, the richest in meaning, the most explanatory and declarative. If man doesn't accept *this* mythical word, it can only mean that he has abandoned the mythical

---

[11] In truth, the people of the Bible saw this a little before our time! There are numerous passages in which we are told that man ridicules God and the sacred surrounding him without effect one way or the other, but our modern Christians seem to have forgotten that.

universe. He now has a mode of thinking alien to myth. He is demythecized. Thus we see that it is in the degree to which Christianity has been put at the top of the sociological and psychological categories of religion, of theism, etc., that the abandonment of Christianity by modern man leads to the view of the secularized society, and of man as come of age, scientific, and rational.

However, the creators of systems are still not satisfied. There remain two additional presuppositions. The first is that, in the end and as systems, mankind and society are of a piece. Such cultivated intellectuals as Bultmann and Tillich bluntly adopt this monolithic position. Since modern man is imbued with science and no longer believes past legends and myths, since his motivations are rational, since he reasons and is absorbed in techniques, therefore he is rational and has left the mythical mentality behind him. Since he believes the scientific explanations of the world, he no longer believes in religion—as though the reality were not, in fact, an amalgam of contradictory convictions and attitudes. Since our society is technological, is dedicated to economic growth, and given over to the search for material well-being, therefore it is no longer a sacral world. It excludes the mythical and the transcendent—as though the mixture hadn't always existed in varying degrees.

Finally, this monolithic view of man and modern society leads to the conclusion that the sacred, myth, the religious, theism, are categories corresponding to past, outworn, and obsolete attitudes which can only be nonproductive. Hence one can treat them as museum pieces and can turn resolutely toward the future, a future in which such concepts and categories have no place, and more importantly, a future which they can neither produce nor usher in. Thus, a priori, those concepts and categories are exhausted. They cannot appear in new forms.

This is very interesting, for it shows that the Christian philosophers and theologians, in their very claim to be putting an end to dogmatism, continue to be just as dogmatic. That, in turn, explains their inability to grasp and comprehend the facts of modern man and of modern society.[12]

---

[12] Books by Christians imitating Cox in the fanfare of success are innumerable. They set out to show that Christianity should adapt to the situation as one of opportunity and truth. We have already cited Combaluzier. See also J. K. Hadden, *Religion in Radical Transition* (1971); C. Duquoc, *Ambigüité des Théologies de la Sécularisation*

The intellectual progression which has led from post-Christendom to the idea of a secularized society (or to the secular city) reflects a defect of method and not only a philosophic urge. In particular, there is a complete lack of critique with regard to presuppositions and preconceptions, hence a complete breakdown with regard to the concepts employed.

In declaring that modern man is no longer religious, one is very careful not to say what religion is, or the sacred, or myth. If a definition is occasionally hazarded, it is always an ad hoc definition after the fact and with justification clearly in view. There is still a complete subserviance to uncriticized presuppositions. Thus it is assumed that society is evolving, that it has little in common with the past, and that we are involved in situations which are entirely new. One seldom takes the trouble to specify what is new, but is content instead with featureless generalities about science and technology.

Especially is it accepted, without further ado, that man has changed fundamentally, that he, too, has nothing in common with his ancestors, and that therefore he is beyond the reach of the gospel message. One avoids, for example, taking a closer look at the question whether, in the final analysis, biblical man was not very close to contemporary man—whether the latter's attitudes, behavior and reactions, including those in the religious sphere, are not already accurately described in the Bible. The following elementary question is never raised: we note that modern man does not understand the language of the Bible, does not accept the proclamation of the gospel, etc., but is that any different from what we find in the Bible? Was the preaching of the prophets, then of Jesus, accepted and understood in their day with any greater ease? To the contrary, the entire Bible bears witness to the fact that their proclamation was always misunderstood and was an object of derision, scandal, or indifference. In other words, instead of judging the situation in relation to the Bible, that is, in relation to an exposé at the point of origin of man's reaction to the biblical message, we are judging it in relation to a past which, in the United States, is a recent past. Only fifty years ago the Christian religion

---

(1972), in which is set forth the procedure of the theologies of secularization counterbalanced by the need to take Christianity seriously as a social force. Christianity's future lies in politics, in social action, in what is now known as "Christ's left" (good reporting by J. Duquesne, 1971) with, in particular, *Échanges et Dialogues* and *Frères du Monde*.

was accepted as standard. Now that has changed and so man must have changed. Since it is obvious that society has been completely transformed, the change in man must be the result of that social change. For that reason, man has become rational/scientific, pragmatic/technician, profane/autonomous.

The question is never asked whether the spread and automatic acceptance of Christianity may not have been due to a gross misunderstanding. Whenever that question is broached, it is always in order to say that Christianity had become religious, that it was a great betrayal, that there is a contradistinction between religion and Christianity, and that, if Christianity is now rejected, this is because man has become areligious. Thus in biblical times people strenuously rejected Christianity (until it became part of the religious system) because they were religious, and now it is rejected because man has become areligious.

The same is true in connection with man come of age. We lose our way in a magnificent inconsistency: modern man rejects God the Father, the God-hypothesis, the consolations of religion. He is taking his destiny in hand. He has become adult. When someone says that to me, I assume he is talking facts, because his statements purport to be based on observation (the rejection of religion). Yet, when I produce facts which cast doubt on this adulthood, I'm told that I misunderstand, that we are talking about a model, a project, something that man should or ought to be. He should be adult, and that is the direction in which we should go. But if I'm at the project stage, how can I claim to be drawing conclusions from an observation—for example, that the preaching of the gospel should be modified *because* man has become adult? I could give numerous examples of this confusion.

Thus it is a basic, an entirely elementary, analysis which is missing from these studies, from Bonhoeffer to Altizer. If we really want to know whether there has been a transformation of man in these areas, whether, as is frequently said, man has nothing commensurate with what went before, whether he has finally come of age, whereas up to now he has bowed before the harsh tutelage of the gods and the fates, we need at least to try to understand what it's about. That implies, first of all, the garnering of as many facts as possible. We cannot rest content with a single order of facts, as is the case with all the studies bearing solely on dechristianization.

I can well understand that the collapse of Christianity is of great concern to Christians, but we absolutely cannot infer from this fact a transformation of man in his entirety. Still less can we pin the specific fact on general causes: technological-society man, man the technician, is dechristianized. We need to operate on a broader scale. We need to bring into view a more comprehensive set of facts, without, to be sure, pretending to be able to garner all the facts relating to religion. But, to begin with, one should try to know what it is that one is talking about.

Therefore, I would like to specify the method to be followed here. It is not possible to give a definition a priori of the sacred, of myth, of religion. There are as many definitions as there are authors. For a work on myth which I was impelled to do a few years ago I had collected, between 1960 and 1966, fourteen mutually irreconcilable definitions. The situation has not improved since. It seems to me that it is necessary to begin with a consideration of the indubitable phenomena of the sacred, indubitable because qualified as sacred by those who lived in that world; with the consideration of myths which are indubitable myths and of religions which are obviously religions. It is important not to take borderline cases, in which the phenomena are uncertain and the subjects are matters of controversy.

However, even when a certain set of assured facts is at hand, it is practically impossible to give an exhaustive definition which takes all the facts into account. Thus, for religion, one is tempted to give a definition based on the four major religions: Judaism, Buddhism, Christianity, Islam. Others would prefer to give a definition based on the "primitive" religions, in which they would be assured of a grasp of the religious phenomenon from the standpoint of its hypothetical origin. But all definitions are exclusive, in the sense that they isolate, as far as possible, the object under consideration by rejecting everything else. New phenomena do not enter into the definition. It seems to me that in extremely fluid areas such as this we have to try a different path, not that of an analysis of established characteristics for the purpose of arriving at a definition, but that of forms and functions.

Any religion, of whatever kind, fulfills a certain function. It is not irrelevent with respect to man. Likewise the sacred and myth have had a function in human society and on behalf of man. They have been useful. Otherwise man would not have clung to them. Therefore the important thing is to discern what that function was. (Ludwig Feuerbach, for example, began correctly by attributing to religion the function, among others, of assuaging the anguish of man, who cannot bear to be alone on the earth.) It will then be possible to assert that whatever fulfills the same function belongs to the same category of phenomena.

If, after examining everything which those primarily involved agree to call religion or myth, I discover a function (complex) on behalf of man and society; if, then, I discover phenomena not expressly called religion or myth but fulfilling exactly the same function, I would be entitled to say that, while the vocabulary has changed, the substantial reality is identical, and I find that I am really in the presence of a religion or of a myth.

This will be confirmed by a study of forms. There, too, we know that certain forms are inherent in religion, and that there is a certain structure in the sacred. If the phenomena whose function has led me to classify them as religion or as sacred have, in addition, the same forms and structures, I am fully confirmed, even though the fact under consideration is not at first sight a myth or sacred.

However, merely because I start with functions, it must not be concluded that I am applying a functional sociology. There again, it is exclusivism and dogmatism which have rendered functionalism impossible, and the same is happening to structuralism today. Yet the basic idea was excellent. The only way to avoid abstractions is precisely to keep functions and structures in mind. So that is the path we shall follow for an examination of the sacred, of myth, and of religion in our day.

III

THE SACRED TODAY

There is no need to restate a general theory of the sacred. Many others have already supplied that. I shall limit myself here to locating a few points of reference.

First of all, I would like to say that in my view the sacred is not one of the categories of religion. Religion, rather, is one possible rendition of the sacred. Surely it cannot be said that "every religious concept (this term is broader than religion) implies a distinction between the sacred and the profane." That distinction itself is a mark of the sacral concept of the world. A sacral society is one in which everything, including whatever is not sacred, is judged *from the standpoint of the sacred*. The profane is not the sacred, but it can exist only in a society which orders everything with reference to the sacred. The fact that man treats a given element as sacred does not mean that the rest is not sacred for the world is a whole. What it means is that the rest is located with reference to the ever present sacred.

I shall not, of course, get into the debate over the objective existence of the sacred itself, or over man's fabrication of the sacred out of whole cloth, in terms of illusion, invention, fantasy, or primitive ecstasy. I am drawing no conclusions about those possibilities. I simply note that there is a whole order of experiences which is absolutely essential (to the extent to which no one has yet been able to escape it), which cannot be reduced to rational categories, to "ex-plications" (which always presuppose duplication), and which is experienced even when one means to curtail and eliminate it.

I note, also, that man always ends by referring, most often unconsciously, to this order of experiences, and that it is from that standpoint ultimately that he assigns meaning, purpose and limits, both to the world in which he lives and to his own life. On the other hand, it is a sphere of the greatest disinterestedness, for, in referring to this, man is not pursuing a goal. The goal will appear when he attempts to lay hold of the sacred and, in so doing, gives it a sociological form. Yet, at the same time, it is a sphere of total interest, for the whole person is involved and ultimately finds there his meaning and his nonmeaning. Only with the greatest difficulty can all this be designated and described. Man never assigns a clear and explicit "sphere" to the sacred, yet we always come upon its secondary trail in every age and in every activity, over and above what man expresses openly and pretends outwardly to be.

Any attempt to pinpoint this experience requires that one be on one's guard against all the simplisms. There is the romantic simplism, which says that a sacred is expressive of an emotion in the face of the great spectacles and forces of nature. There is the rationalistic simplism relating the sacred to whatever is set aside for use in worship. Then there is the political simplism, according to which the sacred is a means whereby the powerful and the heads of state establish and maintain their authority. The materialistic simplism describes it as a fantasy on the part of a person powerless to grasp the real—we could go on and on.

On the other hand, we must also be on our guard against complex and ultimately nebulous designations of the sacred as: "what is decisively important for man," "that from the standpoint of which man is going to judge everything," "that which cannot be called in question, which is beyond man's reach, and about which man tolerates no discussion." That may all be true, but it is much too broad, too uncertain. In the last analysis, such approaches aim at something far beyond the sacred and are totally lacking in precision.

Inescapably, if man sets up a sacred, there is some reason behind it. Yet I always find it hard to believe that, if "primitive" man had a great capacity, a great intelligence as a worker, a speaker, an artist, an organizer, he was afflicted with downright stupidity the moment some other type of expression was involved, such as the religious, the mythical, the sacred, the magical. Such a total break at that point is very improbable. Therefore, I think the sacred must have had a meaning just as real as the fabrication of the first tools.

1. Functions and Forms

If we bypass the fearful sacred, the *tremendum* as such, we perceive that the sacred establishes a certain type of relationship with the world. Man's movement toward sacralization has its source in his relations with the universe. In a world which is difficult, hostile, formidable, man (unconsciously, spontaneously, yet willingly, to be sure) attributes sacred values to that which threatens him and to that which protects him, or more exactly to that which restores him and puts him in tune with the universe. What was achieved in the early ages, this integration into a threatening and reassuring totality, in which man restored his life forces, has been destroyed. It has to be reconstituted, perhaps for the first time in history. In that consists the depth of humanity's crisis today. Man is in search of whatever is going to assure him of this universal communication, this life-giving force, and this refuge in which he can be restored.

But this search, this new sacralization, can (like the other) be carried out only in terms of the most all-embracing, the most profound, the most moving experiment that man could make. The sacred has to relate to man's necessary condition, to that which is inevitably imposed upon him, to that which he must experience without any possibility of remission. He has to attribute an ultimate quality to that condition because it is inevitable. He has to place a value on it because it has been imposed upon him. He has to transmute it into the order of the sacred because he cannot conceive of himself outside of that order. It is a despairing call for mastery over that which escapes him, for freedom in the midst of necessity.

One is always impressed with the restrictive character of the sacred, imposing taboos, limits, prescriptions. In reality, however, the institution of the sacred is an affirmation by man of an order of the world, and an order of the world with which he is familiar, which he designates and names. For man, the sacred is the guarantee that he is not thrust out into an illogical space and a limitless time. We always have a false meaning of freedom whenever we think that a given restriction on our actions is a restriction of freedom, when it may be a condition for freedom. To be able to do "anything at all," "whatever comes into my head," is not livable. I can exist only in a certain order, and my freedom exists only if it operates in a certain order. The sacred is the order of the world.

To be specific: thanks to the sacred, man possesses a certain number of points of reference. He knows where he is. It saves his continually having to make exhausting decisions. He has stable coordinates. Thanks to the sacred, he can be oriented in the world and know where and how to act. He is not in a deadly weightlessness, nor a crazy kaleidoscope. Everything in the world is not identical and indifferent. The sacred designates for him a set of guides and discriminations, ready-made to facilitate life in this universe.

It can be objected that these are false points of reference and unfounded discriminations. However, even if I concede that there may be no sacred as such to which man's loyalty is restricted, even if I concede that the sacred is a pure creation of man, at least I'll say that this order which man imposes on the world appears false and ridiculous to us because we judge by other criteria, but that is not the way things are in that man's perspective. I'm not at all certain that the world order imaged by our modern science is objectively that which *is*. That, too, is a matter of an appearance obtained by a set of methods which we consider exact and superior. The fact is, we have no assurance that they, in their turn, might not be judged and ridiculed on the basis of some other point of departure. Our only guarantee is the efficaciousness of the experience. Now, for the "primitives," they claimed to have the same guarantee through the sacred!

So the sacred, in the process of establishing an order, has a function of discrimination. Everything operates in pairs (pure/impure, permitted/forbidden, etc.). It places in front of and around man a certain number of boundaries, of limits. Thus it defines a domain in which man is free, together with a forbidden, or rather, an untouchable domain. The domain is one of actions, rites, places, and times. The points of reference and the limits always have a very firm, and finally, a very pragmatic quality. It is always a matter of knowing what it is possible to do, and sometimes how and where to do it. From then on, the sacred defines a certain order of action, for it is precisely that action which cannot be carried out thoughtlessly. It is appointed in a given space. The sacred is an organization of action in a space, and at the same time it is the establishment of a geography of that space in which the action can be undertaken. It is a veritable general topography of the world, involving all aspects of the latter, material and spiritual, transcendent and close at hand.

By reason of that fact, the sacred is a bestower of meaning, for obviously the two aspects, meaning and orientation, must not be separated. The sacred gives orientation thanks to the topography, but in so doing it attributes a significance to the acts which I perform. The latter cease to be senseless. They are arranged according to a set of signs which make it possible each time to perceive the meaning of what I am doing. So the sacred defines an order in space, thanks to which I receive meanings (which, moreover, make perfect sense; meaning is possible only in relation to a certain order).

However, the sacred also has to do with time. What seems noteworthy here is that the sacred always appears to play a reverse role in relation to time, because the sacred time is that of festival, of transgression, of ecstasy, hence of disorder.

But this reversal, as I consider it to be, needs to be rightly understood. The sacred time is inserted into the sacred order as a period of legitimate disorder, of transgression included in order. In other words, the sacred time does not usher in an era of anarchy, a lunatic history. It is not the absolute beginning of something *other*. It is the insertion into the course of time of a limited period, determined in advance, during which transgression is the rule, just as taboos had been the rule previously. It is a time between the times, a silence between words, a plunge into the absolute origin, which one must *come out of* in order to begin. It is a plunge into chaos, which one must come out of if the order is to have force, virtue, and validity. It is a delimitation of the time during which the dark powers can act, an opening into that which man distrusts but cannot eliminate.

At this point, let us avoid explanations which are too modern (a time in which man lets himself go, after having been too repressed during normalcy, etc.). It is better to stay with this feature of the delimitation of the moment of the dark powers, whatever they may be. Thus the sacred time is also an element in the overall topography. It releases a set of forces, and supplies a set of reference points to guide the action and to make it efficacious.

Finally, the sacred has a third function, that of integrating the individual into the group. The sacred cannot exist except as a collective. It has to be received and lived in common. Conversely, the group has no solidarity unless everyone participates in the same sacred. I am not saying that it is a means of solidifying the group, because that implies a conscious intention, something never found in the institution of the sacred. But it is indeed a function. A group never exists on the basis of clear intention. The form which constitutes the group is the opposite to a contract. The latter can take place only after there has been a sufficiently powerful motive for concluding a contract. If such motives are purely voluntary, the contract, like the group, is very fragile, for nothing is less enduring than the will.

A genuine, strongly cohesive group presupposes an urge or a reference to a transcendent, an imperative received and recognized by all, and to which all have recourse. That is the only thing that can establish a lasting group in the face of all the reasons which all the members constantly have to withdraw, to go their several ways, and to despise the others. If today we are able to display a very great independence toward our groups, if we think to be very individualistic, that is possible only because we are living in a very "protected/protecting" society. Whenever there is no social security, the solidarity of the family or of the neighborhood becomes a matter of life or death. The converse is also true. Whenever there is no longer any solidarity of the family or the neighborhood, the individual is so threatened that social security becomes a necessity. In the world situation prior to this century, it was impossible to survive without a number of groups responding to every need.

However, no group can survive with sufficient power solely on the basis of conscious interest. In other words, man can live thanks only to the group. Yet that necessity neither establishes the group nor strengthens it. Man is not the mechanism he is too often described as being, who automatically pursues his interest in all areas. It takes a higher urge, a commonly recognized experience, a reason which eludes all reason. It takes a motivation which we not only feel inscribed within us but which also imposes itself upon us, like the love urge. A social group can exist only if all its members are included in a common "reason," are subject to an imperative recognized as transcendent. They must be living in a community relationship, not one, of course, which is constant or openly recognized, but one which is latent, and so basic that it can bloom outwardly only in rare moments. Yet everybody shares in this order.

Thanks to the sacred, and to that alone, there can be harmony between the individual and the group. Through participation in, through insertion into the sacred, man is led to accept and adopt all the group behavior. The most excessive, the most whimsical, the most illogical demands are responded to as a matter of form, either because they are expressions of the sacred or because they are understood through a diffusion of sentiment from the sacred. Human sacrifice, self-sacrifice, deification of the king, cannibalism, deviant sexual practices, etc., are all normalized. The sacred brings about normalization through the justification which it supplies. Everything, in fact, which participates in the sacred order is justified in such a way that there can be no further moral problem.

Morality is a product of those societies in which the sacred fades out and tends to disappear. It is a weak substitute for that which had been radical, ultimate, and established beyond dispute. The more morality is rational, the further removed it is from the sacred, and the weaker it is. Anyone participating in the order of the sacred feels so completely righteous that he can have no remorse. If, on the other hand, he disobeys, it isn't a question of the "evil" he may have done, of sin, of remorse. It is, rather, a question of being struck down by the group. Once he has put himself in opposition to the sacred order, he cannot survive. It isn't just a matter of the group's having been contaminated by the impure, or infiltrated by the forces of evil. It is, rather, that the order which man had established for himself must be total if it is to be an order. If a person who has denied that order continues to survive, that is proof that the order is not an order, whence the irremedial character of every attack upon the sacred. It is the entire group which is called into question in such a way that it can be shattered only if the desacralizer survives. That is why, in the myths containing such stories, the powers of the group and of the entire order of man, of nature, and of the divine intervene simultaneously. They are all considered to be under simultaneous attack.

Given the functions which the sacred fulfills in human society, we can understand certain of the forms it assumes, certain of its aspects which are universally recognized. First of all, the sacred appears as the expression of the unpredictable, dark and destructive powers. It is a mysterious domain in which numerous unseen forces are presumed to act. It is the concentration of all that threatens and saves man. It has to be that if it is to be order, if it is to set limits and provide meaning and justification.

If man had clearly ascribed these functions to himself, he could not have taken them seriously. It is not because there is thunder and lightning that man invents the sacred. Man made the thunder the source of meaning and of limitation because the world has to have an order, because action has to be justified. With a spontaneity, an "instinct," as inescapable as those he could have for hunting and fishing, man "knew" that he could not justify himself, that he could not tell himself that he was right (this approbation has no value and fails to reassure him because it leaves him in complete uncertainty). Neither can he say to himself that it is he who establishes an order in the world whereby he can locate himself. He hasn't the means for doing that. That is why the development of techniques is desacralizing, insofar as through them man is able to establish *his own* order.

Thus the concentration of powers is linked to the function itself which the sacred was to assume, and they are powers with which there can be no compromise, no accommodation. Every transgression is impious, that is, inexpiable. No pardon can be looked for from within the system. A man cannot ransom himself: the powers are inexorable. The order of the world depends upon them.

A second form or quality of the sacred to be kept in mind is a remarkable combination of what we would call absolute value, rites of commitment, and embodiment in a person. These are human formalizations of the dark powers, but it is especially important not to dissociate those three aspects. What constitutes the sacred, what makes it visible, tangible, and an expression of the body social, is this combination of the powers. There is no sacred in a society unless absolute value, rites of commitment, and embodiment in a person are *conjoined*. Each of these factors is related to the other two.

The absolute value is one of the sure signs of what a given person or group holds sacred. There is the untouchable, or again, that which cannot be called into question. This defines the boundary of the sacred. One can argue or joke about a given idea, a given behavior, or criticize a given reality or person. Then, suddenly, one is brought to a halt by an icy coldness or a flush of anger. One has just attacked what the other holds sacred. No argument, no friendship, no understanding or good faith can survive such an offense. In this matter one may not laugh. Criticism is not acceptable. The very being of the person seems under attack. He reacts because he has the feeling of being uprooted. The nerve of a tooth has been exposed. The reaction is vital. Even if he has no clear knowledge of what the sacred is for him, even if he can't explain it, he is laid bare at that point.

It is exactly the same for the sacred of "primitive" peoples. How many ethnologists have had this experience. They touched the stones which had been set up, the sculpted posts, the masks, all those things which are supposed to be sacred, and no one objected. Then, in a corner of a closed cabin, hidden in an angle of the woodwork, is an unnameable package containing nothing in particular. This they have no permission to inspect or to disturb. It is the heart of the sacred, from which everything is ordered. In this sense we can, of course, accept the idea of an ultimate sacred reality which cannot be altered or called into question.

But this absolute value (which can be maintained, incarnated, in anything whatsoever: an object, a human being, an animal, an idea, a place, a principle, a sociological reality) has to be combined with rites of commitment. These are more often referred to as rites of initiation, and of course that is what they are, rites of transition and initiation. Only after one has received a certain training, declared oneself and finally been "accredited," can one enter without prejudice into this sacral world and participate in the collective sacred. But it is too often forgotten that this all involves a mark, or marks, often physical. The young initiate is "marked."

At that point he is committed. He can no longer escape from the world order into which he has just been inserted. He becomes a participant in the rites, ceremonies, and forms, and through them he participates in the entire order, in which henceforth he has a role to play. Thus he is committed. He cannot renounce the sacred, nor violate it. He cannot think of not sticking to his role. The ultimate value of the group must become *his* ultimate value. He integrates all of society's sacred into himself. He is *within* that order, and he becomes one of its units who must be active.

Finally, the sacred implies a person who embodies it, for the sacred must be incarnate. This person is not of the same order as a sacred object, or a sacred idea. The person in question is the one in the group who concentrates in himself all the "virtues" implied by the sacred. He is the living sacred in motion, actualized in the present. He is not in himself the point of reference of the entire world order, but he is the point of reference for all the people, to show them how they should act, how they should appear, and how they should behave toward the sacred.

Thus the sacred exists only when there are the three elements in combination. The rite of commitment implies a commitment to the sacred value, and at the same time it implies a fixation on the exemplary person as a model. The exemplary person is the most committed of all through more exacting rites and in close relation to the sacred value. The sacred value has no meaning unless people are marked to obey it and unless there is a man to incarnate it. Under those conditions the sacred can truly be an order of the world and not a metaphysical abstraction for dilettantes.

In addition, and this is the last form of the sacred I would like to call attention to, it was shown long ago that the sacred is organized around opposite poles which, though conflicting, are equally sacred. This implies an "ambiguity" of the sacred, as Roger Caillois has shown. The sacred is the coupling of pure/impure, holy/blemished, cohesion/dissolution, profane/sacred, respect/violation, life/death. It is important to remember that it cannot be said of these polarities that one term is sacred while the other is antisacred, or desacralizing. The sacred is the relation between the two. Just as there has to be a south and a north, a right and a left, for direction and for mapping a route, so the antithetical categories taken together are the sacred. Thus it is the sacred of respect and order which implies the sacred of violation. The latter would have no meaning were it not for the former. Likewise, the sacred is both "condition of life *and* gate of death," as Caillois well puts it.

This organization around antithetical terms (which was discovered long before the application of the structuralist method) is a specific characteristic of the sacred. The same word often covers opposite things. Thus the sacred is that to which sacred respect is due and at the same that which is condemnable and ought to be expelled from the social body. The word covers two extremes between which there are no intermediate stages nor gradations (a person is totally pure or totally impure). Yet between the extremes there is a link, a relationship, a tension, an equilibrium, so that the one cannot exist without the other. It is around the axes thus established that the whole order of the world and of the society is organized. To us this may seem absurd and irrational. Perhaps it is, but the important thing is that there should be axes of orientation and criteria of discrimination. In other words, that the world should not be a horrible chaos in which All and Nothing would be equally present and equally possible.

2. Desacralization

Thus man constantly, and everywhere in the same way, has tried to establish an order, which implies something sacred. But the latter has frequently been called in question. That is, a principle of organization, once it has been put into operation, can, at a given moment and at the cost of much effort, be challenged and repudiated by someone, by a group located outside that world order. Thus Georges Gurvitch claims that such was the role of magic with respect to religion. Historically in the West we have known two attempts: Christianity, which called in question and desacralized the pagan sacred, and the Reformation, which called in question and desacralized the medieval sacred. In both cases there was an intent to desacralize radically. From the standpoint of the creator-God, who was at the same time a liberator, Jesus Christ, Lord of history and an incarnation of the love of God, a sacral world order was no longer necessary. The sacred has no place, no reason for existence in the biblical revelation. Primitive Christianity attacked the sacred of nature and the sacred of power in the Mediterranean world. The Reformation attacked the sacred of nature and of power which had been reinstated, and it also attacked the sacred of the church.

What is absolutely decisive in this double attack, which had been as profound as possible, is that, on the one hand, the sacred was irresistibly reinstated (which would go to prove that it is a human creation and an unavoidable necessity of such depth that it cannot be uprooted and of such vitality that it cannot fail), and on the other hand, what had been the instrument of desacralization became itself sacred. Thus Christianity for two hundred years succeeded in destroying the pagan sacred of nature and the sacred of power, in the name of Creation and of the Incarnation and of the Lordship of Jesus Christ. Yet, what was to become the sacred after that?—the church, the revealed truth, the very thing that had been the instrument of desacralization. With that as a beginning, the remainder was reinstated. The natural order of Creation and the power of the emperor as the vicar of Christ became sacred.

We must understand that with the ambiguous and conflicting (the pure/impure) structure surrounding the sacred, the process is, in fact, inevitable. Also, the sacred and the desacralizing agent are found inevitably to be building blocks of the social world. The sacred is such that it necessarily absorbs that which desacralizes.

Such was the experience with the Reformation. It attacked all the reinstated sacred, as well as the sacred of the church and of dogma. It did this in the name of Scripture as containing the revelation, and it set in motion an actual violation of moral regulation. It restored freedom to the person with respect to the economy, for example.

Then what happened? The Bible became the "sacred text." It joined the game of the sacred. At all levels, the profaning actions became sacred actions (smash the statues of the saints, lend money at interest, and exploit natural riches, as God said to do). In addition, the ensuing conflict, the wars of religion, were typical of sacred conflicts. From that point on, everything was reinstated. The Protestant princes became sacred personages (and the republics became sacred as well). The Protestant church and morality are typically sacred. As far as nature is concerned, that is not treated as sacred in itself but, for one thing, its use becomes sacred and, for another, Protestants elaborate a natural law based on a specific sacred in nature.[1]

Now we are witnessing a new enterprise of desacralization, in which we are currently involved, and which concerns us in this book. The tendency, since the end of the eighteenth century and throughout the nineteenth century, toward desacralizing and "dereligionizing" (the two are not identical) is well known.

One thinks right away, of course, of the action of scientifically minded persons and of philosophers, and that is not without its importance. The scientific process of the period, which tended to refer everything to the observable and the tangible, was a solid foundation—too much so! It was forgotten that the instruments which made the observations possible were limited, and that after

---

[1] Especially interesting is the demonstration by Jean Baudrillard (*La Société de consommation*, 1970), showing that from the Middle Ages to the twentieth century there has been a long struggle of desacralization, of secularization, against the "soul" and in favor of the body. The values of the body were subjective values. Today those values have the freedom of the city. But "the body, instead of being an instance of demystification, has simply taken the place of the soul as a mythical court of appeals, as a dogma and a plan of salvation. Its 'discovery,' which for a long time was a criticism of the sacred and a struggle of man against God, takes place today under the sign of resacralization. The cult of the body is no longer in conflict with that of the soul. It follows upon it and inherits its ideological function." Here again we meet up with the process seen above, in accordance with which the desacralizing factor becomes the bearer of the new sacred. The body is the object of a religion. All the advertising, all the ideology connected with beauty care bear that out.

all it was not impossible to make other observations with more delicate instruments. Moreover, in order to be able to apply the scientific method, it was necessary to delimit the object precisely and to isolate it. In consequence of this delimitation and isolation, everything not included in that field of experience counted for nothing. Ultimately a method of reasoning was established which made it possible to take into account a very great number of phenomena and thus to advance toward an understanding of nature—*an* understanding, which was mistaken for *the* understanding. This purely rational method excluded everything not susceptible to that type of reasoning and explanation.

For those various reasons, science appeared to be in outright conflict with religion, and to be a profanation of what man had held sacred up to that point. Now, with the emphasis on efficiency which began to gain ascendancy, it became obvious that religion up to the present has shown itself remarkably inefficient. Science, to the contrary, was ever more efficient in all the spheres which were set forth for man's action and admiration. In addition, the sacred, that dark and mysterious domain in which unseen powers were supposed to act, also showed itself to be weak and without foundation. The terrible threats and the vengeance which profaners had always dreaded were never carried out.

Science quietly took over areas formerly held to be untouchable. It brought light into the darkness, and it stopped at nothing. Sacrilege never seemed to be struck by lightning. The illuminated darkness was not filled with powers or monsters, but only with bodies subject to algebraic calculation. One could calmly affirm that it was the suspension of reason which had given birth to monsters. This approach extended to all the available spheres, and history, like nature, ceased to be a place of mystery and miracle. Instead, history was seen as a rational chain of events linked together by discernible causalities, and involving the interplay of observable forces. All the rest which did not fit in with this systematizing was treated as nonhistoric, as legend and untruth.

At that point a philosopher entered the picture to reduce everything to rationality, and a sociologist established the ages of humanity. Accordingly, the age of religion became an age of infancy, a period of images and illusions. Now that stage was over and done with, was radically superseded. Thanks to the sciences, humanity became adult, and the mark of an adult was reason. We had entered a new era. Progress was irreversible. Yet let us remember that, by a singular turn of events which can be called prophetic, this same sociologist in this era of rational science claimed to set up a new religion, to recover a "Virgin Mother," and to found a cult.

Be that as it may, this intellectual, scientific, and philosophic evolution, which is so commonplace that it is needless to dwell on it, would surely not have sufficed to pull society in the direction of desacralization by rationality alone. It took events, group trends, common experiences which rendered man open and susceptible to that kind of thinking which was then vulgarized and made intelligible even to Monsieur Homais.*

Now those events did take place. It is, of course, impossible to assign priorities and to make a final determination whether the thought preceded the event or vice versa. Let us recall some events. One fact of importance which is too often neglected was the death of Louis XVI. The king had remained the sacred person in full force. The sacrality of Majesty, the *arcana imperii,* had persisted in the popular subconscious in the eighteenth century exactly as it had been in the twelfth century, or even in the seventh century before Christ. The condemnation and execution of the sacred person par excellence, the focal point of the sacred forces, the instigator, the initiator of vital powers, was a mutilating, uprooting experience and a loss of psychic moorings. A great psychoanalyst was of the opinion that the French people had not yet recovered from the shock in 1793 and that that explains their reactions.

Along with that and more socially, perhaps more profoundly, the people as a whole were able to experience directly the results of the desacralizing science through the development of technology. We must remember that the negative reactions of individuals against technological innovations during that period (the introduction of steamboats, railroads, etc.) were not in the first instance motivated by considerations of personal advantage but were reactions in the category of the sacred. It was the fear of transgression, of the unleashing of secret powers, of the *implementation* of what had previously been thought untouchable and unnameable. But, as always happens in those spheres, the turnaround was for that very reason all the more total, and one passed from one extreme to the other because the sacred of transgression is but the obverse of the forbidden sacred.

Thus the untouchable domain, when it is profaned, becomes the

* Tranlator's note: Monsieur Homais, a bourgeois character in Flaubert's *Madame Bovary.*

domain of its opposite. Perfect purity, when it is desacralized, becomes the very rationale of prostitution. The secret, vital experience, once it is brought into the open, becomes an act of the most vulgarized and banal utility. So when the effectiveness of technology had triumphed over the sacred terrors and hatreds, it brought about this same reversal. It was the release of man along a path of efficacious rationality, the unbridled use of means, the increasingly rapid conquest of the most profound. The latter *had to be* profaned because nothing *could* any longer remain outside this expropriation. That would be another threat and another judgment. Yet the people of that period were unaware that this frenzy of exploitation was itself a sacred. Oh no, it was all clear and easily explained.

Finally, in addition to a number of other factors which we cannot deal with here, let us remember that this was also the era of urbanization. For many reasons, an increasing number of people left the country and crowded into the cities. They were workers for the most part, and some merchants. That had its desacralizing effect at two levels.

First, man is breaking his relationship with nature, with the vital resources, with the natural cycles, etc. The sacred was always an experience connected with nature. Man was part of this whole which had been given him. The sphere of the sacred always related to the world of nature. There had been no sacred except in relation to, and in respectful reserve toward, the phenomena of birth and death, of germination and the lunar cycle, etc. Man who leaves that milieu is still imbued with the feeling and imagery derived from the sacred. However, these are no longer revived and rejuvenated by experience. The city person is separated from the natural environment and, as a consequence, the sacred significations no longer have any point of contact with experience. They soon dry up for lack of support in man's new experience with the artificial world of urban technology. The artificial, the systematized, and the rational seem incapable of giving birth to an experience of the same order, the more so since they are linked with the desacralizing movement, and since man is being trained by that means.

A second level at which urbanized man becomes part of the desacralizing trend is that of the structure of his work. Work in the country mediated the sacred order. Through such work man could share more profoundly in the sacred, which thereby became a constituent part of his experience. In contrast, the new type of industrial, mechanized work was essentially rational, without mystery or depth. It failed to mediate the world of nature. It did not involve learning from an independent power. It was not a risky cooperation with unknown forces whose menacing graciousness predominated, in the end, over our own actions.

In our day, mechanized work obtains clear and unambiguous results which can be calculated in advance without reference to an extraneous Wholly Other. Any interference from that direction could only be troublesome and negative. Moreover, the work of the beginner is in the same category of simple, legal relationships with sure and certain accountability, and results explained without recourse to mystery.

Work had once been filled with those secret things, with those hidden participations in a unitary world from which one snatched a fragment and became a Prometheus in so doing. Now, by contrast, work is a process of the global seizure of a world which, the more it is worked the more it is robbed of its depths. In this way man is experiencing desacralization. He is quite prepared to listen to and accept the message of pure rationalism, the demonstration that profanation is a good representing progress. Since he is experiencing profanation every day and is performing it himself, why shouldn't he accept it?

Thus man today relates to a world which is clear, simple, and explicable, a world needing only to be put in order and which is capable of being put in order. It is a world transformed into an object from which man thinks to withdraw himself so as better to act upon it. He expels it in order to control it. He isolates himself from it in order to calculate its techniques. There really is no more sacred. Undoubtedly some peasant superstitions still persist, Catholic ceremonies and beliefs of the past, all of which are ultimately doomed.

Corresponding to this progress of man, there is organization and lucid opinion. Politics as well is to be stripped of its participation in the sacred. Everything is completely explicable. No longer is it necessary to appeal to some mystical body, to some miraculous charisma, on behalf of the authority of the law or the sovereignty of the administrative power. Power is a matter of system. Again, organization is all that is needed.

Thus man thinks of himself as new, released from the crushing burden of the ancestral sacred. Now he is subject only to reason and will. That being the case, it is indeed true that what was formerly sacred, which had been destroyed, expelled and profaned, can never again be what it was. It is indeed true that the order of experiences which had been integrated into the sphere of the sacred, but which is now explained and rationalized, can never rise again from those ashes which are now scattered and swept away. It is indeed true that the former religions are dead and will never live again. For Christianity, this means that it cannot remain, nor ever again become, the religion it once was. It has to be itself, faith in the revelation of the Wholly Other, or nothing (unless some other path should lead it to a new adulteration and the chance to become some other religion). The sacred which has been profaned cannot, even in rapture, ever be sacred again. That would involve an act of the will which the wary unconscious rejects whenever lack of experience forbids its participation.

This is what sociologists and psychologists, between 1930 and 1950, loudly proclaimed as the "secularization" of our modern world. In truth they were a little late. The phenomenon we have described was characteristic of the nineteenth century.

3. The Sacred Today

On May 3, 1961, Premier Khrushchev, addressing himself to Abdel Nasser, said, "I am warning you in all seriousness. I tell you that communism is sacred." [2] He repeated that on several other occasions. Premier Khrushchev knew what speech was all about. He displayed great skill in it and was not given to using words carelessly. When he said solemnly that communism is sacred, it is unlikely that that was just a manner of speaking! Communism has entered that invisible, intangible, dreaded, and mysterious domain in which lightning and rainbows mature, and the Grand Master was attesting to that mutation.

The truth is that for nearly a half century we have witnessed a massive invasion by the sacred into our western world.[3] Rational man has not been able to adhere to his rationality. In the end, the world is revealed to have a number of false bottoms. The more man

---

[2] There is a remarkable constancy in soviet communist thought on this point. Secretary Brezhnev declared on October 28, 1971, "For a soviet communist, everything which bears on the life, activities, and *name* of Lenin is sacred. . . ." Coming from a technician, that is quite something.

[3] There is a splendid statement by Norman O. Brown (*Life Against Death*, 1959), who was one of the first to observe the phenomena we are studying: "We must not be misled by the absolute antinomy between the sacred and the profane into interpreting as secularization what is merely a metamorphosis of the sacred."

penetrates into himself the more he is led to question the systematic certitudes so painfully acquired during the nineteenth century. We are detecting the remote depths which can no longer be concealed, and we have learned that our lucid intelligence rests on a base of mystery. We have seen reasonable man caught up in waves of mystic insanity and acting like a barbarian. We have witnessed the exasperated search for universal communions, from surrealism to jazz to eroticism. The fact is that man cannot live without participation in the sacred, and we are seeing his protest.

But man cannot retrace his steps. The forms and meanings of the sacred today can no longer be those of an enduring sacred. Man is forced to create something to serve as a sacred. Is it substitute or reality? I can't say. In any event, it cannot be said that man is no longer religious just because Christianity is no longer the religion of the masses. To the contrary, he is just as religious as medieval man. It cannot be said that there is nothing sacred now just because we claim to have emptied out the sacred from nature, sex, and death. To the contrary, the sacred is proliferating all around us.

However, we must realize that the sacred is no longer located in the same place as before. It is obvious that man defines the sacred in relation to his own life milieu. That has to be the case if the sacred is really to be the unimpeachable, inviolable order to which man himself submits and which he uses as a grid to decode a disorderly, incomprehensible, incoherent world that he might get his bearings in it and act in it. It is in his own milieu that he has need of an order, of an origin, of a guaranteed possibility for a life and a future. It is for this milieu that it is important to have rules of behavior deriving from the sacred. Moreover, it is the milieu which provides man with his most universal, most rich and most fundamental experience, which gives the sacred its substance, its corporality, and which prevents its becoming a dry intellectual construct.

It is, then, the milieu which is invested with sacred values. That milieu had once been the natural milieu. It was in relation to the forest, the moon, the ocean, the desert, the storm, the sun, the rain, the tree, the spring, the bull, the buffalo and death, that the sacred was ordered. As long as nature was man's milieu, nature was the origin and object of the sacred. Man constructed his myths and religions in relation to nature. The sacred was the humanized topography of nature. In a secondary way, to be sure, there was also a sacred related to the group. When the group expanded to a certain size, sacred personages appeared, such as the king, the priest, or the magician. Yet it must not be forgotten that the group was immersed in nature, was impregnated by it, and established in relation to it. The nature/culture polarity was a couplet rather than a contradiction. Lévi-Strauss has shown how man attempted to structure his group in terms of the classification which he established in the universal reality of nature. That was where his experience lay. That was the most direct manner in which he was present to the world. Finally, it was an attempt which did not vary greatly throughout scores of centuries because the milieu of man's active experience remained the same.

The novelty of our era is that man's deepest experience is no longer with nature. For most practical purposes it no longer relates to it. From the moment of his birth, man lives knowing only an artificial world. The dangers which confront him are in the domain of the artificial. Obligations are imposed not by contact with nature but solely by contact with the group. It is not for reasons of survival in the natural milieu that the group formulates its rules, its structures, and its commands. The reasons are entirely intrinsic. The relations of the group with other groups have become more unremitting and imperious than formerly and in any case more imperious than the relations with nature had been. Nature now is subdued, subjugated, framed, and utilized. No longer is it the threat and the source, the mystery and the intrusion, the face and the darkness of the world—either for the individual or for the group. Hence it is no longer the inciter and the place of the sacred.

Man's fundamental experience today is with the technical milieu (technology having ceased to be mediation and having become man's milieu) and with society. That is why the sacred now being elaborated in the individual and in the collective consciousness is tied to society and technique, not to nature. The sacralized reality will have less and less reference to natural images and relationships. Formerly, when power participated in the sacred it was *always* in a sacred of nature (having to do with the power of fertility, Lupercalia, destructive powers, and revelatory powers, etc.). It was with reference to nature that the social power was exercised. Today, however, there is no longer any reason to make use of that reference. It simply has no meaning or content. It is the political power in itself which becomes the source and the instigation of the new sacred. Society now becomes the ground and the place of the forces which man discerns or feels as sacred, but it is a society turned technician, because technique has become the life milieu of man.

The trouble is that this technical milieu is no more comprehensible (even though technology in itself is), no more reassuring, no more meaningful than the "natural" milieu. Man in the presence and at the heart of this technical milieu feels the urgent need to get his bearings, to discover meaning and an origin, an authenticity in this inauthentic world (Enrico Castelli). He needs axes of comprehension, of interpretation, of the possibility for action—that is, the sacred. Thus the desacralization of nature, of the cosmos, and of the traditional objects of religion is accompanied by a sacralization of society as a result of technology.

This corresponds exactly to what we discovered above, that the desacralizing agent becomes the center of the new sacred. The power which instigated the transgression of the old order cannot help being sacred itself. It enters the sacral world and finds itself endowed with an unquestioned presumption, which is all the more blinding for having triumphed over the first presumption. J. Brun emphasizes this very mechanism when he writes that the masters of desacralization in our modern era (Marx, Nietzsche, Freud) "are henceforth held to be beyond suspicion. One sacralizes them, consecrates them. They have become the new sacred monsters, so that what we are witnessing is a reinstatement of the very sacred which we claimed to have exorcised." Moreover, he shows how our political manifestos and petitions take on a sacred quality "replacing the encyclicals," and that all our intentions to desacralize, "if they denounce the sacred as an expression, still imply it as a requirement." [4]

A second quality of the modern sacred we would like to emphasize is a result of the foregoing. In the world of the sacred, man is related to the world directly. There is a lack of distinction of subject from object, an immediacy of relations, an experience of totality. That was brought about in certain contacts between man and nature. Currently we are seeing a suppression of the distance between man and object, the restoration of an immediacy. But it does not have the same meaning as before. The irrational in which man places his hopes is in no way a surpassing of rationalism. It does not represent a new grasp of reality which would at last assure man of his being and his world. The reason is that this immediacy is a result of the very structuring of society into which man is integrated and assimilated, and to which he finds himself reduced.

---

[4] J. Brun, lecture: "Désacralisation et Nouvelles Idoles," Semaine des intellectuels catholiques (1971).

One is forever seeking to make the integration more complete, more precise, in the hope that ultimately it would involve the whole man.

There is no more distance, but that is not because of an insertion into the sphere of the sacred. It is because of an insertion into the social mechanics. Man's singular fate was that, in imposing on nature his lucidity, his analysis, and his language, he dissociated himself from her and entered a situation which he finds intolerable, that of an absence of communion. He continually has had to restore, and even to reorganize, the sacred. So by a remarkable turnaround we are witnessing in our day a reverse process. As a result of having imposed his reason, his technology, and his procedures on society, man finds himself forced into an extremely intimate association with society. Society can no longer live, move, or grow without a soul, and it can have no other soul than that of man. That is a need, and how can this need be denied by the great and powerful body which is filled with all the promises and threats?

Society can fulfill itself only by acceding to the sacred, but the latter exists only in immediacy with man and in the sacrifice of man. So here we are in this equally intolerable (for the present) condition of a sacral communion by means of the progressive absorption into something artificial, the very thing which had served to disengage us from the primary absorption in nature.

Symbolism is one of the essential expressions of the sacred. In symbolism we confront the same problem. We are persuaded that modern man no longer responds to symbols. He displays nothing of the symbolic and no longer operates by means of symbols. However, all we can really say is that our symbols which have been consecrated by long tradition no longer symbolize anything. They are outdated and fail to convey meaning. The symbol of the water of baptism or the wine of Holy Communion is as void for contemporary man as the phoenix or the grail.

Obviously we cannot here go into a detailed study of symbols, symbolizing, and the process of the obsolescence of symbols,[5] but there are two aspects I would like to emphasize. First, a symbol is

---

[5] On symbol, I would refer the reader, above all, to the works of Enrico Castelli and Paul Ricoeur. According to Ricoeur, symbolic language is one in which a primary meaning refers to a series of secondary meanings through a succession of shock waves. It is a language which fans out into evocations instead of converging on an expression.

surely not a conscious creation of man and his group. People never say to themselves, "Look, we're going to take this as a symbol for that." There is no express agreement or code which has been worked out to link the symbol with the group and with the truths signified. The emergence of a symbol is connected with a lived experience matched to a set of raw, accepted, and undisputed truths which are frequently rooted in the organization of the ancestral mind. They are designated as archetypes by Jung, and they are sometimes mythical. If there is an archetype of red, red will become a symbol according to the circumstance—of the military power, of the Roman consul, of the wild offering of the Khmerian elephant hunters, or of the will to revolution. The result does not come about through a knowledge of the archetypes, nor through any clear awareness of the correspondence between symbol and reality. The symbol imposes itself as such on a person in a given group at a certain stage of its evolution. Its function is to express in an unmistakable manner a truth which is known and lived in common. It is such that it could not be anything else. It alone expresses that truth. The truth, in turn, can be expressed exclusively by that symbol.

But progressively, in the evolution of the group, the symbol loses its potency. The symbol wears out to the degree in which the raw, experienced truths evolve. The symbol can vitalize that truth for a while, but not indefinitely. There is an increasing discrepancy between the accepted truths and their fixed symbols. That brings about a consciousness of the symbol. Man becomes aware that it was a symbol and not the current, indisputable truth. At that point, a certain amount of systematic analysis will keep the symbol alive, but it is ruined in the very process of being justified. The moment there is an awareness that this object, this color, this deed *is* a symbol, the moment one *knows* it, it has already ceased to be a symbol. Conscious awareness and analysis destroy the symbol, which no longer communicates as such. It has now become a discourse understood only by specialists and, if necessary, by the faithful who must have it explained to them, which is the very opposite of a symbol.

That granted, however, it cannot be said that modern man no longer has a feel for symbols. To be sure, he no longer has direct knowledge of the meaning of the fish or the swastika. Yet the latter is very instructive, for it has become a symbol once again for modern man, but with a meaning entirely different from the meaning it had three thousand years ago. Symbolism is not abandoned today. I would say, to the contrary, that the symbol has again become an essential mode of expression for moderns. Without going as far as Marshall McLuhan—for whom all modern thought is already and will increasingly be mythical and symbolic because of the impact of the media, particularly television—we nevertheless are forced to acknowledge that it is thanks to the symbols living in the mind or the heart of modern man that advertising and propaganda have so much influence. Vance Packard's studies of advertising symbolism are well known,[6] but advertisers do not manufacture the symbols. Modern man is already living that symbolism; thus its use can be effective and can give rise to the search for "motivations." These latter are never anything but the individual's reaction to the appeal of common symbols.

Likewise, despite its too systematic character, the sexual symbolism of various technical objects established by Baudrillard (the system of objects) is essential for an understanding of the order of relations existing between techniques and modern man. Obviously, modern man knows nothing of automobiles and refrigerators as symbols, yet the automobile and the refrigerator would hardly have their lure, would not occupy the place they do in life, if they were mere objects of convenience without a meaning. They must, and they do, symbolize a profound truth of life.

Thus western society shows itself very destructive of worn-out symbols and yet an avid consumer of living symbols which link this new world to the deepest roots of one's being, and which restore the sacred to its imperial position.

4. What Is It?

The modern western technical and scientific world is a sacral world. We have seen that this sacral world implies an order and a transgression, a topography of the world, but that, today, it is a topography of the society and not of nature. I shall set forth as a proposition[7] that the modern sacred is ordered entirely around two

---

[6] This has all been restated and magnificently demonstrated by Jean Baudrillard, *La Société de consommation* (1970).

[7] I shall do this after having made the necessary analyses, to wit, that the axes of the sacred which I am about to indicate correspond, item for item, with the functions and forms of the sacred which we noted above.

axes, each involving two poles, one pole being respect and order, the other transgression. The first axis is that of "technique/sex," the second is the "nation-state/revolution" axis. Those are the four factors (I say exclusive of every other) of our modern society. Just as every sacred is always organized by opposing pairs, so we find the same structure at the present time.

It would seem, at first sight, that technology is not susceptible of such sacralizing, since it is rational, mathematical, and explicable at every point. It is hard to see how it could be part of a world so radically contrary to it. Nevertheless, the fact is that technology is felt by modern man as a sacred phenomenon. It is intangible, the supreme (in the cabalistic sense), unassailable operation. All criticism of it brings down impassioned, outraged, and excessive reactions in addition to the panic it causes.

To be sure, much has been said about money as sacred, and of course that is true. This is mentioned so often that I have no need to go over it here, but there are two things I would like to point out: first, this is not a trait peculiar to our times or to our society. Money has been sacred from the very beginning (cf. my study, *L'Homme et l'Argent*). This sense of the sacred has taken different forms according to the age, but money has always been part of the domain of the powers. Hence its sacred quality is not a new phenomenon. It is simply that it has been susceptible to greater emphasis because of the expansion of the reign of money, its universalization, and its unbelievable power at the very time when the other traditional sacreds were tending to fade out (in the nineteenth century). It is indeed a fact that the ideology of money, the religious fervor for capital (in no way the same kind of sentiment the miser might have for his gold pieces), the exaltation of its role and of its virtues have been, in the nineteenth century and at the beginning of the twentieth century, the most obvious expression of the sacred. The splendid passages of Marx on capital as a vampire, or on money as capable of everything, or on the need for money becoming the only true need (in the total sense) suffice to characterize this growth of money as sacred.

My second observation is that I have the impression that, since 1929, this sacred has been tending to diminish. It is no longer the major axis of the world. Assuredly the religion of money still persists, for it never fails to ensure existence in this "consumer society," but the mechanisms of capitalism on the one hand, and of the technical society on the other, have become so complex that money is less and less directly obvious. It is less and less clear to the collective mind that money is the guarantee of the future. There is social security. It is less a certainty that money dominates society, science, and the state. It is less obvious that money guarantees us against the new threats which we face.

Obviously, one can do many things with money, but less and less can we do everything with it. Furthermore, there has been a crisis of confidence in money since 1929. It has been the object of such general criticism from the point of view of socialism and of various humanisms that the collective conscience and public opinion finally have been affected. If money remains as a power, if it still forms part of the sacred, it is no longer the order of the world, in spite of all the efforts to keep on explaining everything by it. Average opinion is less and less responsive to such a generalization. If money is still a god, it is a god on the wane, who is no longer loved except in secret and with a bad conscience. It is no longer the glorious divinity parading its triumphs. Rather, it seeks to conceal them. Progressively it finds itself being replaced in the hearts of the faithful by other social powers and other beneficent divinities, while its priests—bankers, money changers, and capitalists—are pointed to as wicked magicians. Money today is no longer the center of the profoundly sacred. Even if it still is wanted and glorified by the crowd, it is not around money that human space is ordered in its interior/exterior correlation. It is not this world's axis.

In the world in which we live technique has become the essential mystery, and that in diverse forms according to milieu and race. There is an admiration mingled with terror for the machine among those who have retained notions of magic. The television set presents an inexplicable mystery, an obvious miracle constantly repeated. It is no less surprising than the highest manifestations of magic, and one worships it as one might worship an idol, with the same simplicity and fear.

But the force of habit, the repetition of the miracle, ends up wearing this primitive adoration thin. It is scarcely met with any longer in European countries. There the proletarian classes, workers or peasants, take pride in the little god who is their slave, be it motorcycle, television set, or electric appliance. It is a pride of condescension, an ideal of life which is incarnate in those things which serve. Still everyone has the sacral feeling that no experience is worth anything unless one has these powers in his home.

The thoughtful proletarian carries this much further. With him, technology is seen as a whole, rather than in its occasional manifestations. Technology is the instrument of liberation for the proletariat. It need only progress for the proletariat to free itself a little more from its chains. Stalin named industrialization as the sole condition for the realization of communism. Every advance in technology is an advance for the proletariat.

This is indeed a belief in the sacred. Technology is the god who saves. It is good in its essence. Capitalism is abominable, sometimes demoniacal, in its opposition. Technology is the hope of the proletariat. The proletarian can put his faith in it because its miracles are at least visible and progressive. Much mystery still attaches to it, for if Karl Marx could explain just how it was that technology would liberate the proletariat, that is certainly not at the level of the proletarians themselves, who know absolutely nothing of the how. For them it remains mysterious. They have simply the formula of faith, and their faith is placed enthusiastically in the instrument, so mysteriously active, of their liberation.

The nonintellectual bourgeois classes are perhaps less responsive to this worship, but the technicians of the bourgeois class are without doubt more strongly infatuated. For them, technology is indeed sacred. They have no rational ground for such a passion for it. They are always flabbergasted when someone asks them why they have this faith. No, they don't expect to be liberated. They ask nothing of technology, and yet they sacrifice themselves and devote their lives frantically to the development of factories and the organization of banks. The "welfare of humanity" and other twaddle are commonplaces which no longer serve as a justification and have nothing to do with the infatuation. Of course they do not believe in a sacred. They smile when the word is spoken, but they fly into a mystic rage when one contests the validity of technology, and from that point on they call down doom on the contesting person.

It could be that the technician performs his techniques because that is his profession, but he creates it adoringly because, for him, it represents the domain of the sacred. No reasons or explanations are involved in his attitude. This somewhat mysterious, yet completely scientific power, which covers the earth with its radio waves, wires and paper, is to the technician an abstract idol which gives him a reason for living, and even joy. One indication, among others, of man's sense of the sacred in technology is the care he takes to treat it with familiarity. It is well known that laughter and humor are frequently a person's reaction in the presence of the sacred. That is true of primitive peoples, but it is also the reason why the first A-bomb was called "Gilda," that the giant cyclotron at Los Alamos was named "Clementine," that batteries are called "water pots" and that radioactive contamination is called a "burn." The technicians at Los Alamos rigorously banned the word "atom" from their vocabulary. All that is significant.

Given its diverse forms, it is not a question of a religion of technology, but rather, of a sense of the sacred, which is expressed differently by different people. In the end it finds expression with everybody as the marvelous instrument of power, linked always with mystery and magic. Whether it be the workman who turns up the volume on his transistor because that gives him a pleasant confirmation of his superiority, or the young snob who hits 125 mph in his Porsche, or the technician who is fascinated by a rise in statistics, whatever their bearing, in any case technology is sacred as the common expression of the power of man. Without it he would feel poor, alone, naked, deprived of his makeup, no longer a hero, a genius, an archangel, which a motor allows him to be at little cost. When all is said and done, technology is for contemporary man that which assures him of his future, and for that reason it is itself the very order of growth.

As a counterpart to this attitude, man sees his origin as always having been *Homo faber*. That throwback of technology into the past, that proclamation that man became man only when he was *faber,* that is, technician, is probably one of the surest marks of this sacred, for it is always in his sacred that man sees his origin. In a world peopled with gods, man is a fallen god who remembers his heavenly past, but in a world peopled with machines the only origin he has is the beginning of techniques. His manner of representing his own starting point, his primal, exclusive characteristic, shows right away where his sacred lies.

With that as his point of departure, he reconstructs his history in terms of technology. There again, the manner of recounting history is indicative of the sacred. It is no longer a history of great heroes, of wars, of charismas and gods. It is a history built up little by little on the progress of techniques. From the standpoint of this origin it couldn't be otherwise! But make no mistake, that is not a secular history. It is a different sacred history. And finally, at the present time all social phenomena are established in relation to technology, whether from serious motives or not.[8] Technology now more often

---

[8] In his admirable little essay, *L'Asphyxie et le Cri* (1971), Jean Onimus, who stresses the explosion of religions among the young, rightly draws attention to a remarkable

arouses apocalyptic ecstasies or visions of the kingdom of God (Alvin Toffler!) than rational reflection. The pseudo-explanatory reactions coming from the technician's trauma are revealing from the very fact of their ecstasy, which discloses the presence of the sacred. But it is a sacred of order, of organization, which commands the respect of the human partner.

Every sacred of respect implies its transgression. It may seem strange and paradoxical that I have presented sex as the sacred of the transgression of technique, strange from two points of view. In the first place, it seems quite obvious that there is no relation between the two phenomena. How can you compare the activity of the creative technician, the servant of a universal mediator, with the activity of a man who has separated sex from the procreative instinct in order to gain from it his own special identity? In the second place, how can you speak today of sex as sacred when sex obviously has been desacralized? Sexual liberty, claimed and achieved, clearly shows that western man, especially the young, have put an end to sexual taboos, have transgressed the prohibitions, have made sexual activity a physiological activity without mystery, one which is normal and free from complexes. People go to bed together the same as they dine together. Alvin Toffler tells us of the young for whom going to bed together is a quick way to get acquainted. In a civilization such as ours, it is necessary to cement human relationships quickly. There isn't time for the subtle

---

characteristic of the religiosity of young people, namely, its technical nature. Not only is all theological substance eliminated, but every element of thought as well. What is sought is a technique for creating an atmosphere of intensity, a community participation, ecstasy, an emptying of the social self. The various yogic practices and Zen Buddhism produce religious effects without speech. They are "ways of breaking through the structures of speech, of liberating the consciousness through the brilliant and decisive assumption of the absurd. . . . We see cults reborn which were thought to be outmoded, such as that of the sun worshipers of the Hawaiian Islands who, naked and fasting, worship the star of the day, or the astonishing cult of Sun-Ra which travels around with its orchestra representing itself as the incarnation of light. . . . Cults compete with one another and are judged by their results. Their followers recount their experiences and make comparisons. Competition is not on the level of ideology but on the level of techniques. As everywhere, the container is in a fair way to replace the content. Method drives out meaning. A set of standardized recipes is about to replace religion. It is a genre composed of drugs, festivals, means of escape, communion and inward renewal." But in reality, this *does not replace* religion. It is itself a religion which has taken on certain characteristics of our technological world and which is being added to the traditional religious techniques.

approach. One makes use of every means for being casual as rapidly as possible, for being *friends*. One means is sex, taken as a point of departure rather than as a fulfillment.

The pill and Freudian desacralization have rendered the sex act and the entire domain of sex meaningless. Here let us take note of an important fact. Desacralization and demythicizing produce insignificance. Loss of the sacred robs actions of their value and meaning. What differentiates the animal act from the human act is precisely the attribution of meaning, for that attribution corresponds to a new organization and hence to a new ordination. Now that is effected only through the sacred. The sex act treated as sacred had a richness and a depth which it apparently no longer possesses. The display in public, the indifference, the ephemeral quality in this sphere are manifestations of desacralization.

Formerly in primitive religions, and recently in bourgeois morality, sex was sacred. The whole system of taboos, of collective judgments, of secrecy show clearly that a sacred dwelt there. It was perhaps the most important sacred of all, for it was from the standpoint of that artificial construct that the profound personality of man was created, together with the social structure. But everything we do today proves beyond the shadow of a doubt that this sacred has disappeared. We are living manifestly in a situation which is profane, indifferent, and without significance, all of which is translated into a sexual life which is barren, a source of keen discouragement, and finally a search for more elaborate sexual techniques to make up for the emptiness of the meaning through the aggravation of the act.

That is doubtless all true, but it seems to me not to be the whole story. We are looking at only one aspect of the phenomenon. If sex is, in fact, desacralized, that means that what was formerly a domain of the sacred, a domain of prohibitions and taboos, has now become a means to the sacred. Our age has resacralized sex instantaneously, in the very act of desacralizing it.

The important thing here is not at all the maintenance of certain traditional aspects of the sexual sacred, referred to by Harvey Cox as vestiges of the past and which he finds symbolized in the importance of *Playboy* and Miss America. That is without interest. It is, rather, that the exacerbated claim to sexual liberty, the publicly flaunted frenzy, is so serious and so fundamental today. This is not just a need to satisfy bottled-up drives, nor an attempt to combat old, out-worn prejudices (sexual morality has been fairly well, if not totally, disintegrated for a century now). The seriousness with which it is taken, the furor aroused by any display of opposition, shows the depth of the problem.

Sex is no longer a natural, free sphere of activity. It is an instrument of strife, a struggle for freedom. Sexual freedom?—not at all. It is a struggle for freedom pure and simple, of which sexual freedom is merely a sign, a concrete manifestation. It is a struggle to declare oneself autonomous and capable of living within oneself. It is a struggle against an order. It isn't a question of desacralizing the sexual domain, but of desacralizing the order by means of sexual transgression.[9]

In May of 1968 I saw in a faculty council room a very significant inscription: "This place has been desacralized. These chairs have been fucked on." Thus sex was a means of destroying the sacred, of transgressing the social order, of which the meeting hall of the mandarins was the high place.

However, like every other transgressing force, it too becomes sacred. Only the sacred can destroy the sacred. Human life is sacred, and so are the assassin, the executioner, the soldier, and the phenomenon of war. The strife over sex has nothing to do with the platitude, "Why make a mystery out of something natural? We should free ourselves from ancestral prejudices." If that were all there were to it, I am reminded that since the eighteenth century the bourgeoisie had a remarkable success to its credit in this matter. The eighteenth and nineteenth centuries were probably the only ones in which, in the bourgeois class, sex was effectively naturalized, physiologized, and stripped of mystery without loss of

---

[9] The success of films like *Decameron I* and *II* depends precisely on the alliance between the erotic and the religious. It is not only the erotic quality which attracts the public, but the fact that the sharp criticism of Christianity through derision is carried out in an erotico-religious complex which is peculiar to religious experience and emotion. That is exactly what the public is looking for. Moreover, this is only one illustration of the well-known fact of the profound connection between the two drives. Quite characteristic of religious thought in this field is the book by Walter Schubart, *Eros et Religion* (French edn., 1971). The author attempts to show that there is continuity between sexual love, love of neighbor, and love of God. Thus, not content to show the relation between eros and religion, which is a given fact, he would also justify it and transform it into an ought-to-be. The knowledge of God begins with erotic love, and religion impoverishes itself as soon as it loses contact with eros or opposes it. This is quite significant of the resurgence of traditional religions (fertility, for example) under cover of modernization in line with scientific knowledge and with the situation of man in a consumer society. That is to say that the desired eros-religion relation expresses the religious need of man, who wants at the same time to take advantage of all that the technological society offers him.

interest! With this result achieved (which it obviously has been in today's youth) one would not expect the strife to continue. But it does continue; evidently that was not the result which was sought.

Those most consciously involved in the movement make it a revolutionary action par excellence. Unfettered sexuality is revolution. They follow Wilhelm Reich rather than Freud. Sex is the means for transforming life. Today's revolution takes place at that level. Everything is so organized as to take in and assimilate the whole of life. All political acts and words are inevitably caught up in it. The conformity is complete. Sex and violence are the only adequate means of freedom.

What we have here is a means, and a means raised to such a height and possessed of such powers and virtues that one is forced to see it as a sacred phenomenon. All the life and activity of the revolutionary is reconstructed around it. He bestows such prestige upon it that the irrational exaltation which results can belong only to the sacred. Anyone who performs a sexual act (even such a modest one as going to see Swedish films), however banal or however deviant the act may be, is looked upon as having achieved something. He has the sense of having shared in a great adventure. Never has sex been so glorified, so exalted, as when it has been made commonplace.

The relation between sexual liberation and the revolution belongs to magic thought (Reich, typically, is a "magician," as is Miller). That is, it is desacralizing and sacred at the same time. The sexual explosion and frenzy of our time is truly Dionysiac—and that is not just a pictorial manner of speaking. The sacred Dionysus is once more in our midst. It is a sacred of transgression, a transgression of the order.

But what is today's order? In the end there is just one order for the entire body social as well as for the individual, namely, technology. That is the great organizer of our times, and we have seen its sacred character. It is in relation to technological order that the sexual explosion is taking place, not in relation to a bourgeois order (which is meaningless) or a "moral" order. Furthermore, the fear of being "caught up in it" is linked to the power of assimilation (not analyzed, but felt, experienced, lived) of the system of technology. If one invokes sex, if one throws oneself into the sexual exaltation, it is in order to break the iron ring of technological organization associated with the vampirizing of man by technology.

Moreover, sex and technology have already been seen as

mutually related. For example, McLuhan has shown how the symbols of sex and of the machine have been fused together by the contemporary mass media (*The Mechanical Bride*, 1957), and this has been taken up again by Baudrillard. But the person who has given us the closest look at this phenomenon is certainly J. Brun (*Le Retour de Dionysos*), when he shows that techniques derive from Eros, and that the machine is an "exo-organism of Dionysus." "The machine today is charged with erotic power because it was already charged with existential power." He has seen clearly the social character of the technological system on the one hand, and on the other hand the association between technology and sexuality stemming from their common origin. However, he probably has not sufficiently stressed the mode of their relationship, namely, this ambiguity of the sacred, of taboo and order, and at the same time of transgression and unleashing.

For this mechanism to work the two have to be of the same nature. The system is no longer "sexual taboos" and "orgiastic festival." It has become more complex, as has all our society, and at the same time it has been universalized and deepened. The system has become "technological order" and "erotic festival," fulfilling the same functions as the former system. Doubtless it could be said that there is a technological frenzy, a technological orgy, but these are not in the domain of the sacred and transgression. They are one aspect of the integration of man. It must never be forgotten that the sacred order is not external, cold, and administrative. It presupposes adoration, communion, abandon, self-dedication, and a glorification of the sacralizing power. There is no sacred order unless there is "devotion," and this is indeed what is signified by the technical vertigo which has laid hold of modern man. He is "devoted" to technique, but the latter is simply the creator of order. Whatever the vertigo, however great the devotion, the order sooner or later becomes intolerable, all the more so because man is implicated in it totally. Hence it has to be broken by some means completely alien to the order, yet similar to it in origin.

That is exactly what is happening. What experiences could be more mutually alien than sex and technology? Yet we have cited major studies which have shown their related origin. That is also why the sexual sacred of transgression is making its appearance in the most technological country. It is not simply a protest of "nature" on the part of crushed and frustrated man. It is a total calling into question, a fundamental rejection of everything derived from technology, which is more abhorrent for being not only powerful but also sacred. Everything connected with it is rejected: consumption, bureaucracy, growth, power, sophistication.

Yet, at the same time and as part of the same movement, those very characteristics are transferred to the sacred of transgression. Sex becomes the manifestation of power. Sexual practices are more and more sophisticated, and sexual consumption becomes excessive. This represents a reciprocity of qualities between the sacred of order and the sacred of transgression. We alluded above (chiefly through Baudrillard) to the sexualization of the technical object. Here we are observing the technicalizing of sex. The game of the sacred appears complete.

We said that the other major axis of today's sacred is that of the nation-state and revolution. The nation-state is the second ordering phenomenon of our society. That and technology are the only two. But we have to consider the nation-state as a complex, not just as the state or as the nation.

That the state is one of the sacred phenomena of this age seems hard to dispute. Here again, I urge the importance of not using the term vaguely or loosely, but in the most strict sense possible, in the light of studies of the sacred by sociologists and ethnologists. The state is the ultimate value which gives everything its meaning. It is a providence of which everything is expected, a supreme power which pronounces truth and justice and has the power of life and death over its members. It is an arbiter which is neither arbitrary nor arbitrated, which declares the law, the supreme objective code on which the whole game of society depends.

Surely the mystery of its power and its share in the sphere of the sacred didn't just happen in our day. It is a commonplace of the sacred that the king should have a sacral origin, charisma, and a legitimate power of life and death. There is no need to stress the libraries of books which have been written on those themes. Yes, political power has always belonged to the sphere of the sacred, has always been a manifestation of the sacred of order and respect.

However, what appears new and strange today is that political power no longer presents the same aspect. It is no longer incarnated in one man, the king. It is abstract. The modern state is a rational, juridic administrative organism with known and analyzed structures and areas of competence. Where is the hidden mystery here? Where will one find the *tremendum* and the *fascinans?* And yet, in the nineteenth century, after the period of the desacralizing determination to reduce the state to its role of management and law, we have seen the sacred rise again irresistibly.

The executioner state is total. It demands every sacrifice and disposes of everything. It is a machine which is both farseeing and blind, a perfect stand-in for the deity. It was not fascism which arbitrarily and stupidly made a sacred out of the state, pasting it onto a different reality for decorative and propaganda purposes. Rather, the other way around, fascism was made possible because the modern state had once again become sacred. More than anything else, more than economic or social conditions, more than class or other struggles, it was the fact of the sacredness of the state which incited and brought about the fascisms. Otherwise, how explain the fact that the Bolshevik state became the same as the fascist state, though it arose out of very different economic situations and ideologies, and had opposing aims? How explain the fact that the modern state structure imposed itself on all the communist nations, and recently on China and Cuba?

That is where the *mystery* of political power is today. In its universality, in its combination of transcendence and proximity, we once again encounter the classic sacred. This was already forecast by a twofold ideological movement during the very period when, through the "enlightenment" and the French Revolution, it was thought that one was advancing gloriously toward an era of the decline of power (liberalism), an era of desacralization (elimination of the charismatic king) and of rationalism (institutions and administration). By the twofold ideological movement I mean Hegel and the anarchists. By the one, the state was seen as the fulfillment of the dialectic of the Idea, from which history gets its meaning. By the other, it was looked upon as the Beast of the Apocalypse, the focal point of all oppression. The frenzied anger of the anarchists toward the state, their blind vengeance against all its agents shows the extent to which it was sacred to them.

Both sides were ahead of their time. The state became sacred again during the war of 1914—the state, let us remember, not the political power, but our state, the god of war and of order. What makes it sacred is not that it sets itself up as God, but the fact that the people accept it, live it, and look upon it as the great ordainer, the supreme and inevitable providence. They expect everything of it, accept its every intention, and inevitably and inexorably think of their lives and of their society in relation to it.

Such is indeed the sacred. Without it our state is *nothing*. No purely rational loyalty suffices for the modern state. It demands more than a reasonable participation on the part of its citizens—for example, at voting time. That would correspond to the aim of the lay state and the legal state. But it is love and devotion which are required. The state is the sacred toward which our utmost in adoration is directed. Am I exaggerating? We shall study the matter in detail in connection with political religions (see Chapter VI).

The state is constantly increasing its demands, together with its areas of competence, so that it can no longer be tolerated except as a mystique—and it is indeed through a mystique that the citizen responds. The more the state asks of the citizen and endangers him, the more he is ground down, the more his response is one of adoration. That is all he can do under the circumstances. This, again, is an obvious sign of the sacred—that which terrifies the most arouses the greatest intensity of awe. But this sacred is incarnate in a human activity, namely, politics.

In contrast, and during the same period, there developed another sacred grandeur, the nation. From the nation as a simple fact in the eighteenth century, there emerged, in the nineteenth century, the nation as an ought-to-be. All peoples must constitute themselves as a nation. It was the era of nationalism, in which peoples enclosed within an empire were under compulsion to liberate themselves, as in the case of the Austro-Hungarian empire. Conversely, peoples separated into principalities should unite to form themselves into a nation, as in Italy and Germany.

Then, in the twentieth century, came the sacred nation (in truth this appeared prematurely and prophetically in France in 1793—albeit temporarily—in the absence of the older sacred order which, however, was not yet dead). The nation today has become the criterion of good and evil. Everything which serves the nation is good. Everything which harms it is evil. Evil becomes good by virtue of the nation. It is good to lie, kill, and deceive for the nation. One's own national spy system is eminently good, while the spy systems of other nations are an absolute evil. The classic values have meaning only through their integration into the national framework. One is reminded of the famous remark of Barrès, to the effect that justice, truth, and beauty existed only as *French* justice, *French* truth. The modifier is more important than the noun, or rather, it takes the place of the noun.

How can we fail to call the nation sacred under these conditions?

The nation is the supereminent truth which gives the values their value. It would be easy to show that it has all the earmarks of the sacred, in particular, irrationality, fascination, provocation, and adoration. It was a common saying that the fatherland is sacred. One talked about the *sacrifice* of the dead in combat without realizing the significance of that concept, for of course the national sacred, like all sacreds, is built on its ration of blood, death, and suffering. It made its appearance at a time when wars, having become national, were wars of wholesale killing, involving huge segments of manpower and resulting in heavy slaughter.

This had to be justified by a grandeur beyond all reason. Only the sacred could gain acceptance for such atrocities. Roger Caillois has clearly demonstrated that *modern* warfare recovered one of the characteristics of primitive tribal wars. War is an "epiphany of the sacred." This had disappeared since Rome, and probably earlier. But, while among primitive peoples war partook of the nature of the sacred of transgression, now it is part of the sacred of order represented by the state and the nation, and it is because it has taken on an all-embracing, terrifying quality that it enlists the people as a whole and becomes everybody's sacrifice. Precisely in that sense is it an epiphany of the sacred.

There is an unbelievable paradox here that almost no one seems to comprehend. It is rationally irreconcilable that a modern state, the organizer of the good, of the great society, of progress, should at the same time express itself through the most horrible butchery. The relation between those two obviously conflicting traits can be explained only if both are expressions of the sacred and are mutually related through the sacred.

Finally, this sacral status will be carried to the summit, to the point of incandescence, through the fusion of the state with the nation to form the nation-state. There is no need here to trace the route by which that came about, nor the reasons for the combination. The fact itself appears certain. In all western countries (including the U.S.S.R. and the United States) the state is taking the nation in hand. It assures the whole of its indispensable services. It combines all the national forces and concentrates them. It resolves all national problems. Conversely, the nation finds its expression only in a powerful state, which is the coordinator if not the centralizer and the orderer. The fusion is complete. Nothing national exists outside the state, and the latter has force and meaning only if it is national.

At the same time that this is a political and economic phenomenon, it is also the fusion of two "sacreds." Their combination produces a power which is unimpeachable. The state is completely justified by the nation's sacred, and the nation is completely glorified by the sacred of the state.

Opposed to this sacred order, however, there necessarily appears the sacred of transgression: revolution. The fact that revolution belongs to the sacred is seen beyond a doubt in the exaltation exhibited by young revolutionaries. In May 1968, for example, nothing was sensible, nothing reasonable, nothing open to discussion. All was explosion, delirium, unreason. The most illogical speeches were listened to as though they were the height of wisdom, all in the name of revolution. The latter is a plunge into chaos, out of which a new, young, and purified society is supposed to emerge. The revolution thus proclaimed as sacred has neither doctrine nor critique. It is obviousness, loyalty, and communion. Those Christians who immediately saw it related to their faith were not mistaken. For some, May 1968 was Pentecost; for others, the beginning of the apocalypse. In both cases, the one of mystic fusion, the other of terror, it was an expression of the sense of the sacred.

The revolutionary talk goes on at its level of incandescence and absurdity. No reason can prevail in the face of this existential loyalty. The revolutionary shuts himself up in a self-consistent universe from which nothing can dislodge him, neither reflection, nor fact, nor experience, nor argument. He is as insensitive to reality as he is to intelligence. He takes his stand within a global discourse which explains everything in a way which is not commensurate with reality but is entirely satisfactory to him. The word "revolution" is the answer to everything. Transition through revolution is the solution to every problem. It is useless to think anything through. Revolution is all that is necessary. To look for content, sense, or plan is completely *blasphemous*. The young revolutionary accepts nothing which might diminish his absolute in the slightest degree.

This social attitude made its appearance at the very moment, historically, when the two sacreds of a political nature were being constituted, the state and the nation. Until that time, revolution was but little spoken of and, in any event, the revolutionary phenomenon showed no mark of the sacred. It is exactly at the moment when the state begins to aspire to the sacred, when the nation becomes the supreme value, that revolution simultaneously takes on an identical aura. That which was decisively constitutive of the modern state, the execution of the king, was the votive and consecrating act of revolution. Then revolution carried through the sacrifice of the founding of the new city. The sacred grandeurs were born together.

But right away they set themselves up as opposed sacreds, the one of order and the other of transgression. Revolution becomes more and more divine and sacred (with an identical face; compare the face of Rude's Marseillaise on the Arc de Triomphe with the face of Revolution at the barricades by Delacroix—it is the same). This happens in proportion as the state demands more and more love. It was normal for the sacred of order to imply devotion, but there is brought about at the same time a rejection which can no longer be anything but execration. Since the state demands love, and can live only by devotional participation, since it presupposes the entire citizenry to be in communion, the struggle against it has to be carried out at the same level; that is, it can no longer be a reasonable contest. It has to be a fierce hatred, an imprecation, which explains the revolutionary speechmaking with its extravagances, its inconsistencies, and its lack of realism. The revolution becomes an affair, no longer of opinion or of doctrine, but of total rejection of the sacred love. From that point on, one is lost in tactics and strategies. The only matters open to question have to do with rites and procedures. The presumed soundness of the movement is a given absolute, since it is a sacred of transgression in opposition to a sacred of respect and loyalty.

The revolutionary movement bears this character of opposition to the sacred within itself. It is an execration of political power in general and of the modern state in particular, but in practical reality it can consist in only a conquest of that power. Here the ambiguity of the sacred comes into full play, and it is because the revolution is sacred that it has this ambiguity. The sacred passes immediately from respect to transgression, from transgression to respect—yet it is the same sacred, as we noted in connection with the Roman *sacer*. Thus revolution, a sacred of transgression, creates an equally fundamental sacred of respect the moment it manages to seize power. It has not changed. There has been no betrayal. It is just that the sacred which gave it its sign has modified the sign.

So, in opposition to the sacred of order of the nation-state, a sacred of transgression is set up, which is revolution. But that entails a certain transformation. Revolution is no longer a separate, isolated act, an apocalyptic explosion in an otherwise cloudless sky. There is no longer *a* revolutionary movement, in contrast to periods of calm lacking in history. Revolution is no longer *an act* of conquest or of the destruction of the power, as a simplistic imagery depicts it. To the degree to which it belongs to the sacred, it is an endemic condition. It is the ongoing sacred of transgression expressing itself through periodic transgressions which we call rebellions.

The rebellion itself is the immediate, momentary, contemporary act of transgression, but it is only that because it takes place within a mythological, universalized revolution. In the eyes of the rebels, this universalized revolution is an irresistible movement of history. The revolt is within a mythical discourse on revolution. Completely meaningful acts of rebellion receive their value solely in relation to the revolutionary sacred, which is not the revolution at all, but a sacred state.

The stress in recent years on the "revolutionary" festival is characteristic of this situation. To say that the "revolution" is a festival is completely false. But if we think of the festival as one of the specific, traditional expressions of the sacred of transgression, then in that sense the statement becomes correct. It is because the revolution is in the domain of the sacred that its periodic expression can be analyzed as a festival. It is not merely a substitute for the missing festivals of former times. It does indeed fulfill the same role and the same vocation, but these are sacred.

Lastly, the final trait reveals to what point that appraisal can be verified. The constantly proclaimed objective in recent years is participation, or self-management. It is characteristic of the relation between the sacred of order and the sacred of transgression that the latter, like the festival, has the purpose of reintegrating man into the order. The order has to be broken, but not for the sake of annihilating it. The purpose is to reinstate it as a sacred and to reincorporate oneself into it. The fact that the revolutionary statement now ends in formulas means precisely that the sacred of order is to be regained, and that it is not a question of doing away with it. The two are not merely contradictory. They *are* contradictory, but in such a way as to be bound to each other, which is what used to be expressed by the *institution* of the festival through the delimitation of the transgression in space and time. That no longer takes place, but insofar as it is a question of the two forms of the sacred, their "contradictory" relationship is expressed by the linkage of the revolutionary requirement of participation (in what?) in the sacred of order, and finally in the nation-state.

Those are the two axes of the modern sacred around which our social world is ordered. Within this social world, myths and religion are developing around the four "poles" of the sacred, as translations and explanations of that sacred. In reality, there are not separate, disjoined elements: a sacred, myths, and then "secular religions." We find, to the contrary, in these secularized societies, the same religious organization as in the traditional societies. There is a system of relationships between the sacred, the myths, and the religions of the social world, which form a coordinated whole.

IV

MODERN MYTHS

1. The Return to Myth

The time has passed for looking at myth serenely, as either legend or, as Littré defined it, "a story related to a time or occurrences which history throws no light on, and containing either a real occurrence transformed into a religious notion, or an occurrence fabricated with the help of an idea." It was calmly affirmed that myth had to do with formal deities, and that it was a way of expressing the relation between those deities and men, whence the historical form in which it is usually found. Whatever the definition, it was something belonging to the past. The gods were dead, and their histories no longer concerned us. The nineteenth century, the century of reason, was free of myths. Only poets (the fakes!) worried about them.

Yet, along came depth psychology, then the sociology of history, to give a new meaning, and consequently a new vigor, to those dust-covered stories repeated in the Greco-Latin mythologies. No longer are they a childish fabrication to color simplistic religion. What we have before us are subtle expressions of profound and complex tendencies in man. The deities brought into play in those myths are no longer merely gods of thunder or of the weather.

They are personalities rich in complex qualities. They take on unexpected dimensions. Kronos and Zeus mask a mystery—a mystery of man. By a strange reversal, what now seems childish is not the imaginary myth but the rationalistic philosophy which called it in question through a failure to understand it. Cicero is seen to be more simplistic than Homer.

The analysis of the myths themselves led to a much deeper understanding of a certain ongoing quality in man, a certain relation of man with the universe, a certain structure of soul. Research was carried out in various directions, but it all came together in a central group composed of Jung, Caillois, Eliade and Dumézil.[1] At the same time it was seen that these myths fulfilled diverse functions, and that one could, for example, distinguish between explanatory, etiological myths (whose purpose was to throw light on a place or a people, or on the origin of a custom or an institution), and ontological myths (which explained some profound, permanent reality of man and which displayed man's reflections about himself). Along this line, it would appear that there was perhaps no other means of expressing those reflections, that from his remote beginnings, man had discovered a special language which alone was suited to his greatest depths and to a direct expression of the inexpressible. Surely we are no longer asking the same questions about the truth of myth. "Myth is seen as sacred history, and therefore as a true history, since it always refers to realities. The cosmogonic myth is 'true' because the

---

[1] See, for example, Jung, *Modern Man in Search of a Soul*; Caillois, *Le Mythe et l'Homme*; Eliade, *Traité d'Histoire des Religions*; Dumézil, *Les Mythes romains*, etc.
We are not involved here in a general analysis of myth, still less in a bibliography, from Caillois to Dournes (*L'Homme et son Mythe*), from Lévi-Strauss to Ricoeur, from Sorel to Bultmann. The range is enormous. It does seem to me assured that myth is not an antique, outmoded expression, attesting the feebleness of nonscientific man. Either it should be treated as an original experience, not to be reduced to any other, designating a project of existence, not as a counteraction to weakness but, to the contrary, as an attestation of man's capacity to take up his project (Dournes)—or else it should be treated as a logical instrument of mediation between contradictions, a means of establishing order in the midst of chaos, to be distinguished from scientific thinking only by the level of reality to which it is applied, and consequently making no sense as a message for life but only as an operative logic (Lévi-Strauss). In both these extreme interpretations of myth, we note its permanence and its contemporaneity. A demythicized universe would be without life. In truth, this universe is unthinkable in the etymological sense!
Finally, on the importance of myth in our society, one can refer to the excellent work of P. Crespi, *La Coscienza mitica. Fenomenologia del sacro in una società in transizione* (1970), in which the analysis checks with my own.

existence of the world is there to prove it. The myth of the origin of
death is likewise 'true' because man's mortality proves it . . ."
(Mircea Eliade, *Aspects du Mythe*, 1963).

That was the first stage. But soon the perception of myth became
more and more basic, and research took off in every direction.
"Myth" was taken as word, a word in process of being born,
explosive; and also as history, as a story, a discourse. From that
standpoint one could indeed, in a certain sense, accept Littré's
dead definition. Yes, myth was seen to be fable, but fable as "a
word at the very center of history, heroic fable and a founder of
civilization. Thus civilization has a basis for existence made more
reliable through the reflection within itself of the myth as a
discourse on origins maintained at the heart of things. That
reflection, in turn, points to a somewhere-else, located outside
human time as an unshakeable guarantee of the reliability of the
civilization" (J. F. Rollin, *Esprit*, 1971). Thus myth was not only a
fundamental expression of man, but also the founder of society, of
civilization. Then there was the series of researches by R. Barthes,
beginning with his *Mythologies*, on myth as language (in the radical
sense in which that term is now understood), and structuralism
generally.

However, these discoveries raised the question of the absence of
myth in our modern world. If it be true that the image expresses
man's permanent drives, and is the founding word of civilization as
well as the justifying word of society, is it really possible that there
should be no myth today? Some answer this by saying that myth is
no longer dominant in the essential sectors of life. But can it be that
man in the first half of the twentieth century lacked reference to the
sacred, to mystery? Manifestly, the twentieth century has only
exorcised such things in appearance, superficially, and precisely in
the area where they don't exist. Moreover, myth is not connected
with belief in formal deities recognized as such. Those are only
presentations, modes of expression, arrows pointing to something
else. Because those formal deities are outmoded is no reason why
myth should not exist.

In fact, it soon becomes clear that myth does exist, but an
understanding of it is no simple matter, and its analysis even less
so. Its domain is poorly defined. Its nature is fugitive, and writers
have heaped up definitions which fail to harmonize with one
another. One of the difficulties certainly stemmed from the
determination to come up with a general definition of myth,
equally valid for Hindu myths, Greco-Roman myths, Semitic

myths, or western myths of the twentieth century. The temptation was indeed great, for if myth is an expression of deep-seated, permanent tendencies, why shouldn't one be able to give it a universal definition? But in being too anxious to generalize, one was led to excessive abstraction, and that deprived myth itself of the very thing which appears most important, its vitality, its capacity to develop, and its forcefulness.

At least three possible trends of "definition" can be seen. According to some, myth is a relation with another world which is inexpressible and unnameable. Thus it is an indirect, oblique way, as though with mirrors, of giving an account of that which cannot be expressed otherwise.[2] For others, it is the expression (pictorially, conceptually, theologically, or juridically) of the major cleavages according to which an institutional system is articulated. Finally, with Lévi-Strauss, one can treat myth as "a sort of bridge providing a logical means of mediating a problematic of culture which man is unable to resolve rationally for lack of sufficient science." It is impossible to do away with the problematic, so it has to be handled in such a way that one can live with it.

One all-embracing definition of myth robs it of just that which makes it a myth. According to this, a myth is the interpretation of a very direct relationship between man and the temporal structure of his life. Outside that relationship his life is dust and absurdity. It doesn't seem to me that any overall definition is possible which would apply equally to our twentieth-century myths and to those of three thousand years ago. I am not in the same situation as man of three thousand years ago. If myth is a mirror of man's reflection, if it is an explanation of man's action, if it is a grasp on and a justification of man's situation *hic et nunc*, if, finally, it is an image of the most mysterious depths of man in confrontation with a given reality, then it cannot, by its very nature, be the same now as then.

---

[2] It is not to be supposed that this concept is bound up with a religious outlook on the part of people who take that line. For example, Lacan offers the following definition (quoted by B. This, *Esprit*, 1971): "Since myth is precisely that which can be defined as giving discursive form to this something not transmittable by the definition of truth, because the definition of truth cannot be based on itself, and because a word constitutes truth to the extent to which it goes ahead by itself, in the domain of truth for example, the word cannot grasp itself or grasp the movement of entry into truth. It can only express it in mythical fashion. It is indeed in this sense that it can be said that, up to a certain point, the content in which the fundamental intersubjective word is concretized as it has been shown to be in the analytical doctrine (the Oedipus complex) has, within the analytical theory, a value of myth."

Myth necessarily appears in specific forms, but its characteristics and reasons are constant and common to all. Since this mode of expression is directly related to its given civilization, it obviously will take whatever form is most suited to man in that civilization. To the very degree to which our civilization is atheistic (not areligious, but simply not recognizing any formal deity to be worshiped as such), myth today will not wear the mask of any active gods, to whom appeal would be made collectively or individually, and for whom the traditional modes of relationship with the divinity are organized. Yet myth always contains an element of belief, of religious belonging, of the irrational, without which it could never express what it is meant to express for man.

Obviously, religious sentiment is capable of focusing on something other than formal deity. If a myth expresses the deep significance of the civilization to which it is bound, if at the same time it is a way for man to integrate himself into that civilization, and perhaps to reduce the tensions between himself and his milieu, then that myth must be related to the nerve center of that natural and social structure, that combination of artifice and givens, in which man is called upon to live. Formerly man was guided in relation to passing time and threatening nature, but that really is no longer the confrontation which haunts man in this century. He has mastered too many things. He is now man alone. What haunts him is his absence of virtue, of certainty concerning himself. Now that natural obstacles are brushed aside, where does his assurance lie? There is nothing to counterbalance his own sovereign action. It is fine to possess the power of the atom, but now to find himself all alone with this thing in his hands, to know that he is responsible for the decisions, with only his own strength to count on—that is an unbearable situation.

Whether the myths be those of reconstituting the environment so that man will not be alone and will be reassured, or whether they be calculated to restore meaning to this adventure by having the past assure the future—in any case, myths are necessarily common to all the people who go to make up this civilization. We might even say that since, as far as the civilization is concerned, all its people are placed in the same situation and face the same question, the image will be revealed to us as myth in the very degree in which it is common to all.

The contemporaneity of myth, its presence in our society, is no longer disputed. Yet there is a tendency to reduce it to a clear sociological function, to rationalize it. Barthes is an example of this when he makes myth the equivalent of Émile Durkheim's "collective representation," a social fixation, a reflection—but a reflection in reverse. "Myth consists in turning the culture back into nature, or at least the social, the cultural, and the ideological into the natural. What is nothing other than a product of the division into classes, with its moral, cultural, and aesthetic sequels, is presented as something to be taken for granted. By means of the mythical reversal, the contingent bases for the assertion become just reasonable good sense . . . in a word, the *doxa* [the lay representation of origin]."

Nothing could be more marvelously hackneyed (for he is merely saying that myth is a justifying system, which quite a number of us have been saying for a long time) and inexact, for he makes no reference to the inescapable content of every myth: the "transcendent" dimension, which brings the cultural right back into the picture. Myth in no way conceals the fact that it is cultural. If Barthes simply claimed to be presenting *one* aspect of myth, that would go without saying. The mistake is in focusing myth on that single function and in explaining it by that alone,[3] not to mention the fact that Barthes himself, for the purposes of his scientific study, follows the myth of the class struggle. We shall come back to that.

However that may be, it is still true that in every critical period of history myths reappear which have as their purpose to assure the maintenance of a certain type of society and to confirm the dominant group in its faith in the system. "The last resort of a certain category of individuals who profit from power and don't want to fall prey to the adversary is to resurrect the discourse on origins and to appropriate it for themselves." But it is just as true to think of myth as G. Sorel does, as a motivating image for the purpose of authorizing revolution and calling the establishment into question.

In any case, and no matter what the sociological substratum, no matter what its use, or the outlook of those who elaborate and transmit it, myth is always explanatory. It explains a situation and

---

[3] Barthes's incomplete grasp legitimizes his method of analysis, which aims at restoring the inversion by breaking up the message into two semantic systems. One is a connoted system with an ideological meaning and the other is a denoted system whose function is to naturalize the class assertion by giving it the most innocent sanction of "natures." That is all well and good if myth is only what Barthes says it is.

a purpose whenever reason is unable to do so, and that characteristic has scarcely changed from the archaic myth to the modern myth. The location and the object of myth have changed, but not its function.

This takes place, of course, in a time of sociological crisis or conflict—which is the point at which reason stops. Science drives myth back, but then immediately recreates it, for science itself raises radical questions which bring back the necessity for myth. Thus, as is the case with the sacred, the domain of myth is shifted. It no longer refers to nature (cosmogony) but to the real problems of the culture of our day. In the face of tragic, threatening, intolerable situations, myth makes it possible to mediate conflicts; for example, "the problematics of culture arising with space exploration, the discovery of the secrets of procreation in a society where ethics are still traditional." "Myth is a palliative which makes the problems of the times livable, and facilitates emotionally the transition to new structures in which man feels more at ease" (Claude Ramnoux).

Problems of the times are brought about through economic growth, through science, through demographic change, through the dissemination of information, so the myths will be related to those situations (not directly, to be sure, but secondarily). Hence their function and meaning have not really changed. In correlation with a given civilization, myth gives expression to the deepest trends.

Myth is not a superstructure in that it is not a mere translation of the material structures. Neither is it an ideological veil thrown over reality to keep it from being seen. Nor is it a summary justification of something felt to be unjust. It is much more than that, and in some ways it is more basic than the material structure itself. In fact, the material structure is nothing in itself. Only as it is reflected in the consciousness of man does it take on importance. Man is situated in relation to this particular economic life, this technological development, this growth of the state. He interprets these, and in so doing gives them significance. More than that, he perceives, perhaps subconsciously, by a reaction of his whole being, the direction of their development, which he wants and fears at the same time. He expresses all this in a myth.

Henceforth the myth is seen both as the stand taken by the human collectivity toward the structures, and as the meaning which it attributes to them. Furthermore, since the economic or political life depends largely on the action of man, the image which he entertains of it and, still more, the image he entertains of the direction of its evolution are of decisive importance for the evolution itself. Myth is seen as the condition of loyalty of the mass of the people to a certain civilization and to its procedures in development or in crisis. It is also an explanation of man's permanence within this civilization.

But of course the myths are themselves influenced by the concrete situation which they, in their turn, are to influence, for the reason that they express in a psychological image the reality of the structures. This explains the fact that the myths, although grafted onto the most profound givens of the individual psyche, can be quite diverse, and vary even in nature, according to the various contexts of civilization. When man is confronted by a radically new situation, new myths appear which have nothing in common with the preceding ones. It is as though there were a new "beginning," which is what is happening today. Another society appears to have chiefly regressive and explanatory myths, whereas our society has progressive and active ones. Yet both are expressions of the same basic tendencies of the individual. It is simply that the individual is situated in a different economic and political context.

In any case, it is quite certain that myths in our western civilization are connected with action, and incite to action. In that sense the definition of myth as "a motivating global image" is certainly the most exact. This myth is indeed a vigorous, highly colored, irrational representation, charged with the entire believing capacity of the individual. It is, for the most part, a subconscious image, because the religious charge which it carries gives it an appearance of obviousness and certitude so fundamental that to become conscious of it is dangerous. Conscious awareness would run the risk of weakening the certitude. The person with a confused sense of it escapes the clarity of seeing the myth as myth. He can continue to take refuge in certitude. It is easy to expose other people's myths and be surprised that they could fall prey to such absurd imaginings, but how we resist an analysis of our own myths!

Finally, myth has to be global. It embraces all the elements of a situation or an action. It furnishes both the explanation and the snythesis, the future and the requirements. The totality of the myth is what counts, not this or that fugitive aspect which might be discounted tomorrow without much damage. Again, it is global because there is no part of the individual to which it is indifferent. Its control is complete. It appeals as well to the reason as to the emotions or the will. Nothing subsists outside its sphere. There is no point which could serve as a fulcrum for criticism. It supplies the entire man with a satisfying image. It is a design which permits of only one interpretation on the part of the person in whom it dwells, and no decisive divergence is possible among those who harbor the same myth.

Nevertheless, at this point we have to distinguish several levels in the construction of myth. Thus, in my view, we have three mythical layers. First, there is the basic line, the subject of the myth itself, the starting point from which the mythical system is organized. Lévi-Strauss has brought this out admirably through a structural comparison of the myths studied in his series of works (*The Raw and the Cooked,* etc.). Second, there are the explicit myths which develop this basic line in a more or less complete discourse. They apply it and illustrate it. Therefore they are rather extensive in their themes and are fairly well elaborated. Third, there are the most superficial elements, a set of formulas, images, ready-made declarations, such as I studied, for example, in *Critique of the New Commonplaces.*

But it is quite superficial to suppose, with R. Barthes, that this last phase, and it alone, constitutes the myth. "Myth can be read in the anonymous pronouncements in the press and in advertising about any heavily purchased article." That is true, but only as a passing, incidental reflection of deeper myth. Barthes's work in *Mythologies* is unsatisfactory. What does the piecemeal currency of myth indicate and signify? When does a mythical account really reveal itself as myth? In any event, it seems to me that the myth is complete only when the three levels are discerned in it, and when they can be related to one another.

It soon becomes apparent that myth presents three qualities. First, it is neither conservative nor revolutionary in its essence. Revolution can be opposed to myth when the latter reflects a situation of domination. On the other hand, revolution can very well produce myth and "introduce it into the course of events as its ghost."

Second, we cannot go on multiplying the phenomena designated as myths. According to some authors, everything is a myth: youth, profit, class struggle, the fatherland, freedom, the university, the state, sociology, enzymes, vacation, the automobile, pollution, etc. It has to be admitted that, generally speaking, there is a semblance of truth in these more or less incoherent statements. What is missing is the effort to show inner coherence. Youth is not, in itself, a myth, but it is part of a mythical system, a totality which is the myth. Therefore, when the mythical character of a given ideological reality comes to light,[4] one has to ask what it is connected with, of what totality it is a part. But, conversely, one has also to ask whether a given concept of truth, accepted as completely assured or as explanatory on the scientific level, may not belong to the category of myth—concepts like class struggle or even scientific objectivity. If it is possible to connect these truths with a mythical system, then we must retain their aspect of mythical truth, but not as truth accounting for reality, nor as a point of departure for explaining everything.

Third, myth is an anonymous discourse. No one is talking to anyone. "When myth is being told, individual auditors receive a message which, strictly speaking, comes from nowhere. That is why it is assigned a supernatural origin" (Lévi-Strauss, *The Raw and the Cooked*). Yet there has to be someone to tell this story which comes from nobody. Someone picks up "the trail of origin." Someone puts himself in the place of no one, yet without destroying the anonymity. From this fact, and it cannot be otherwise, myth is "a word from the origin about the origin, of which no one is the author, but which is addressed to all" (Rollin).

In our century this has taken on a special tonal quality. The anonymous account brought to all by someone, who assimilates himself to the anonymous, is no longer that of yesterday. Anonymity can no longer be assured by ancestral tradition in a society geared to the future and rejecting continuity with the past. The anonymity is now assured by the mass media. The someone who carries the story to all, the someone who is completely known and completely anonymous and is assimilated to the "no one" speaking in the myth, is, par excellence, the television announcer.

That is where we find, not the birth of modern myth, but its guarantee of mythical authenticity. The transformations produced in the modern psyche by the mass media, the disconnected order of the discourse, the reappearance of global mythical thinking, the rejection of rational logic, the instant seizure of the real, etc., that has all been thoroughly shown, demonstrated and explained by Marshall McLuhan. This is surely the best possible refutation of the idea that contemporary man is rational and scientific, and that we are in a demythicized society. Our historic situation involves a recourse to myth. Our means of acting in the world, and on reality, produce myth of themselves. How could we escape it?

---

[4] As is excellently done, for example, by J. F. Rollin for vacation camps and the Club Méditerranée, in "Civilisation Méduse," *Esprit* (1971).

2. What Myth Today?

That which is the deepest, the broadest, and the most decisive, on which every edifice rests, is perhaps also the most passive. It enjoys a greater share in the common belief in group values, and it is less direct in its demand for action. If it didn't exist, myth could not be constructed. It is also the most widely distributed. It dwells in everybody. Again, it is the most durable because it develops along with the structures of civilization. It is coextensive with civilization, and only disappears with it.

Today we could say that the two fundamental myths of modern man are history and science.[5] There is no need to go into a lengthy analysis of their origin and characteristics. That has been done many times. Let us simply consider that they are the bases for all the beliefs, ideologies, actions and feelings of twentieth-century man. History has been transmuted into a value, which makes it the judge of good and evil. "History will judge," said Marshal Pétain, and Nikita Khrushchev declared that history will decide between the U.S.S.R. and the U.S.A., and it will be a judgment of God.

We are here in the presence of a significant mutation. It is known that history traditionally had a sacred meaning. It wasn't a matter of describing events, but of gaining from them an exemplary, meaningful account. History was one of the instruments of myth. Traditionally it had no value except in its integration into a myth. Now we have changed all that. We have secularized history. It now consists in a recounting of events without reference to the eternal, and in a tracing of their unfolding without looking for a meaning. It is desacralized.

But, by an amazing turnabout, at the very moment of the desacralization of history, we see constituted the myth of history.

---

[5] I am in complete agreement with Tillich (*Philosophie de la Religion*, French trans., 1971) in his concept of myth as combining a logical grasp with an aesthetic grasp of the Unconditioned. Myth would lay hold of the true and the real, but at the same time it would account intuitively for the substance of the Unconditioned. It develops necessarily in three directions: the myth of being, the myth of history, and the myth of the absolute idea. The three elements constitute a "triad." The remarkable thing is that if one looks today for that which matches all these characteristics, one necessarily comes up with science and history, which, as ideas, are the only ones claiming to explain being (or origin), history (or salvation), the absolute idea (or fulfillment). The genuine expression of mythical power in our day is in the logical and intuitive grasp of science and history.

No longer is history integrated into a myth. No longer does it serve a sacred. It *is* the meaning, in and of itself. It is no longer referred to the eternal, because it contains within itself the value of the eternal. Perhaps one of the most remarkable general phenomena of our time is that by which the desacralized universe becomes sacred through the very fact of being desacralized.

This new characterization of history explains the lack of harmony, the rupture between history as known, understood, explained, and narrated by the historians (a process which Vayne in *Comment on écrit l'histoire* has admirably elucidated), and the mysterious, grand goddess who inhabits the thinking of contemporary philosophers and the brain of the average person. It is impossible to harmonize the account of historical science, which conveys neither meaning, nor lesson, nor value, nor truth, with the "belief-discourse" about history, which is nothing but that. Thus, when the historian and the philosopher pronounce the word, they are not at all saying the same thing.

To be sure, there is a relationship between myth and history. Myth is always a recounted history, but Vayne has clearly shown the sense in which the account of the historians is nothing but a myth. While the history which is the point of reference for television and the newspapers, which is the atmosphere in which all our reflections are steeped, which modifies our manner of seeing and understanding both morality (relativity of morals) and God (who has become relative to history), is simply a history about man and his destiny, it is at all points a myth. It is a new discourse about origin. It is modern man's way of recapturing his origin and of establishing himself. His life is legitimized by his status in history. He is justified in everything he does, for all is in history. The one vocation is to continue to make history possible. Those are all specific characteristics of myth.

But more than that, there is the problem of meaning. We have said that history of itself has become significant, and that has two sides: it is endowed with meaning and it gives meaning. The second depends on the first. The major problem stems from the fact that history no longer receives meaning from something outside of history: God, truth, freedom, etc. History itself is all-inclusive. Nothing any longer is extra-historical (and that indeed is mythical). Hence it has to get its meaning from itself. The meaning cannot be obtained from a philosophy of history, which would again have an external reference. It can come only from the very structure of history itself.

If history has a structure, then it has a meaning. That is what made dialectical materialism a success. The dialectical movement of history guarantees the meaning. Through it we have the key to man, to his past and to his future, and everything gets its value from that dialectic. There is no need to look elsewhere, because elsewhere, by definition, is not subject to this dialectic, and consequently it could have nothing to do with history. It could not even exist, since it is impossible to conceive of anything existing not subject to history. Conversely, if from its very structure history has an intrinsic meaning, then since everything is inserted into history, everything receives meaning through that insertion—each life, each decision takes on value and truth because it shares in the meaning of history.

This basic myth, this general line which underlies all modern myths, also displays the completely mythical quality of being valid for all degrees of awareness, irrespective of social categories. The philosopher and the journalist, the average person and the member of the proletariat, young and old, white and black, fascist and leftist, everybody and at all levels of intelligence and interpretation, submit without hesitation to this implicit verity, which is both diffuse and conscious, and which has become the *ultima ratio* of the wisdom of our time. How could we refuse to qualify it as a myth?

The second fundamental myth is science. We find the same constituent factors as in the preceding case. On the one hand, there is the transition from a sacred science to a desacralized/desacralizing science. There was science as the preserve of the magi and the cabalists, the secret-sacred whose remains are observed by modern research into the secrets of the Great Pyramid or the Inca civilization. Then is brought to light a method of comprehending and apprehending the real which implies that the real is no longer sacred, and that the method can no longer be secret. From being esoteric, science became exoteric. It was constituted within itself, without reference to the outside, and everything it examined became desacralized.

Following upon this, there came into being a discourse about science, and that is the second aspect. One witnessed an increasing gap between what scientists were doing in their laboratories, the patient research, the cautious conclusions, the abandonment of explanations, the refusal to generalize, the challenging of causalities, mathematical abstraction as a representation and a method— and, on the other hand, the grandiose, grandiloquent discourse about science, such as was heard at the time of sputnik, or of the first landing on the moon. Occasionally a scientist ventures into this area, as Monod *(Chance and Necessity)*, following upon Teilhard and Lecomte du Nouÿ, has unfortunately done. But then the scientist is no longer behaving like a scientist but like any average man who yields to the magnetic attraction of myth.

Specialists are beginning to ask whether, in the last analysis, "scientific discourse might not be understood as the contemporary form of mythical discourse. But how could we, during the time in which it is being written, read the text of science as myth without the risk of reading the truth into it as its cause, instead of knowledge as its end from which it gets its charter?" (P. Boyer). That is just what is done by the discourse about science, which people call science. Lacan gives us a similar warning: "The amazing fecundity of our science needs to be questioned about how it relates to that characteristic by which science would hold up: that she would have nothing to do with the truth as cause."

That may be the way it is with scientists themselves in their work, but it is not at all that way with the exultant glorification of science. There, of course, science has the truth as its content, certitude, principle and end. It is the revealer of ultimate truth. Associated with this faith is the absolute conviction that science's capacity is universal, a belief which is likewise bound up with the mythical. The transmutations, the fabulous adventures, the unrealities which appear normal in myth, and which guarantee its authenticity, have now left fables and dreams to enter this image of science as a domain in which everything is actually possible, so that we can no longer be surprised at anything.

I am not referring to science fiction, where the author and the reader play a game of unreality together, while retaining the question: "After all, why not?" I am thinking rather of rhapsodic works like *Future Shock*, in which the author firmly believes in the reality of what he is writing: all is possible to science. But all is never possible except in the universe of myth. Moreover, the latter, like science itself, has its own strict rules and structure.

This belief in the universal capacity of science is now associated with the faith that science is man's destiny.[6] He lives (and cannot

---

[6] Moreover, one can reflect on the fact that the myth of science ends by turning against science itself. It is in the name of this myth that we now see solid scientic research called in question, and doubt cast on the possibility of indefinite growth. The myth of science assures us of happiness and truth. Science brings none of those benefits, therefore. . . .

live otherwise) in the scientific cosmos. Science discloses his origin,
justifies his present, and assures his future. Of course the scientist's
science does none of that, and doesn't pretend to. But it has such
prestige and produces such magnificent results, it stands for such
great value, that, in generalized global discourse, this can be
brought out only in the form of myth. Science is thought of as
undertaking everything, in conjunction with history. We expect
everything of science, as of an awe-inspiring and benevolent
divinity, which plays a central and mysterious, yet well-known role
in the story which modern humanity is telling itself.

But this mythical discourse compromises science itself, just as, in
a parallel case, it compromises the historian's history. Here we
must consider one of the aspects of the penetration of myth into the
scientific mind itself. Thus, in the sphere of objectivity, Roszak
(The Making of a Counter-Culture) seems to me to be the first to
present the problem *under this aspect:*

> Are we using the word "mythology" illegitimately in
> applying it to objectivity as a state of consciousness? I
> think not. For the myth at its deepest level is that
> collectively created thing which crystallizes the great,
> central values of a culture. It is, so to speak, the
> intercommunications system of culture. If the culture of
> science locates its highest values not in mystic symbol
> or ritual or epic tales of faraway lands and times, but in
> a mode of consciousness, why should we hesitate to call
> this a myth? . . . What is essential here is the conten-
> tion that objective consciousness is emphatically *not*
> some manner of definitive, transcultural development
> whose cogency derives from the fact that it is uniquely
> in touch with the truth.

To the degree, in fact, to which objectivity stems from pure
methodology, then becomes a state of consciousness, an attitude,
an ethic, it becomes a value judgment, an exclusion of every other
mode of apprehending truth. That relation to truth introduces us
into the mythical. But more than that, objectivity presents itself as
a value which synthesizes all science. It is just that to which the
mythical discourse lays claim, in the view of Roszak, with which I
agree.

This myth of science is the other great myth of modern humanity. Its universal reference, which one finds in all the attitudes, all the research, all the recognized certitudes, all the assumed positions, makes it the "profound motif," the arcanum, like history. On those two profound motifs, "belief-images" are constructed, one degree more superficial, in which are interwoven the two major themes of "history-meaning" and "science-salvation." These "belief-images" are the detail of the basic myth, mingled with particular speculations and explanations. We cannot go into them all. They are multiple facets of one and the same reality of common belief. We shall take up class struggle, happiness, progress, and youth.

To speak of class struggle as a belief-image forming part of the collective myth is surely a terrible insult and a profanation. Still, when we try to specify, we are obliged, first of all, to observe that the classes do not exist, at least not in the way one would have them exist. With Marx, one never knows whether the class is a "model," an abstract construct for the purpose of bringing out the movement of history, or whether he supposes that what he is saying about it corresponds exactly to sociological reality. In the latter case, it must be noted that he varies considerably in his appraisal of the structure, the number, and the definition of the classes.

Since that time the situation has grown worse, so that it is impossible to make a valid statement on what a class is, or to segregate the members of the society definitely into classes. To be sure, one can always say that there are the rich and the poor, the exploiters and the exploited, the oppressors and the oppressed. Alas, in saying that, one has indeed affirmed a constant in human history, but that corresponds to nothing that Marx claimed to be saying about the classes. To reduce the class struggle to the conflict between those two groups of people is very satisfying, for it is easy to see what one is talking about, but then one is neither talking about classes nor a class struggle. It is completely useless to employ those terms and to pretend that there is anything whatsoever of the scientific in it.

The conflict between the rich and the poor in no way permits of a scientific explanation of history or of politics. No scientific strategy, nor any rigorous tactic, can be obtained from it. But if one is not talking about that, one is not talking about anything! These classes, in this society, are quite indistinguishable and unclassifiable. It is needless to produce a demonstration which is already at hand.[7] The thinking of Roger Garaudy is simply a final embodiment.

But if there are no classes, how can one speak of the class struggle? How could that be made the focal point, the key to all history and to all politics? Yet, in opposition to this factual attitude, in opposition to this result acquired the hard way through painstaking observation, there is set up a monumental belief, an indisputable dogma, to the effect that everything depends on class struggle. With serene seriousness the best French intellectuals explain language, the economy, political relations, the use of leisure time, pollution, the role of television, the lack of communication, problems of growth in the third world, racism, militarism, and modern music in terms of class struggle. It is the master key which fits everything because it has no form, no substance, no content. Of course, the impregnable fortress of class struggle enables one to defy and bombard the adversary, and the master key makes it possible to disclose why it is that the sociologists have not managed to perceive these much touted social classes.

It all goes together perfectly, too perfectly. The ability to explain everything should put us on our guard. The only thing completely explainable is what man himself manufactures. I know exactly how many squares there are on a chessboard because a craftsman like myself made it. To the very extent to which the class struggle explains everything, I have to suspect it of being a pure concept, fabricated to explain everything.

But it is a pure concept derived directly from the two great mythical structures of science and history. It is a scientific explanation of history. As a pure concept, it lives by a blind, rigidly uncritical belief on the part of the masses of people for whom this class struggle is so certain that it needs no proof or demonstration. It is an assumed fact, and everything that happens, no matter what it is, nourishes that faith. When Georges Sorel spoke of myth, he at least knew that this class struggle had to be carried to the point of myth in order to empower an effective action. We have arrived at that point, but reality escapes us. The myth, by virtue of which one acts, is still there, in all its dreamlike perfection. Such is the situation. How can we fail to characterize it as a "belief-image"?

---

[7] I think I have read seriously just about everything which it is possible to read about the classes and, except for some blindly dogmatic writings, all I have been able to find is a complete skepticism.

The "belief-image" of happiness is likewise founded on science. The recipes for happiness hitherto proposed to man were based on individual experience, on an exercise of the reason or of the body, and almost always, even in the case of Epicurus, on a discipline. What is now being substituted is a collective, materialistic possibility, namely, a happiness guaranteed through scientific progress.

All have a right to it. All are actually promised it. There is no need for any sacrifice, any education, any decision, any responsibility. Happiness is due everybody, and it consists in a growth in collective riches, for this happiness is purely material. Thus what was only a vague dream for the masses and difficult research for intellectuals has completely altered its character in our society. It is a precise image, capable of realization and shared by all.

The myth of happiness is what makes it possible for man to feel that life is worth living. Without that promised happiness, why live? Justice, truth, virtue—all fade into the darkness of vanity before the triumphant conviction that the realization of happiness is the one thing to be taken seriously. All activity should be given over to that exclusive end, and it is impossible to conceive of life and the future except under the auspices of happiness.

Here, again, we note that the myth is gloriously shared by all, and connected by all to scientific development. The sole difference between communists and the bourgeoisie is a disagreement over what means are best suited to furnish man with this plenitude of happiness. The power of the myth is enough to legitimize without hesitation all crimes and all sacrifices. The elimination of the bourgeoisie is all that is needed for the totality of the people to achieve happiness. The nazi officers entering France in 1940 could say, "We are coming to bring you happiness."

Every expression of doubt about this myth, however slight, is enough to cause the doubter to be looked upon as an enemy of mankind. Do you doubt that American civilization, in its orientation toward the achievement of happiness, is justified by that alone? You are "un-American." Do you doubt that the Number 1 problem of the world is hunger? Do you think that the happiness of eating, extended to the masses in India or South America, could be paid for by a higher price than life is worth? You are an enemy of mankind. If you talk like that, you are a bourgeois with a full stomach. This is an assumption of myth which makes it possible to classify as wicked all who do not share it.

That brings us to one of the major mythical aspects of our time:

the "power-image" of progress. This is located at the pivotal point of the two fundamental beliefs—science and history—and it shares as much in the one as in the other. Science cannot but lead us from progress to progress. That myth was born with the explosion of marvels before the bedazzled eyes of nineteenth-century man. Then there is history, which unveils for us the slow, secret, mysterious advance of man, driven, from his origins onward, toward a fulfillment better and better implemented, better and better understood, albeit through hesitations and even retrogressions.

It is a movement of freedom and democracy, from the beginnings of history to its flowering in the nineteenth century. It is a movement of reason, triumphing over the darkness in science itself, as hailed by Auguste Comte. It is a movement of work, which now has reached its point of triumph and its hour of truth in the ceaseless struggle against the exploiter. Those are three examples of one and the same belief in progress, bearing simply on different symbols.

Should the diversity of the symbols have awakened a doubt in the minds of the believers? But precisely because it is concerned with a myth, the mind can entertain no doubt. Otherwise the myth would cease to exist the moment it was called into question, and destitute man would be brought face to face with an agonizing reality. Reference is sometimes made to the belief in progress. That expression is inadequate. There is indeed a belief, but there is more than that. There is an image, both precise and rational, which calls forth the belief and incites to action. It is a rational attitude, because the entire past guarantees this progress, and even the memory of a single lifetime provides unmistakable evidence of the expansion of our means. This simple experience, shared by everybody, should be expressed in one word and must lead us onward toward the future. The past assures us that the movement will continue, and at that point the element of belief is introduced. Teilhard de Chardin is typical of this building operation of the myth of progress, to which he was completely enslaved.

If we are so well equipped in reason and faith, the question has to be asked whether it is at all possible not to share in the belief. This apparently irreversible movement, this characterization of history at our own level—can we refuse to grasp it and to be grasped by it? Such a thing is even less possible as the movement itself is more rapid. No longer is man's progress seen over millennia, but in the course of a single lifetime. How could I escape taking up a position for or against?—and how be against, since progress is inevitable? Here we have the third element of myth, the spur to action.

But myth is also characterized by its extrapolation from what is to what ought to be. The progress we see as being so unmistakable is the progress of machines, of technology, of material means as a whole. The progress of institutions is less certain, and the progress within man himself is probably nonexistent. Neither intelligence nor virtue seems very superior now to what it was four or five thousand years ago. The best we might be able to say is that we know nothing about it.

Now it is precisely the man in the grip of the myth of progress who does know about it. He knows with a certainty that man's progress goes along with progress in things, and that his inventions are proof of his greater intelligence and truth. Indeed it has to be that way, for otherwise the whole thing might turn into a catastrophe. There isn't the slightest doubt in anyone's mind that man today is better, more intelligent, and more suited for self-government than the Athenian of the fifth century. If we project this toward the future, we have the same certitude that the man of tomorrow will have all it takes to resolve the problems we are unable to overcome.

Thus, not only does progress exist, it is also undeniably good. It has improved the human lot and is headed in the direction of the good. What lunacy, therefore, to think to pass judgment on it, or to oppose it! What lunacy and what evil! Myth always makes it possible for the person possessed by it to judge from the height of his certitudes any outside observer. Anyone today who has questions on the subject of progress is the butt of the most bitter and contemptuous judgment, a judgment brought unanimously by those of the right and of the left.

For let us not forget that, by an outworn tradition, we designate the person on the right as a reactionary. He believes in progress as much as the others, only his kinds of progress are different. His is progress toward the spiritual, toward individualism, toward the human. Here again, let us especially not forget that the bourgeois is the initiator of the myth of progress. If, in the name of one of the incarnations of the myth of progress, the person of the left can accuse his adversary of wanting to return to the liberal nineteenth century, the person of the right, in the name of another progress, can accuse communism of wanting to go in for a far worse retrogression toward the integrated society of primitive times.

These are family quarrels. The important thing is to make

history, and that goes by the name of progress. This incarnate act of faith does away with all problems except those relating to means.

History's myth of progress is always accompanied by the myth of youth. Civilizations turned toward the past had the myth of old age. We have surely changed, and that change itself is weighted with profound significance. The sameness of this youth, which is everywhere alike, takes the pungency out of the discourse in its praise. Though rationally based, because youth represents the maximum in working energy, the maximum capacity for progress and the greatest strength for the battle, the myth nevertheless cannot stop at that. It is true that we need the young in the face of superabundant technical progress, for only they can adapt to the endless innovations. It is true that scientific research always calls for a newly trained, hence a young, personnel, and that the need for increased production requires the young even more. Of course. But from that, one passed on solemnly to the well-known tautology that youth is the hope of the future, and in this attitude one is leaning automatically on the myths of progress and happiness.

At this point, I wish we could sense how closely interwoven our myths show themselves to be, and the fact that this is one of the characteristics of all mythology. Myths reinforce one another, explain one another, and together form a unified pattern. The nation is formed by and for youth, and the latter is the driving force of progress. The only true face which can be shown the world is the face of youth. That alone inspires confidence and friendship. A political regime which exhibits such beautiful young people cannot be anything but good. The visage of youth has been displayed the same in *Life, Match*, and the *R.D.A. Revue*,* just as it was displayed the same in the communist magazines, in the nazi magazines, in the fascist magazines, and in American magazines forty years ago. Youth is everywhere the same. It is photographed the same, is used for the same causes, and answers always to the same myth. We were that youth.

Strictly speaking, nothing has happened in two generations to justify the myth. But the myth has no need of material proof in order to grow. Despite the evidence of the facts, the myth of youth is more alive today than ever. The tomorrows filled with song are obviously those of youth. Whenever a problem of civilization seems

---

* Translator's note: *R.D.A. Revue* is the magazine of the German Democratic Republic.

insoluble, a voice is raised to remind us that "youth is coming."
What we cannot do, youth will do.

Youth itself believes this. It conducts its own myth. It spreads
itself, adorned in these images. Poor youth! What a convenient way
to get rid of it, by tying it to its own myth, from which it has no
right to escape! It must fulfill its role. It must carry the burden of
our hopes. It must enter the mold prepared for it. The moment
youth is in bondage to the socio-political structures, it is elevated,
in jest or in compensation, to the level of myth. The elderly declare
that they believe in it, and in fact they really do.

3. Genuine Myths?

The myths we have just described are, in the last analysis, the true
motivating and psychological foundations of our civilization. They
are clearly to be differentiated from ideologies, for they are not,
first and foremost, political nor politicized. They are expressions of
the very being of the collective and universal civilization in which
we are living. In them we see our image and our future. That is
what we want ourselves to be. That is how we think of ourselves. In
the last analysis and limiting ourselves to our own times, there
would not appear to be any myths other than those. Apart from
those great themes, what are called "myths" have scarcely any
validity. Either that term is applied to everything, because sufficiently vague and pretentious to suit the journalistic style, or else
it is an incorrect analysis of contemporary civilization by which we
speak of the Marxist myth, or the liberal myth, or the imperial
myth.

Still, we were saying that there are different levels of analysis.
More exactly, the basic myths which we have just hastily described
condition some lesser images in their turn. Like all the religious
myths of antiquity, these are composed of tertiary myths which
have their own individuality but which exist only through their
reference to the essential myth, of which they are really only facets,
and to which they lend a brilliance, a color, a reality. They provide
the basic myths with a resurgence of vitality, although dependent
upon them for their force. At this level we can enumerate (and each
would require its own explanation) the myth of the machine, those
of hygiene and health, the myth of the bourgeois, those of justice
and peace, that of the actor or star, of the hero, those of oil and of
productivity. There are many others.

Marxism, for example, is a part of these actualizations and illustrations. It is not one of the basic myths of our time, but a secondary image which is much more superficial and temporary. It exists only to the extent to which modern man is radically imbued with the belief-images of work, progress, technology, etc. They are what guarantee its dissemination, and supply it with warmth and passion, the very function of secondary myths. Marxism is nothing more than an expression of these deep-seated forces. Moreover, it gives only partial expression to them, and if it seems more satisfying than any other ideology, that is because it nevertheless expresses them better than any other current formula.

Furthermore, it is quite useless to try to determine how these secondary myths arise or gain circulation. The mechanism of their creation in no way explains their appearance. Their cause, and also the thing which gives them their vigor, is the need to express the basic myths in terms of current reality. The basic myths do not crop up as such in the expression, but (and it is the very nature of myth which requires this) they need to appear always in a new disguise, because the outward tinsel of the myth wears out rapidly and needs to be renewed and freshened up. That is why the description of these spangles, brilliant today and tarnished and discarded tomorrow, is deceiving, because one fails to perceive their lasting inner significance. It has to be agreed that soon what had been taken for myth is just absurd tittle-tattle, in which no one any longer believes. The current situation keeps supplying these endlessly, for the detail is constantly being replaced. That the hygiene myth, based on the myth of progress and youth, should afterward be expressed in terms of soap-equivalents and detergents, that the hero myth, based on those of progress and the fatherland, should be registered in a Johnny Halliday or a Che Guevara— those are only matters of circumstance, occasion, and coincidence. One must pass on quickly to what follows, for the myth cannot long remain fixed in its formal incarnation, to be life-giving for a time, only to become disappointing and commonplace in the end.

But a scruple can come to mind. We should ask ourselves whether, after all is said and done, these collective belief-images we have tried to define are indeed myths in the technical sense of the term. The question is not entirely without interest, given the deep-seated nature of myths and their basic role in human life. If we look at the mode of formation of the foregoing images, we can actually say that this mode is very close to that of myth. However, one cannot really characterize the phenomenon by its mode of formation. Neither does the fact that it is shared by a great many people suffice for treating it as myth. A certain structure, a certain function, a certain signification defines myth. Can we, by comparing these with the ancient myths, discover a relationship after having noted at the beginning the inescapable difference?

First of all, it is clear that myth cannot be private or personal, and that it describes an exemplary, universal action. Over against myth, man cannot but encounter a truth which determines the structure of the real, and also a human behavior. The action expressed in the myth, and the reality disclosed by it and carried to the level of truth, are to be reproduced just as they are incarnated in the hero of the myth. The first set of characteristics is exactly duplicated by the belief-images we described. All show the essential structures of the real revealed to man, not as such, but as truth and treated as truth. They describe actions which are strictly exemplary: work, youth, the pursuit of happiness, revolution, progress, which are quite truly the only givens that in our day inspire "histories" (those myths of detail of which we were speaking) and incarnate themselves in heroes. Every myth, in fact, is incarnated in heroes who speak to all people. Their story is significant and symbolic, universal and exemplary.

In order to know to what degree these belief-images are myths, we need to recall who are the heroes (in the most ancient sense) of our times: the hero of work (the stakhanovit, or the worker), the hero of the nation (the fighting man, the unknown soldier), the hero of the movies (the eternal young lover, the ever new conqueror of love), the hero of science (the obscure scientist, the human guinea pig, the benefactor of humanity), the hero of the revolution. These heroes, who call upon us to imitate them, exactly determine our myths.

In these we will recognize another characteristic of traditional myth, namely, they are addressed to the person as a whole. The myths are assumed by the total man. At one and the same time they are a vision, an image, a representation—then a belief, commanding loyalty of heart and soul to this assured verity of our progress or of our work. Finally they are an idea, a way of thinking and even a doctrine, for is not all this founded upon reason? Ultimately they issue forth in action, and bring man precisely to the active imitation of the heroes. No part of modern man is left neutral or indifferent in these myths, as in the great religious myths at the beginning of history.

Religious? It seems correct to say that one of the chief functions of myth was to make possible the abolition of time and space. More exactly, man in the grip of the anguish of time adhered to a myth which allowed him to master time, and to share in a "glorious time." At first sight it would not appear that our belief-images are of that type, and yet they do play the same role. More than at any other epoch, western man now has an agonized awareness of the passage of time and of the irreversible character of history. Long before Valéry, and without any great thinker's having to become involved in it, nineteenth-century man knew that all destiny was historical. It is to that anguish (and not to the perhaps different one of the Greek and the Semite) that these modern myths respond. It is precisely time which they make it possible to master, and in a sense to abolish.

The myth of progress as man's seizure of history in order to make it serve him is probably the greatest success ever brought off by a myth. The myth of work as an affirmation of man's transcendence and everlastingness in the face of, and in relation to, history; the myth of happiness as the joy of participating in a glorious time, which is outside the time in which we now participate, hence both a reality and a promise at the same time—all that appears to be at the very heart of these creations of the modern consciousness. In truth, it is all simply the mythical response to the person in the new situation.

But that gets us into a complex debate. It is usually assumed that, because man's basic situation has always been the same from his most distant origins, therefore man's reactions must be similar, and the myths created five, six or ten thousand years ago and registered in our most profound depths, remain in us as unchangeable archetypes never to be replaced. At the very most, they might take on some new form provided they retain those mythical precedents. It looks to us now, to the contrary, that over the past one hundred and fifty years there has been such a mutation of the milieu in which man is called upon to live that, for the first time since the beginning of the historical period, the situation has changed. Just as the great mutation of fire and of iron produced its myths, so also the mutation we are experiencing today must be registered in the deepest reality of man in the form of myths appearing as a defense and as an explanation. Thus these myths display the same characteristics as those of the origins of mankind or of the origins of civilization, but they necessarily display new characteristics as well.

Like all myths, they tell us that something has been clearly revealed, that an event has really taken place, one which is decisive for one and all. Like all the myths, they explain to us how that happened. This "how" suffices. It takes the place of a fully satisfying explanation. It replaces the "Why." Myths of work, of progress, of youth have no other rationale, and they are, in fact, in one way or another revealers of a mystery.

Yet it is no longer the same. The origin which these myths are telling us about is no longer the same origin, nor is the event which they are interpreting the same. It is no longer the origin of the world and of man, because that is not a real question for people today. It is no longer the origin of the gods, for the traditional gods are indeed dead. It is no longer the advent of fire, or of the city. The origin, the advent, which enchants and at the same time obsesses them, is the machine, electricity, the dominion over nature, abundance. If myth is always a return to zero, it can certainly be said that it is not always the same zero.

In the western world today, our zero is in the neighborhood of the year 1780, in that marvelous time when all the hidden forces of nature were about to be let loose by a sort of magic, to be placed in the service of man. The myths of work, of progress, of history are constantly telling us how that happened. They are constantly causing us to relive this innovation and to participate in this dawn. This takes the place of the "why," and of all justification. At the same time they are showing us that it was truly an origin and not a fulfillment.

Here we have the difference, perhaps a unique difference, between these myths and those of tradition. The latter involved a return to the past exclusively. Perfection was always to be found in times gone by, and there had been a fall. Our myths, on the other hand, place perfection in the future. The future is the certain fulfillment of the past. Modern myth is what permits us to lay hold of the origin and the fulfillment at the same time. It guarantees the latter by means of the former. It presupposes, much more forcefully than through the past, the total participation of the individual, for it no longer involves him simply in a new beginning, but in an abundance greater than that at the beginning, and one for which each person is in some degree responsible. The projection into the future renders the myth still more active, more compelling, and more satisfying than the primitive myth, all the while guaranteeing an even greater mastery over time.

To be sure, when we speak of a zero point, we do not mean that these modern myths are completely new and cut off from traditional mythical elements. We could easily find mythical precedents for these replacement images. The myth of a lost paradise to be found again at the end of time is very directly related to the myth of progress and to the myth of happiness. The myth of youth most certainly has its roots in the myth of the goddess *Juventas*, who is the bearer of hope and is always sacrificed. The myth of the nation relates to the myths of the founders of cities, and to those of power. But those lines of descent do not enlighten us much, for the real question is not that of possible survivals from traditional myths, but rather, the question of what takes their place in our world. What are today's power-images, whereby the man of today tries to explain himself and in virtue of which he acts? That search, merely sketched here, shows us what it is that conditions man's action today, what he can be absorbed in, the future he pictures to himself, and which could even be our future in fact, since our myths commit us to making it that way.

4. Additional Observations[8]

This analysis, done some time ago, is now confirmed by the enthusiasm of our intellectuals for utopia. The fasion burst into the open in 1968. Sociologists, intellectuals, men of letters, philosophers, politicians, everybody today has recourse to utopia. It is the great cliché which allows one to look as though he were taking the situation seriously into account, without letting it be seen that he is caught in a trap: the leveling society, the totalitarian recycler? the consumer society? one-dimensional man, alienated and turned into an object? Oh, come now! But yes indeed! Luckily we can avoid all that, thanks to utopia. It is an unparalleled project which makes it possible at one stroke to escape the unwieldiness, to avoid seeing the reality with which one has been too happy. It is a project which permits man to overcome obstacles and to ignore the traps. What good would it do to describe in detail this utopian talk, which today is repeated ad nauseam?

Nevertheless, in order to understand how it relates to myth, we have to grasp at least two characteristics of this revival. First, there is quite obviously a certain excess in this utopian thought. It isn't a

---

[8] The preceding pages are, with a few additions, a reproduction of my article "Mythes modernes," which appeared in *Diogène* in 1958. I am adding here three supplementary notes.

matter of repetition, in spite of the new glorification by Fournier. The renewal stems from objective conditions. Goldschmidt (*Platonisme et Pensée contemporaine*, 1970) was able, very skillfully, to write that utopia was now *replaced* by three phenomena: "the transformation of the eschatology of salvation into a belief in historical progress, the ascendancy of technology over the economic and social life, and a third element, which remains properly utopian in as far as it sets desire over against the existing order." According to Goldschmidt, this last element inspires works of the imagination, science fiction, and modern art.

But this splintering does not really bring about a disappearance of utopia. Mannheim and Marcuse both have announced the end of utopia, but in a totally different sense. For Mannheim (*Ideology and Utopia*) it is truly a decline (brought about by realism, scientific thought, etc.). For Marcuse, on the other hand (*La Fin de l'Utopie*, 1968), it is a question of fulfillment. Technology is making possible the consumer society, which, when rationally organized, guarantees man's material life, an egalitarian and democratic administration, etc. What is done away with is the word "utopia," insofar as it designates a project of social transformation which is impossible, because the means are at hand for the realization of these projects. Only a few minor defects still stand in the way (repressive organization and exploitation, which can and will be eliminated by technology).

Thus, on the one hand, technology and science appear as the real, which tends to reduce, if not to eliminate, utopian thought. On the other hand, utopia is open to question when it comes to realization. But "the [utopian] imagination is no longer satisfied with escape fiction. It wants to take over" (Goldschmidt), and it rejects the consumer society and repudiates all the techniques. "The only thing left to them is to subdue the enslaving universe created at all levels by technology."

Thus one finds oneself caught up in a remarkable inconsistency which is eliminated by the utopians (looking, of course, to possible realization) thanks to two procedures. On the one hand, one idealizes technology. One refuses to see it for what it is and reduces it to a wonderful working sketch. One doesn't even bother to describe it at all, but is content merely to invoke it. On the other hand, one omits the intervening period and the how. One passes from the current situation to the situation in which idealized technology will finally function without any drawbacks. This is where the imagination really triumphs, as it "avoids the real and tries to destroy it." But it triumphs by taking a specifically myth-producing step. This is all the more true if we observe, with Goldschmidt, that this movement, which rejects future predictions, long-term planning, and projections, turns to the past in search of analogies. The more the belief in progress asserts itself as an accomplishment, the more it becomes utopian, insofar as it is forced not to take into account the (technical) real to which it owes its substance. It never manages to get into that.

The second characteristic is also marked by inconsistency. Here, following Goldschmidt, we have to rely on the study by Karl Popper (*The Open Society and Its Enemies*, 1966), which distinguishes a "piecemeal social engineering" from a utopian social engineering aimed at a global society, the latter being inapplicable because pretending to a total mutation. Yet regimes like those of Hitler and Stalin have precisely actualized the possibility of this global mutation. However, as Goldschmidt shrewdly observes, if utopia would take reality into account in order to make use of the implementing possibilities, the global utopian technique would be changed into piecemeal engineering—with the frightful result observed in Stalinism and Hitlerism. Nevertheless the conviction of the carrying out of the global utopian technique remains.

In the face of this open possibility, the intellectuals, who are incapable of any effective political action or of any utilization of techniques, exhibit their impotence even more. It is they, and they alone, who are the creators of global "politico-social" systems. Thus they are necessarily thrown back on utopia, which is their way of imagining that they have a grasp of the real (since the utopian technique is capable of realization). The current development of utopian thought is thus exactly the product of the encounter between an observed fact (the total impotence of the intellectual in the current system, combined with his intense desire to play a historic role) and a belief (in the possibility of accomplishment, thanks to the technique of the utopian project).

This effort ends precisely in mythical thinking. It is both a justification of the situation of the intellectual "class" and a pretension to the total, radical, irreversible and unmitigated overthrow of our society. One doesn't go into detail. The more unreal the thinking, the more absolute it can be. That is indeed what characterizes our utopians. They retain the stamp of classic utopia, but with the mythical belief that in this way they are about to change life and transform the world.

So this utopian "thinking" is basically mythical, yet with a substantial difference in comparison with the myths. In this case we have the *intentional* construction of myth. People understand more and more that they cannot survive in the current situation by pretending to overrule fact, except through the mediation of a figure of speech, of a story to be believed as a source of courage and as an excuse to go on. For that reason utopia displays the two faces we discerned in myth. On the one hand, it is a justification of the existing situation and, on the other hand, it is a recourse for man who is unable to change that situation, and who in this way gives himself reasons for continuing to live in it. Utopia is the "Negro spiritual" of modern intellectuals of the West. It is a consolation in the face of slavery, an escape from something one is unable to prevent, a spiritual dimension, a separation of a free intellect from an enslaved body, a reinforcement of faith.

In this case it is faith in man, in history, and in science. The utopian story is rooted in the two great mythical essentials. It exists, one can bring faith to bear on it, only to the extent that it is an outcome of history and is guaranteed by science. Precisely what is important is not utopia as such, which introduces nothing new. It is the phenomenon of the belief of the intellectuals, who are running away in this fashion. The complexity of the modern world is such that (even with the aid of Marxism) one cannot grasp it, analyze it, or comprehend it—so one substitutes the marvelous blueprint of utopia. It is clear and simple, since in it all human relations have finally become comprehensible—thanks to mythical symbolizing.

Confronted with a civilization on which one has ceased to have any hold, which is beyond our capabilities of action, one sets up utopia as a means of action. This makes possible the conviction that one is about to change people's beliefs and thereby to transform the facts. In the midst of a society given over entirely to means, to efficiency, to techniques, a society in which ends have practically no place or value, one goes resolutely for ends. One asserts the radical perfection of the end, and in a crisis situation one invents whatever makes life possible and the crisis tolerable. Utopia allows one to live and to get one's bearings in this present world by escaping from it. Thus it fulfills precisely one of the roles of myth.[9]

---

[9] Do we have to be reminded that all the utopians today are leftists, and even Marxists, very often onetime members of the communist party?—and that nevertheless Marx was not easy on socialist utopians! For him utopia was the height

Formerly, whenever I analyzed the modern myths or the secular religions, I was reproached for "attacking" only the left by taking only leftist beliefs as examples of myth. The same could be said as well in connection with the sacred. There is the sacred of nationalism (it must not be forgotten that nationalism was in fact invented by the left, and that it was constantly the left which, more than the right, asserted its nationalism in crises, in 1871 and in 1940, for example), scientism, eroticism, progress, technology, etc.

In the first edition of *Mythologies*, R. Barthes explained, at length and dogmatically, how it was that the left could not be a creator of myths or, more exactly, why it was that a socialist society could not be productive of myths (and I'm sure he would likewise have insisted that it could not base itself on a sacred). The basis of the demonstration is well known. It is Marx's doctrine of ideology and of the false conscience. I would not be so ingenuous as to present it again here. In a socialist society, the moment there would no longer be a divorce between thought and action, no longer an exploitation of man by man, no longer a rupture between man and nature thanks to a mode of operation which was once again just, there would then be no more false conscience or ideology. Hence there could be neither a sacred nor myths, which are a product of the false conscience, and are a part of ideology. There simply couldn't be.[10] Just like the savant Cosimus, who brought to perfection a bicycle after impeccable calculations. When he was about to fall,

---

of the nonscientific: "As long as the proletariat is not sufficiently developed to constitute a class, as long, consequently, as the proletariat's struggle with the bourgeoisie still lacks a political character, these theorists are nothing but utopians who, as a way of providing for the needs of the oppressed classes, improvise systems and flirt with a science of regeneration" *(The Poverty of Philosophy)*. One could retain exactly that same judgment today, by modifying the premises as follows: when the proletariat is no longer a social class and the political struggle no longer anything but an illusion.

[10] One example, out of hundreds, of this Marxist shame is the following passage from Nizan, "Pour un réalisme socialiste": "All reactionary literature stands in dread of reality. It runs away from it or disguises it. It is the expression of societies with something to hide. It is the very definition of idealism. Revolutionaries have nothing to hide. They keep coming back to reality. . . . The story of Aragon is sufficiently exemplary. It is that of a man who came to realize why there was a literature of the transformation of reality the moment he joined the ranks of those who were really working to transform reality. That is socialist realism" (1935). Those words were written at the time of the Stalinist frenzy, at the time of the most total lie ever perpetrated for the purpose of concealing reality, of the most brazen negation of reality. So revolutionaries have nothing to hide! We have learned, to the contrary, that revolutionaries have much more to hide than anyone else!

he proclaimed that, according to his calculations, he couldn't possibly fall.

So, in view of the politico-social realities of the past half century, we can note without qualification that in the socialist countries and the movements of the left the maximum in myth has been produced and used, and the most conspicuous sacred of our time has been set up. The fact is there. How could it have happened?

That question allows us to introduce some precisions on the subject of myth. We must not deceive ourselves. Myth is not the result of fabrication on the part of the intellectuals or the elite. It is always an expression of the most active force in a society, the force creative of the future. We have seen, however, in accord with a majority of authors, that myth is very often conservative, a means of justifying the status quo. At this point we have to make a distinction between the time of the creation of the myth and the time of its utilization. It is always the social force on the rise which invents the motivating collective images which can be believed and accepted by the mass of the members of a society, because that is always the force which formulates a project. Without a project there is neither a return to an origin nor an explanation of the past. The two factors inevitably go together.

Thus the myths which we easily characterize today as bourgeois date from the era of the bourgeoisie, a revolutionary group trying to seize power and, at the same time, bearing within itself the hope of the oppressed poor. At that time it constituted the entire left. But when it became an established class, when it had set up its privileges and had taken up a defensive position, it used these myths as a means of justification.

Like it or not, there has always been an inability to explain the fact that it is the dominant class which creates the dominant ideology and which imposes it on the dominated classes. How is this imposition accomplished? How could it become an object of faith? Why are the alienated incapable of producing their own ideology? In reality, one has either to think them too stupid or else to rely on simplistic formulas (the dominant class is the one which is productive of dominant ideas, etc.) which explain nothing.

And yet, propaganda has its limits! It has to be noted that, historically, the myths of the bourgeoisie were born during the period of its rise and its conquest of power. We have to realize that the proletariat, the left, created substantial myths during its period of oppression and alienation. It seems to me that Marx's formula should be exactly reversed. It is the dominated class, but in its period of conflict and seizing power, the group which bears society's future, that creates myth. That is the time when belief in myth is possible. It is not the dominant class which can believe in ideologies, and have faith in its own histories, when there is no longer a battle to be fought.

Hence we are forced to conclude that the class on the rise brings with it its myths which are revolutionary. But when it has become dominant,[11] its myths likewise become dominant. At that point it tends to retain its power, so that the myths become conservative and instruments of defense. What is more, those myths had held out a future for the society, but the people who made the promise are now on top. From that point on, by retaining the same myths, they present themselves as the guarantors, the bearers, the fulfillers of the collective hope. Myth becomes the justifier.

However, there is another point to consider. It is also possible for the dominant class to seize upon a myth created by the rising class, in order to give it a new direction and to use it for its own justification (thus leisure is a creation of the left, but it has been transformed into an ideology of the right, with vacations, the *Club Méditerranée*, etc.; there are many other examples).

But it is never the dominant class as such which fabricates, circulates, and believes in myths. Thus it is that, just because it is the bearer of the hopes of the masses and of the future of the society, the left is the great purveyor of myths and of the accompanying political religions. That is not a vice. This is not an accusation. The left is the great religious force of this age. Marxism is the great producer of myths. Still, we have to be aware of the fact and not shift the responsibility when it happens, or say that it is through some mistake or deviation. To the contrary, it is through force of circumstance.

That also means, to be sure, that if the sacred, myth, and religion are what prevent man from coming of age, then it is the left and Marxism which bear that responsibility today.

One final point requires an explanation. It may be that the reader fails to see clearly the relation (or the opposition) between the sacred, treated in the preceding chapter, and myth. Isn't it just a

---

[11] In this connection I have consciously employed the terminology of "class," characteristic of the class struggle. I have done so in order to place myself within the Marxist perspective on the problem, and also because, in my opinion, it is indeed true that classes and the class struggle really existed in the nineteenth century.

matter of the white hat and the hat that is white? Could I not, for example, have referred to the myth of the nation-state, or of sex, or of technology (I did that in an earlier writing through carelessness and error)? Conversely, could I not have spoken of the sacred of history and of science?

Here we have to take into account two points. First, myth can be formulated, developed, believed only in a sacral world. It is one of the expressions of the sacred, one of man's points of reference for getting his bearings in the world. It is a way of inserting himself into the sacred time, into the zone of the sacred, and of explaining and at the same time expressing it. Without a sacred there can be no myth. Without the revolutionary sacred, there can be no utopia.

Wherever a thought-pattern is developed, one can be sure that there is a sacred domain. Therefore one should try to detect this sacred, starting with the myths. From the standpoint of method, one can, in fact, work back from the myths, the known accounts, to the sacred. The reverse route is impossible. Behind and beyond the myths one discerns the sacred of which they are an expression. It is by a kind of geography of the myths that one can discover the axes of the sacral world.

With regard to distinguishing between them, it seems to me that one could work that out on the following basis, and this is my second observation. The sacred is a qualification attributed to a completely tangible reality. This tree, that spring are sacred. The organization of the sacral world is an organization of the actual world in which man lives. Myth, on the other hand, is a fictive statement about a reality in connection with a given portion of that world. Hence the sacred keeps man constantly at the level of the real, whereas myth leads him into a fictive universe. The myth of history or of science is completely different from the sacred attributed to sex or to revolution.

In the extreme case, one might conceive of all the real as located in the sacral world, in the sense that each element in it has its proper place in relation to the great axes of the sacral domains. Likewise, on the other hand, *everything* could become the object of mythical discourse, which would be an expression of the sacred while, at the same time, fulfilling the specific function examined above. This is a function, moreover, which it could not at all fulfill were it not for the fact that the inventive and believing minds had previously been immersed in the sacral and sacralized universe.

V

SECULAR RELIGIONS:
Current Religious Attitudes[1]

1. How Put the Question?

We must come to an understanding. What are we saying when we speak of religion? The remarkable thing is the constant oscillation between two convictions, of which the first is radically false but never avowed, while the second is a mere hypothesis treated as though it were an undisputed fact.

On the one hand, we witness the endless confusion between Christianity and religion. Modern "areligious Christianity" has not improved a thing. The fact is that, in times past, one expounded Christianity, for apologetic purposes, as the most advanced of all religions, as superior, as "the pinnacle of religions." This was carried to the point of the conviction that Christianity was "the" religion. What conclusion does that lead to, now that the intellectuals are asserting vigorously that Christianity is the opposite of

---

[1] Let us remember that the expression "secular religions" and the corresponding analysis were in the first instance the work of Raymond Aron in 1943. Many have used it since without going back to the source.

religion, that it is areligious? All it says is that modern man has ceased to be religious, since he is no longer Christian. The two go together. In a pinch it was acknowledged that man had known other religions, such as Islam, Judaism, and one now adds Buddhism. But we note that the great traditional religions are on the decline, at least in power and authenticity if not in membership (it is common knowledge that Islam is on the increase). That confirms us in our conviction. Once again, we must remember that every theory of modern areligious man is based solely on this assimilation of Christianity with religion.

The proof that Christianity is not a religion, that it is the very opposite to a religion, has become a *leitmotif.* The Bible teaches us that there is an irreducible opposition between God's revelation about himself and man's elaboration of religion to satisfy his own needs, his religious instinct. However that may be, it is sociologically interesting to observe that the very philosophers and theologians who maintain, on the one hand, that Christianity is not a religion declare, on the other hand, that modern man is not religious. Their one and only proof for this is that modern man is no longer Christian. So, in their subconscious, they are giving unswerving obedience to the basic Christianity/religion link.

Doubtless one knows very well that there are also other religions: the ancient pagan religions, now over and done with, the surviving African, Indian, and Melanesian religions—but that seems of little importance, and the surviving ones are due to disappear. The fact of the matter is, as I wrote elsewhere, "We are faced with a sort of intellectual paralysis which prevents our escape from the former categories. The moment modern man ceases to be Christian without turning to Buddhism, he must be religionless."

Contrary to this stance (which is certainly unconscious) there was another, the naturalist stance. This held that man is by nature a religious animal. The signs of this religious attitude on man's part are evident historically from the very beginning. No nonreligious civilization has ever been known. Religion appears to be an expression of man's nature, springing from the very depths of his being. For a long time, Christianity made use of this opinion or hypothesis as an apologetic argument (man a religious animal, Christianity the peak of religious evolution, therefore . . .).

Today that conviction has few adherents. One is disconcerted to see that this religious evolution is not continuing along traditional lines, and a lack of imagination fails to discern its appearance under new forms. But there is also a conformity to an overall change of outlook. We are no longer interested in *Homo religiosus,* nor even in *Homo sapiens.* Our interest, is, rather, in *Homo faber.* The moment we are no longer interested in *Homo religiosus,* as a result of sociological conditioning, *Homo* is no longer *religiosus.* In any event, it was merely a matter of an uncertain characterization changing with the changing mode.

While all this throws light on the convictions of modern intellectuals, it tells us nothing about what is meant when we pronounce the word "religion." If we give up defining religion by the traditional content of the term, can we fall back on etymology? That would be to adopt too narrow and unsure a view. Actually, religious phenomena have been designated in different societies by terms whose etymologies do not refer to the same essential data. When we depend simply on the Latin word *religio,* there are, as is known, several possible etymologies (*religare* and *relegere*), with an assortment of meanings for each.[2] So that is not the right course to take. As far as encyclopedic definitions go, that of Littré or that of Robert, they all lapse into a limited view of history. We could multiply definitions without accomplishing very much.

Do we have to be reminded of the controversy between Romain Rolland and Freud? For the former, the source of religiousness is "the sense of the infinite and of eternity"; while the latter declares that he never knew anything of the kind. Freud's theses are well known. God, the heavenly and almighty Father (note that, like all the others, Freud falls into identifying religion with Christianity), is simply the projection, in fantasy, of a real father, answering to the desire of the child to be protected from danger and to have his anguish assuaged. With regard to the sense of the infinite, it is the sense of the almightiness of the I, and that is not the true source of religion. The latter is a consoling illusion which makes life possible and gives us an escape from its unhappiness. "The idea of giving life a goal exists only in terms of a religious system." This goal of life is happiness.

In *The Future of an Illusion,* Freud does not go much beyond Feuerbach and Marx. He pursues, I think justifiably, not a definition of religion, except very superficially, but rather a determination of its usefulness to man. The theologians also come back to this functional definition. For example, religion is "the complex ensemble of operations aimed at reducing a distance

---

[2] The entire etymological problem has been admirably set forth by E. Benveniste: *Indo-European Language and Society* (1973).

between earth and heaven, time and eternity, the finite and the infinite, impurity and purity, the limited and the unlimited . . . operations of prayer, of sacrifice, of worship" (G. Crespy). "Religion appears the moment people accept the existence of forces or persons free of the limitations we experience: inadequacy, the shortness of life, localization in space, the agony of death. . . ." [3]

All that is certainly correct, but it scarcely throws any light on the yes-or-no question whether or not modern man is areligious. Crespy will say, on the one hand, "In a certain sense religion is part of man's nature (to the extent that he is a nature), for it is based upon the discovery of impotence, of a weakness, of an irremediable failure to be." Yet he also writes, on the other hand, that "religion's power is due to man's weakness, to his lack, and the question is whether that lack if incidental or basic." The mere fact of his putting the question shows that, for Crespy, the situation is not "irremediable," and this is precisely the conviction of all who proclaim that modern man is no longer religious. He has no need to be, because his state of weakness is over and done with. He has become strong. He has taken his destiny into his own hands, thanks to science and technology.

I will confine myself to two observations on the subject. First,

---

[3] I would be very close to accepting the definition of religion through the Unconditioned, in Tillich. If religion is an orientation toward the Unconditioned, which is not one particular reality among others but the depth-dimension possessed by all reality (or again, the ground of being), then it is indeed true that religion is not only in the culture but in All. If I do not hold to that definition, it is because it strikes me as too all-inclusive, and as failing to take into account the specifics of the religious.

There are, in any event, three possible approaches. Must we confine religion to the person who, because he has a religious mind, is capable of discerning this Unconditioned?—or is there objectively an Unconditioned in everything?—or, finally, is there religion whenever a given exceptional reality lays claim to the Unconditioned? Tillich does not seem to me to make this clear (for example in *Philosophie de la Religion*, French trans., 1971).

I'm quite prepared to accept Tillich's statement that one cannot discover the essence of religion from the starting point of experience, that sociological or historical study is not the thing which will teach us what it is. However, the concept of the Unconditioned seems to be too broad, and necessarily too arbitrary, even if Tillich limits it afterward by saying that one cannot find the Unconditioned anywhere except in religious acts. How define all those acts as such?

Without doubt Tillich is right to affirm the union of religion with culture, by reason of their orientation toward the complete unity of the forms of signification, but he ends in a demonstration of religious universalism. Unbelief is then merely an attitude, and is that solely in its intention. Every cultural act is really a believing

what we have in all this is a fairly simplistic and limited view of "religion." Its functions are reduced to a schema which is difficult to accept. Afterward, without knowing where to look, one is going in search of the scientific-technical triumphalism, which declares that man's weakness is over and done with—as though, to the contrary, we didn't find ourselves plunged, thanks to science and technology, into difficulties, problems and agonies, and subject to stresses and maladjustments, which give triumphant man a sense of panic and helplessness in the presence of new fates which he himself has unleashed.[4]

In order to try to understand the current situation, it appears necessary to go back to the traditional functions fulfilled by the recognized religions, with the forms and the mental attitudes adopted.[5] Feuerbach had seen the situation correctly. Thus we can discern several factors. On the one hand, religion works on fear, on anguish, on finitude. It provides consolation, hope, and an ability to override limitations. Through religion man ceases to be limited. He no longer loses forever those who are dear to him. He is bound to them, and to his own life, by ties that do not depend on him, on his weakness. He receives a set of guarantees and securities.

---

act. It is impregnated with the signification of the Unconditioned. Otherwise it would ultimately be devoid of meaning and substance. One comes right back to the attitude, which is all too familiar and too facile, according to which the unbeliever is religious without knowing it.

That is why I do not hold to Tillich's concept. It finds the religious everywhere, and the question put to us by contemporary society, and which the intellectuals put to themselves, is resolved by a too simple metaphysical formula. The question is in fact voided, without anything being explained, and without our having made any progress.

On the other hand, if I confine the Unconditioned to "that which presents itself as . . . ," then that formula reinforces my analysis, because in our day science, the state, technology, for example, each asserts itself as the Unconditioned. But, though this is true, it is really too facile to allow us to conclude their religious character on that basis.

Finally, the last criticism I would direct at Tillich in this area is that, quite obviously, he still confuses Christianity with religion.

[4] Very interesting in this connection is the book by Alvin Toffler, *Future Shock*, in view of the fact that this fanatic admirer of science and technology keeps coming back to the idea that thereby man is put through a (medical) test, a "shock," an agony, which until now far surpasses his ability to live and adapt. In that context the modern religious renewal is to be found.

[5] Mircea Eliade's admirable *Traité d'Histoire des Religions* (1955) is useful for this analysis. To this should be added H. Sunden, *Die Religion und die Rollen (Eine psychologische Untersuchung der Frömmigkeit*, 1966); also P. Chalus, *L'Homme et la Religion; recherches sur les sources psychologiques des croyances* (1963).

These guarantees not only operate in connection with the present, but also in connection with the future. Every religion is both an attempt to influence the future and a prediction of what must take place. By reason of that knowledge, of those certitudes and consolations, religion is an inexhaustible movement (which one could call dialectical, if he so wished) of anguish and comfort.

But the comfort, in its turn, generates anguish, since the powers to which one appeals for comfort are never either completely known or fully mastered. So religion brings about another crisis, that of "responsibility." The religious person feels himself vaguely responsible for tragedies and disasters. If he had been in full accord with the gods, nothing of the sort would have happened, since the gods are the very ones who protect from those dangers.

It has often been said in recent years that it was Christianity which weighed man down with the sense of sin and crushed him under the load of an unlimited responsibility. That is incredibly ridiculous, yet, alas, many Christians today accept it as a legitimate charge. Before Christianity ever entered the picture, there never was a joyful pagan, happy to be alive, completely naïve, innocent and free from guilt. It is true that there have been a variety of religious points of view, but most of them are oppressive, and have man living in terror. As far as guilt is concerned, Christianity merely altered the content.

In another aspect, religion can be characterized by the creation of a global interpretation of the world and of life. There is no religion without an attempt at an explanation. This is not at all systematic in nature. It does not play an intellectual role. On this point there has frequently been misunderstanding. Whenever we are confronted with the famous three stages of man, in which science as an explanation of the world should replace religion, which is a *less good* explanation, the mistake is made of placing the two on the same plane. The global explanation, the schema, provided by religion does not have an intellectual purpose. It is to enable man to "get his bearings." Man cannot live in an insane, illogical universe. Things have to make sense. This can be fictitious as long as some sense is there. Religion depicts a history, and supplies a view of the world whereby man can locate himself. Thanks to it, he has points of reference for living and acting.

Thus religion has an existential and pragmatic aim. That is why science as such, and to the extent that it really remains science, cannot take the place of religion, for it does not fulfill that function. It is at this point, of course, that religion links up with mythical thinking, expresses itself through it, and becomes rooted in it. Mythical thinking is part of the religious phenomenon generally considered.

Finally, we can add to this summary analysis the factor of ritual. The decisive importance of rites is well known: their realism, their meaning—hymns, prayers, liturgies, incense, vestments, sacrifices, lights. The purpose is to establish communal ties and to relate man to the universe so that he can find his place in the human situation and can better assume it.[6] Those relationships can be directed in richly varied ways. Specific types can be isolated (fertility, maintenance of the creation, duplication of the origin, etc.), but if, in their variety, we expose the rites as such, we find elements and objectives which are identical.

The anguish/comfort dialectic is usually referred to a more or less transcendent deity, and the same is true of myths and rites. Consequently, it can be said that the god is a very important element in religion, but he is not at all the decisive factor. Buddhism is certainly a religion, although Buddha is not a god. In other words, religion is an ensemble of inventions, languages, and practices corresponding to hitherto irrepressible human needs, and leading to a certain attitude.

One of the basic characteristics of this attitude is irrationality. The religious person doesn't reason according to reason, but in nonrational ways. He interprets his life and events irrationally. He falls back on undemonstrated beliefs. He puts his trust in words, in persons, and does not confine himself to verifiable experience. He looks for "whys," for the most part imaginary, and he creates "hows" in an unreal way. He remains imperturbable in the irrationality of his convictions, in spite of contrary proofs which have no effect upon him. He has more confidence in a global interpretive system than in the accumulation of sure proofs. He takes up a position in a fortress of assured, interrelated, and mutually reinforcing dogmas, rather than in the open field of uncertainties and research. That is his irrationality.

However, if we have grasped the fact that man's religious imagination simply could not live in a universe with which it could not deal, and which was both incomprehensible and foreign to it, we can be sure that this irrationality was indispensable. Without it, religion could not have played its essential role. It could not remain

---

[6] See J. Cazeneuve's indispensable book, *Sociologie du Rite* (1971).

uncertain, hazy, wavering. It had to provide certainties, and in that period of human history it could only have been irrational.

That brings us to the question: in our day, when we are dealing with the universe concretely, are explaining a very large portion of its phenomena, are grasping the "how" of many events, does man's religious drive, or religious need, have any substance, or any reason for existence? Does religion still have a role to play? Does man still have an anguish, and myths, which bring him to religion? We know that most theologians today answer No to those questions, but this is not an affair of theologians!

Quite obviously, religions are fulfilling the same functions as formerly. It is a case of a response to the loneliness severely felt by modern man, of a refuge from the panic and agonies of our situation in contemporary society, of compensating for science's failure to resolve everything, of establishing artificial points of reference, because the natural ones have disappeared.

It is true that, *logically*, the progress of science and technology should have had the expected happy result, but in such matters logic doesn't mean much! After an appearance of rationality, coupled with an obvious indifference to Christianity and heightened by the rationalism of the nineteenth century, we have witnessed for a half century now a prodigious resurgence of religions. But they are no longer the same. In evaluating this, I see no need to examine whether the religious sense and need still exist, or whether there is a persistence of the religious in man. For me, that belongs to metaphysics or psychology. It seems to me lacking in certainty, dubious, and always open to dispute. I would rather confine myself to the observation of concrete, still observable phenomena.

There is another function of religion, too easily neglected today, which must not be forgotten. Religions have always *peopled* the world. Man found himself alone on earth. No animal came to his aid, answered him, or was like him; and woman was so quickly assimilated to him in a common situation that she no longer was the Other, with whom he might have endless, mysterious, and comprehensible dialogue to break the loneliness, the wandering, the unknown. Man found himself alone in the world, and he could not stand that situation. He had to have a vis-à-vis, a face-to-face, another, like himself and yet different—another to people this foreign and hostile nature—another to take him in and finally to provide validity and a possibility of peace, because he has finally been understood.

So religion peopled the world with gods and powers, with spirits and demons, with angels and with genii. These are mysteries, but they are accessible mysteries, whereby man need no longer be obscure to himself. Centaurs, satyrs, and fauns are not childish fables. Who is going to enable man to have dialogue with nature? Who will help him go beyond the visible, where his understanding lies? Didn't he need a look from without to give him an understanding of himself? To these spirits, whom he welcomed, he made himself transparent. By peopling the world, they for their part made it transparent and similar to him.

From time to time, to be sure, thinkers in highly developed societies courageously rejected this new peopling. But immediately, as though by some invincible force, by some superhuman abhorrence, man was driven to re-deify that which had served to deny the gods, and the world around him ultimately repeopled itself. Except in the case of individuals, there is no instance in which human groups have not wanted, at any cost, to populate the world by someone other than man, someone who could make answer to a continuing discourse.

It is absolutely essential to understand that we are here in the presence of a need, of a necessity, which man cannot put down. If nature abhors a vacuum, man abhors nature's vacuum even more. May we be spared the feeble explanation of anthropomorphism. We are far beyond that. Here is man in his new milieu, in our modern society, feeling alone all over again, and without a respondent. He directs at the empty sky a discourse without dialogue. He embraces things, which are never anything but objects. He is living anew the horror of silence and incompleteness. The "horizontal relationship" fails to satisfy him.

The stoic statement, that it is all a matter of helping others live, is good enough for some philosopher, but the ordinary person will say: "How about me? Who is going to help me live—the person next to me? What could he say to me that I don't already know? He's too much like myself. I know what I can expect of him, which is nothing different from what I could expect of myself . . . , unless indeed he's a guru, a sorcerer, a fortuneteller or a priest. A person like that would be in contact with the unknowable that I hesitate to name. He could be a mediator for me."

Modern man in these grandiose cities, in these feverish exchanges, in the continual chatter of radio and television, knows the human wasteland perhaps as never before. The chatter has no more meaning for him than the swarming of insects or the chirping, on every note, of millions of birds in a tropical forest. The human wasteland of the big city or the highway is even more disquieting and oppressive because new questions without number come to the lips of modern man and arise in his heart. There is no one to give him an answer. How can he talk with a computer?

So, in this new solitude, which there is no need to describe after *The Lonely Crowd*, in this new confinement, man looks everywhere for someone who will tell him the truth, someone who will enter into a meaningful relationship. In so doing, he duplicates the old traditional movement. He has to people his wasteland with new genii and new superpowers, with mysterious beings from beyond the cosmos, from those otherworldly places which are the joy of science fiction, of *Planète* [a science fiction magazine], and now of pseudo-scientific studies. The situation is the same as at the beginning. The need is the same one our distant ancestors knew. It is the same specifically religious attitude, leading to similar, though not identical, explanations. The heavens studded with antennae and spewing smoke are the same whence comes our hope.

In the tumultuous ferment of the metropolis, man makes up for the absence of any serious relation with others by creating secret micro-groups of election and mystery, in which there is a sharing, a communion and exchange in secret and trembling, together with drugs and novel sex experiences, adoration, incense, and rituals. All this is in expectation of seeing the moment when the one who peoples this world will appear, who is ceaselessly invoked, who will speak.

Without the slightest intention of falling back on the idea that religion is inherent in man's nature, without basing anything at all on a nature in man, we can at least note that religion has always fulfilled an essential function, and we can raise the question whether, in that case, it is not inexhaustibly renewed. Religion is not an "ideology" in the Marxist sense, nor is it a gratuitous and superficial activity. Since it is a collective expression and manifestation, it is obviously sociological, but to see it merely as a "historical stage of humanity" or as a "reflection-cloak-justification" of man's actual condition is childish. Religion has the most profound and seemingly ineradicable roots in the very being of man. Experience shows it to be ineradicable, because the greatest attempts to destroy religion only result in a new religiousness.

Let us recall that Buddhism presents the most astonishing problem in this connection. There is a lot of easy talk nowadays of an "atheistic religion," but it would indeed appear that Buddhism, in the beginning, was not a religion. It has to do with a meditation on life, and with the establishment of a norm of life, not only without reference to God, but also without any concession to religion—or rather, as Panikkar correctly put it: "The elimination of the name of God is for Buddha the religious step par excellence." The remarkable thing is that, "while excluding the existence, the essence, the name and the reality of God, Jainism and Buddhism very soon become authentic religions." [7] The religionizing power is so strong that Christianity (which I am deeply convinced is antireligious) is finally engulfed and is progressively transformed into a religion. Then the movement of scientific rationalism, extended by Marxist, materialistic rationalism, winds up recreating the religious in the world. Religion even inserts itself into militant atheism. Marx, in his famous passage in *German Ideology*, longed to see the disappearance of atheism at the same time as that of religion. Moreover, it is common knowledge that, in his view, Voltaire's anti-Christianity was nothing but a form of religion.

I certainly am not prepared to say that man is forever bound to religion. Yet, up to the present, nothing permits us to say the opposite. To the contrary, everything tends to show that the mechanism of religious creation makes use of enormously multiple elements, and sometimes those which are the most antireligious.

But of course, religion is not an isolated phenomenon, a sort of object to be considered in itself (which it is when reduced to rituals, practices, and beliefs). It is bound up with the whole of a person's life, a whole for which it sets out to provide meaning. To the extent that this life is inserted into the sacral world, religion appears, sociologically, as a "translation-betrayal" of the person's participation in the sacred (if we grant the existence of an objective sacred), or of the person's sacral experience (if we believe that the sacred exists only in the person).

---

[7] On this whole problem, see the excellent studies by R. Panikkar: *El silencio del Dios* (1969); "Le Silence de la Parole," in *Analyse du Langage théologique* (1969). On the difference between the Buddhism of the people and the Buddhism of the monks, and on disciplines of salvation by the renouncers, see Louis Dumont, *Homo hierarchicus* (1966), and the bibliography he provides on the subject. Louis Dumont is surely right in showing that the salvation disciplines are part of the "religious ensemble."

2. Expressions and Signs of the Religions of the Modern Western World

The first order of facts concerns religious expressions (i.e., corresponding to the actuality of religion) of a more or less spontaneous kind. We shall limit ourselves to an enumeration of the patent signs, without getting into the study which each of these indications would merit.

To take the most external, there are, for example, in the neighborhood of three thousand soothsayers, fakirs, fortunetellers, etc., in Paris.[8] Each has a clientele of one hundred and fifty persons at the least. That means that there are four hundred and fifty thousand adult Parisians, and probably a lot more, who consult fortunetellers. Obviously, that is not indicative of the whole of their lives, but when a religious pagan consulted the Pythian oracle, that was not an act of his whole life either. The two are the same.

Similarly, in all the newspapers it is the daily horoscope which is the most read. All the newspaper polls give the same result. They indicate that at least ten million French people follow the horoscopes. After a broadcast on extraterrestrial phenomena in September 1972, thousands of telephone calls came into the television station.

The purchase of amulets is also very significant, the more so since these can have no value as secret power in view of their mass production. The statuette of a Hindu goddess, mass produced in France, has no supernatural power. Yet a great many people buy it (by mail order) and express their satisfaction with it. The directress of the enterprise tells (on television) that she sells for one hundred twenty francs an object which costs her twenty francs. The result is a gross of a billion a year. In the face of such figures, we have to acknowledge that this is no small matter. It is a superstition involving several million French!

As Caillois rightly observes, there always was a department in the large stores where statues of the Virgin and pious medals were sold. Now it is medals with signs of the zodiac (but St. Christopher

---

[8] The growth is obviously difficult to follow precisely. A. Larue estimates that there are in France about three thousand visionaries (only), of which five hundred are in Paris. But there are soothsayers, astrologers, fortunetellers, chiromancers, etc., which gives us the figure of three thousand for Paris. The price of a consultation ranges from thirty to two hundred francs.

continues to have the usual success in spite of his obvious ineffectiveness on the highway). The superstitious element of religion has shifted toward astrology, palmistry, talismans, etc., according to Caillois; but I think there is no religion without superstition, and the latter always remains one of the outward signs of the religious mentality.

The incredible success of the *Planète* movement is of the same kind. Here we are on a higher level intellectually. But what is significant is the entrance into the mysterious, and the desire to proceed to a synthesis between the scientific and the "spiritual"— transplanetary phenomena, spirits, metapsychism, survival, etc. We find in *Planète* all the themes of the most ancient religious superstitions. Here we have a mass phenomenon involving hundreds of thousands of readers who are not part of the pop audience. The people who enthuse over *Planète* are not the mentally retarded, but administrators and semi-intellectuals. It can be said that *Planète* is the exact complement of the most simplistic forms, but for a different public, one that is more cultivated, more inquiring and demanding. These are diverse lines expressing the religious search and preoccupation.

This is shown also in the success of religious bookstores. It is noteworthy that very successful publishers are bringing out collections like "The Enigmas of the Universe," in which are displayed, at an absurdly low intellectual level, *The Gods Who Flee Heaven and Earth*, *The Presence of Extraterrestrial Beings*, and the incredible *Age of Aquarius* (by J. Sendy), which testify to the credulity, the blindness, the shoddy religiosity of the cultivated French reader.[9]

---

[9] In this vast literature a distinction has to be made between works *about* the growth of magism, astrology, etc., and those works and films which exploit that religious enthusiasm. In the first category, we cite the good sociological study of Defrance, Morin, *Le retour des astrologues* (1971); the interesting reporting of M. Bessy, *Bilan de la Magie* (1964); and the excellent press analysis by J. Dimmet, "La Religion," in *Paris-Match* (1967).

On the borderline between the two (i.e., between study and exploitation) are works like those of C. Hansen, *Witchcraft at Salem* (1969); and J. Caro Baraja, *Les Sorcières et leur Monde* (1971); and I am not counting the innumerable books on initiating mysteries, on spiritism. These are coming out at the rate of two or three a week. The success of this proliferation of books is proof of the public's enthusiastic interest in the worlds of mystery, in supernatural powers, in sorcery, in religious aberrations, etc.

With regard to commercial exploitation, there are the collections of Laffont *(Les Enigmes de l'univers)*, or of A. Michel *(Les Chemins de l'impossible)*, which provide an abundant harvest of books, all equally stupid, on extraterrestrial beings (the book by

This thirst for reading about the "strange," having the twofold aspect of the appearance of rationality and science coupled with credulity, is growing rapidly. There are in France about ten collections put out by serious publishers which have an enthusiastic public following, beginning with the too-familiar *Morning of the Magicians* (350,000 copies). One calmly announces the arrival of the civilization of immortality, thus linking up with the most central of religious beliefs. Manuals of magic are proliferating, together with the study of the third eye, books on reincarnation, on philosophers' stones or abodes. It is in fact a resurgence of the lowest superstitions of the religious phenomenon. As Caillois so well puts it: "Saint Christopher and the horseshoe are giving way to flying saucers and magicians." But all is camouflaged under a science which is an optical illusion.

In the same order of phenomena is the enthusiasm of intellectuals for films of diabolism, vampirism, and magic. Polanski is the most striking example. Of course, in the beginning it's a question of pulling one's leg. The first films of vampirism are noteworthy. By reason of their irony and their objective stance, they make it respectable for intellectuals to come and go along with their belief. One isn't really believing in it, because one is making fun of it. One is strong enough minded. One means only to take part in the show, not really to be headed in that direction. Still, at bottom, there's a tiny quaver of belief. Then progressively one drifts to the point of *Rosemary's Baby*, in which it is certainly not a matter of jest and objectivity. The diabolism is the very reason for the success of the film. The public is eager for this mystery, this communion with the devil.

The great skill of the producer is to be able to present a medieval devil acting in the context of a technological, rational, and scientific society. The combination is the same as in *Planète*. It corresponds to modern man's religious conviction of a presence which cannot be acknowledged, of a personalized power at the heart of our world, a world which is the most modern and

---

Von Daniken is side-splitting in its scientific pretense), on *The Third Eye* (Rampa), the early lives, the secret diaries of sorcery, the secrets of the great pyramid, the secret journals of Moses, the moon as a key to the Bible, alchemy, etc. These are all works set forth with a scientific and rational apparatus, in imitation of *Planète*, but in which "the scientific language serves as an optical illusion." As Caillois puts it, "Science has helped superstition to grow by providing it with a glamorous vocabulary."

seemingly the most enlightened. The devil's disciples have become numerous again in our day.

"Mystery" is more than ever fashionable in this rational, scientific world. It is that trend which explains, on the one hand, the success of scientific books offering an answer to the "enigmas" which the religious person has always encountered, and the success of Christian books, on the other hand.

The first of these facts is attested by the success of J. Monod's book: *Chance and Necessity.* It is the religious question pure and simple, anxiety in the face of life and death, meaning, etc., which has driven the throng to this book. They are in search of an answer from the doctor, the scientist, the magician, in whom one can have faith (for there is no question of *understanding* the vast scientific labor which underlies the thinking). It is a faith in the revealing word of the One Who Knows, a strictly religious attitude. There is no difference between the readers of Monod and the disciples of any guru.

The second fact, the success of Christian books, culminated in the vogue of Teilhard de Chardin.[10] Yet it is the more striking in view of the success of books claiming to be theological, like *Honest to God,* or *The Secular City.* Those books have a wide sale in France as well. One gets the impression that dechristianization is itself in doubt. We shall have to come back to that. The fact is that here again we have a sign of modern man's impassioned interest in *everything* religious (provided only it is not expressed in terms which have been dead for one or two hundred years).[11] It is a basic curiosity, together with a waiting for the one who will finally speak the word of our destiny.

In this religious renaissance, to be sure, the hippie movement cannot be overlooked. Renaissance?—or is this, rather, an obscure progress exploding visibly into the open? The hippie phenomena are not a sudden eruption. We have been witnessing, at least since 1930, youth movements exhibiting the same characteristics. But

---

[10] There is no need to dwell on this point after, for example, B. Charbonneau's study, *Teilhard de Chardin: Prophète d'un âge totalitaire* (1963).

[11] What we are writing will surely not satisfy exacting minds who demand figures and statistics. Come on—what is *really* known about these readers? That means little; what counts is the trend. A half century ago the religious book had no readership. Now publishers are putting out collections on religious subjects *at every intelligence level*—from illustrated collections, to comics, to theological works—for commercial purposes. Enough said.

hippie-ism, in its various forms, carries all the religious tendencies to their extreme. It isn't a question, at this point, of describing the hippie phenomenon, but merely of recalling certain of its religious aspects.

How deny that all the following characteristics stem from a religious attitude: the rejection of the rational in order to plunge immediately into a spiritual experience, the search for community and fraternity, the ideal of communion and of nonviolence, the active will to change human life from a spiritual point of view, the return to nature and to the "natural" life, the rejection of an enslaving occupation and of everything that degrades man, the denial that life is meaningless and that it is limited to comfort and living standards? This is all the more true as the religious becomes explicit through the frequent wearing of religious emblems (many hippies wear a crucifix around the neck) and through expressed loyalty to some classic religious tendency such as Zen Buddhism.[12] Surely it can be said that "complete" hippies are not so numerous, and that one swallow doesn't make a spring. That is true. But the young people of the West who are won over, entirely or in part, to the hippie ideal of life are innumerable.

Here again we have the specifically religious. At the core are a relatively small number of conscious believers, who believe by choice and are deeply committed. Then there is the large crowd of imitative believers, who take up with the rituals without knowing much more about it than that, imitating the lifestyles and repeating the formulas. Now that is exactly what we observe with the hippies. The great number (30 percent of western youth?) with long hair, smoking hashish, runaways, conscientious objectors against society—these are the faithful faithless of the religion. They commit themselves to that path through religious need.

But the hippie phenomenon cannot be dissociated from drugs

---

[12] The zest for certain religions of India is not accidental. The relation, for example, between enjoyment and religion is very attractive, *precisely* as an expression of man in a consumer society! It is not in *opposition* to the technological society that one discovers tantrism, but rather, in order to be at home in it! "Pleasure becomes the discipline of liberation (yoga), sin becomes a good activity, transmigration becomes liberation . . . ." "Pleasure from wine, or meat, or woman, is salvation for the person who knows. For the uninitiated it is a fall" (noted by Louis Dumont, *op. cit.*). One understands why, in this society of enjoyment, the current of youth can turn toward that type of religion (and to beliefs like those of the sexual revolution). It is the incarnation of religious need, in a religious form which does not conflict with the major drives of the technological society.

and pop music. I know, of course, that a great many hippies do not use drugs, or more exactly, they no longer do so. The better part give that up the moment they find a higher religious expression, so that they no longer need that recourse, for drugs are, above all, a religious adventure. One could search for hundreds of explanations. There certainly are a variety of motivations, but the heart of the problem is religious need. In a society which no longer offers any outcome to the collective search for meaning, which is oppressive and technicized, one in which mystery and the irrational are pursued, drugs are the great means of recovering human communion. Constant upheaval, technology, and the flood of news make any irrational experience impossible and eliminate any chance for meditation and escape. Such is the central secret of the spread of drugs. All the rest either is derived from that need or is secondary. Among the several factors, the religious need is the one which is recognized by all those specialized in the study of drugs.[13] It is indicated by the achievement of ecstasy, the search for communion, transition into the world of the beyond, etc.

The two principal factors are the following: for certain addicts (marijuana) there is the element of communion. One doesn't smoke alone. The mere act of passing the cigarette from hand to hand is more important than the drug itself. It brings the desired "effect" with only tiny doses whenever the communal factor is working in the group. On the other hand, drugs create mental states and experiences comparable to those described by the mystics—an artificial paradise, ecstasies, visions, confusion of the senses, way-out music. But we mustn't overlook a third factor: the sect. Drug users constitute a sect whose members have their signs of mutual recognition and are deeply loyal. They live in their "holy" world in scorn of the uninitiated.

At all three of the foregoing levels, the use of drugs ends in phenomena closely allied to classic religious phenomena. The spread of the drug habit expresses the need to have those experiences. It fills in for a lack of the religious in our society, or at least for the lack of a satisfying religion which would be sufficiently strong and unanimous.

Along that line, we find gatherings of young people at "pop

---

[13] Everything that can be said on the religious nature of drugs is available in de Felice, *Poisons sacrés, ivresses divines* (new edition, 1969). In his analysis of "drug" religions, he described in 1930 all that we are seeing today in our western world! Likewise, *Les Danses sacrées* (mostly oriental) (Le Seuil, 1963).

festivals." There it is a case both of mystic paroxysm and of collective ritual. The gatherings at Monterey, the Isle of Wight, Amougies, and Woodstock are the exact equivalent of orgiastic religious festivals. Pop music itself is of such power as to evoke the entire subconscious and to create the religious. There again, the attraction, music-drugs-togetherness, works only because there is a higher aim and a more basic need, namely, to escape the materialistic, monetary, low world, weighed down with daily preoccupations and expediencies, and to enter the world of the cost-free and the gracious, the world of freedom and love, the world of the unencumbered. That is exactly what all religions have always done in all societies. For each individual, it is at the same time a matter of getting beyond the self.

The orgiastic delirium also expresses itself in violence. We all know, obviously, the close link between religion and violence. The psychological reasons for this have been a matter of question. The fact is that religion, characterized by a vibrant and explosive faith, goes together with violence. This is true whether, on the one hand, the religions involve sacrifices, the human sacrifices of Behanzin or of the Aztecs, the *herem*, the wiping out of unbelievers, the burning of witches, and the clubs of the hermits of Alexandria, or whether, on the other hand, they involve self-mutilation, flagellation, the acceptance of martyrdom, inward violence (like priestly celibacy, the *perinde ac cadaver* ["just like a corpse"]), or outward violence. I don't mean, of course, that all violence has a religious origin, nor that all religions produce violence, but even so.

The fact that Christianity, the revelation of the God of love, could have so changed as to become, during the dark and bloody adventures of the crusades, a religion of forced conversions, and of the inquisition sets one thinking. On the other hand, how is it conceivable that man should turn against his fellows in extreme violence without motives—and what higher and more justifying motive is there than religion? It is in the name of Truth, of the Absolute, that one person does away with another. Neither the communists nor the nazis could have attained the supreme violence had they not been religious. When man wants to commit violence he has to justify it. Thus there is a reciprocal relationship between religion and violence. Religion *always* produces violence. When violence comes first, it requires the appearance of a religion.

That is why, in the hippie situation, we observe the strange slipping into violence. The hippies have a nonviolent ideology, but groups, entire branches, take the contrary route of absolute violence against the society they have rejected and despised, against the type of person they consider the most hateful. The line is very thin, and the change from nonviolence to violence is almost automatic where religion is involved.

The exaltation of violence in the world appears to us as an expression of religiousness. Georges Sorel saw this, and analyzed it perfectly in his *Réflexions sur la Violence*, in which he connected violence with the circulation of myth and the necessary belief. Who has not been struck by the delirium of violence in our society? It seemed all the harder to credit in view of the fact that for two centuries we had been lulled in the illusion of an end to violence in our social relationships. There were parliamentary government, peace tables, liberalism, democracy, and urban manners. We were in complete euphoria. Primitive savagery and religious sectarianism had been brought under control. The communists and the revolutionary unionists were only wicked exceptions, and they would soon disappear. The Russian revolution and Hitler were accidents.

However, questions began to be asked, and then, here we are! Oppressive and repressive, liberating and counter-repressive—it crops up again everywhere. There is the irrational belief that violence will resolve the "problems." Through acts of violence, revolts, coups d'état, tortures and convictions, one is supposedly on the way to a pure and true, a just and free society. Rebellions without a cause or an objective represent completely irrational attitudes, feebly verbalized from beliefs and displaying mythical interpretations with regard to society.

From the outbreak of the youth at Stockholm, on the night of St. Silvester, 1953, violence has been the normal expression of more and more extensive groups, out to destroy evil and oppression, who want to "slay the dragon," enter the promised land, win their freedom, and smash what seems to them, in the abstraction of our world, the visible sign of evil. There is an exaltation and a happening which ends in a collective crisis of nerves. When nervous resistance and argument fail, violence sets free metaphysical obsession by itself turning into a religious behavior. This applies to the frenzies of the Congolese in 1961, and of the blacks of Detroit or Newark, Carmichael's completely mystical verbal exaltations, or those of *Do It!*, the savagery of the automobile driver, the success of cruel plays, of the bloody and sadistic Arrabal. "Be cruel, be violent," one read at the Sorbonne in 1968. The outbreaks at Battaglia in 1970, or in Mexico in June, 1971, at a soccer game. That isn't political. It is the reappearance of religious delirium.

To be sure, that is not to say that all the violence in our society is of the religious type. It is clear that the violence of the police or of administrations, that of the great economic powers and of "imperialism," have nothing of the religious in them; but the violence specific to our time, which is the overflow of an exaltation, and the means par excellence for the realization of an ideal carried to the absolute limit, especially that of the young leftists—those are acts of the religious people of this age. They believe absolutely. They listen to no reason. Without knowing it, they have an otherworldly outlook which they describe as political. They want to change society by changing life.

They are ready for every sacrifice, and are ready to sacrifice all who do not believe. They form sectarian cliques. They have a yen for spectacular martyrdom and for witnessing through propaganda. They despise all truth which fails to confirm them in their absolute. They confound a rational explanation of the world with belief in old, resurrected myths. Their violence is an expression of the combination of all that. For them, without hesitation, violence is a religious action against evil, because the world, like every religious world, is clearly divided between absolute Good and absolute Evil.

I will surely not say that the increase of violence in our society is by itself a proof of religiousness! It is not a proof; but this type of violence, associated with all the other factors, is part of a constellation which throws light on the need for violence, and that need goes far toward completing the puzzle. To be sure, in diverse societies there are diverse violences. There is a hidden violence, an organized violence (war, the police) and a "primitive," illogical, anarchic violence, which is the only one that could be called religious. This primitive violence is expressed in those societies which no longer have a common ground, an accepted structure.

They take place in our society because the structures are external to the person. They are incommensurable with him, and appear to him hostile. Here religious violence is explained less by the lack of an issue (war, for example) than by the lack of humanization. It is a protest on behalf of man against bureaucracy, advertising, technology, and it is in the exaltation of violence that man is to be defended or restored. This is a mystique, and it is religion.

The religious spirit of the leftists is expressed in two formulas, among others, which covered the walls of seashore resorts in 1970:

"Geismar is everywhere," and "Mao is looking." There we have slogans expressing a God-transfer. The ubiquity of the true Witness, that universal presence which is but the expression of universal justice, through the zealots and disciples as intermediaries. There is an identification of these disciples (who put Geismar everywhere) with the hidden but omnipresent person, coupled with the universal but personal watchman. The eye was in the tomb. Mao is your conscience. He is *the* conscience of the world. He is looking at you and is judging you, for he is the sovereign judge who knows the reins and the hearts. Geismar is the current incarnation of Providence. He is everywhere and can act at every instant. Mao is the principle of Good and Evil, the absolute Father whom no one can escape. *That* is what the authors of those inscriptions really mean, and of course, like all the faithful of all religions, they are ready, through their activities, to assume those divine attributes.

Music, drugs, incense, violence, sexual freedom: festival. It is indeed noteworthy that our modern thinkers, revolutionaries, antitechnologists, renovators of mankind, preachers of liberty, all put their hopes in utopia, as we have seen, and in the "festival": happenings, barricades, confrontations, sit-ins, fancy dress, theater of participation, pop festivals, deafening and intoxicating music, audiences swaying with the rhythm of the drums, a participation which becomes identification. Each participant does himself in with sound, with fatigue, with drugs, with violence, with cries, with impressions received in common.[14] The desire is to get one's bearings, and to establish an intervening space foreign to the rest of the world, an ocean in which to plunge without restraint, so as to blot out everything which is not the festival. The festival, greatly longed for by all the contestants as a way of putting down modern society, is acclaimed as an ought-to-be, and as the revolutionary means par excellence.

Here it is, put into actual practice. It is already experienced, sometimes as a way of creating the new life, sometimes as a political method. The fanatics for festival, who remind us that every society has always had its essential festivals, and that ours is the only one not to have a genuine festival, forget the stern warning of Jean Brun. He shows, first of all, that the current enthusiasm for festivals is no accident, but that it results precisely from the

[14] See the works of H. Lefebvre on the festival of 1968; see also Harvey Cox, *The Feast of Fools*, which welcomes the festival as the religious liberation of Scripture.

structures of the technological society of which it forms a part. Time and space have vanished, thanks to the resources of the media. By reason of that fact, we are living in a simultaneous happening, as McLuhan says. Our society itself produces these raging throngs, and it is creating Dionysian man. Far from its being a reaction against technocratic bureaucracy, it is a product of it and a way for it to survive.[15]

In addition, Brun quite rightly reminds us that the only regimes to give politics a festive quality are the fascist ones. "One may well wonder whether the best definition of fascism may not be that regime which undertakes to make politics into a perpetual festival, in which exaltation and beauty are found only in the throes of struggle and violence." But that doesn't bother our panegyrists and participants. "Festival" is the key word. Everything must be "festive" in order to be revivified. Only in the festival do institutions throw off their rigidity, so that man can have freedom and find meaning and a future. Festival is a panacea as well as a revolution.

What strikes me in all this talk, and in all these experiences, is the unshakable ignorance of the actors. The festival is religious in the end. The sacral world necessarily involves festivals, which are its religious expression. Caillois sees festival as one of the supreme expressions of the sacred. That is obvious, but conversely, festival is always religious. It is that in essence. There is no such thing as a lay or a secular festival. Every time someone has thought to have a rational or a lay festival, the result has been a dismal and ridiculous caricature.[16]

There is no festival without reference to a final value, which is affirmed and transgressed. Whenever some power wanted to institute the festival of reason, it had to divinize reason before the action made sense. If it is not religion, festival is only a sorry entertainment which satisfies no one. It must be a total risk for a total resurrection, the discovery of a freedom from beyond time, a transgression of taboos, the assertion of role reversals, a triumph of the irrational, an abolition of the concrete, a recourse to a Beyond, a plunge into the Great Time, a restoration of chaos. Festival must

---

[15] I shall not stop here to demonstrate what I have already outlined in *The Technological Society*, and which has been perfectly demonstrated by McLuhan and Jean Brun.

[16] For example, the marriages in the town hall, which the Revolution of 1789 tried to make into a festival.

express the religious side of man in order to be a festival with a psychological function (a psychodrama) and a sociological function (release of antagonisms and revivification). Revolution, in its turn, is a festival because it is an annulment for the sake of a new beginning without limits. That is all religion, of the most classic and traditional variety.

When religion becomes degraded, it transforms the festival into a ceremony and the dance of Dionysus into a liturgy. When it outlives itself, when it is merely a social framework, then it ceases to be the expression of a religious need or of a religious instinct. When that happens, religion denies itself and turns against festival. The entire history of religions is made up of this progressive degradation, followed by a return to the source through a rediscovery of the festival.

Thus, when war is held sacred it is called a festival (with the understanding that people are going to die in this festival), just as revolution is treated that way today, and plays the same role. But this yen, this desire, this call for festival is nothing more or less than a deep religious seething discharging its lava.

And of course the religious, which has many facets, is also constituted by the act of transcendentalizing the concrete conditions of life. We are witnessing a violent verbal attack against the consumer society, yet, on the other hand, the latter, and everything that goes with it, is the object of a religious exaltation. Consumption, along with the technology that produces it and the advertising that expresses it, is no longer a materialistic fact. It has become the meaning of life, the chief sacred, the show of morality, the criterion of existence, the mystery before which one bows.[17]

Be not deceived, the rejection of the consumer society is on the same level. The quarrel is really a religious one. The disputants never leave that world. To the contrary, they serve to reconfirm the religious fact. The religious attitude toward consumption is expressed by what Brun admirably calls "the furor over consumption." "Those who criticize consumer societies, and who are

---

[17] It is needless to go back over what we were saying (p. 71) on the subject of money. There is always a worship of money. I have studied that fact in detail in *L'Homme et l'Argent*. A more recent analysis has been done by Norman O. Brown, *Life Against Death* (1959), who emphasized especially the fact that the religious attitude toward money gives the lie to economic theories of the rationality of monetary phenomena. But Brown's psychological explanation of the fact seems to me imaginary.

concerned at the same time to give disadvantaged societies more to consume, are in this sense not reproaching the societies in which they live for consuming too much, but in fact for not providing others with enough to consume. It's very important that they discover the tempo of the increase in consumption if they are not to be brought down by a monumental problem. Consumer societies swamp us with finites. Dionysus aims at the infinite, so he has to find ways to uncover new thirsts. . . ."

An overvaluing of the ephemeral transformed into law everlasting, the transformation of everything into an object of consumption, absorption in living standards, a giddy frenzy attempting to feed on all the possibles in order to attain thereby to true existence and to transcend the human condition—that is what is being expressed by every argument for our society. We walk on the moon. We fly at Mach 3. We split the atom. We create life. We are going beyond the human condition. The techno-consumer is the shaman of our society.[18] But it is a shamanism made available to spiritual nothingness with a bank account.

This attitude toward consumption, which plunges man into ecstatic delirium, is coupled, obviously, with a worship of the thing consumed, especially of the thing offered for consumption. We have seen that modern man had set up technology as a sacred, but the technical object itself receives a different charter. It is toward the technical object that religious sentiment is directed. Modern man places his hope, his faith, his assurance, his happiness, his security, and the development of his personality in the use and possession of more and more technical objects. These play the role of many former religious substitutes.

Curiously, if we consider that the "little gods" were the *deus ex machina,* the needed stopgap, because man was unable to do what had to be done to meet his need, what is happening today is a statement of religious feeling toward those little gods concerning the technical objects which take their place, and which really perform what it had been hoped the gods would do. But that has in no way rendered the statement materialistic or rational. The

---

[18] Baudrillard *(op. cit.)* shows how the daily exercise of the benefits of consumption is experienced as a miracle: "The beneficiary of the miracle sets up an apparatus of signs indicative of happiness, and then sits back, waiting for happiness to happen." Consumption seems handed out by some beneficent mythological solicitation, of which we are the legitimate heirs: technology, progress, growth, etc., and, following Jean Brun (whom he does not cite), he stresses the religious giddiness of consumption.

religious attachment, which was apparently the *support* of the gods in question, is now the seemingly indispensable expansion factor attributed to an efficacious object as such. The bare efficaciousness taken alone is not satisfying, if one stops at that! This is probably one of the most singular workings of the psychology of our times.

Man cannot rest content with the concrete value of the objects of the technological society. He cannot limit himself to entering upon material happiness. He has to have a spiritual satisfaction of a religious kind to go along with it. The separation of the two is not acceptable. Yet that is what all the moralists of the technological society are advocating. Thanks to technology, one is going to assure man of a comfortable material living and free him from time. With that taken care of, this man can give himself to the higher activities of the spirit, of art, of culture, etc.

. This has already been criticized in many ways. On the religious level, a basic observation is called for. Man has always rejected that dichotomy. The religious was always expressed in tangible activities, political or economic. Conversely, quite often tools themselves were sacralized, divinized, through the entire gamut of possible interpretations, even to the complete assimilation of the tool with the divinity. Thus, among certain elephant hunters in Cambodia, the lasso *is* god. It is a phenomenon strictly identical with what we find today. Man cannot separate material satisfaction from spiritual satisfaction. The technical object has become a religious object.

This twofold religious phenomenon (delirium of consumption, worship of the technical object) is found expressed and consecrated by advertising. That is the liturgy and the psalmody of the consumer religion. It would be interesting, and not difficult, to identify the religious vocabulary in advertising (e.g., a recent term: "trustworthy"; a trustworthy machine is truly a god) in order to show how it is planted in the sacred and in the religious structure. Each one could make his own version and appraisal.

But I think it more important to stress the fact that modern man's sensitivity to advertising, and also to propaganda, has a religious cause. Vance Packard's study is surely correct, yet it lacks precisely this dimension. It is because man experiences consumption as a sacred delirium that he is plunged into the Orphism of yet more, and still more, and that advertising arouses such a sympathetic vibration in him. If he obeys advertising (and Oh, how he obeys!—in spite of pitiful denials based on obliging statistics), it is, more than anything else, because he has been sensitized beforehand by the worship of consumer goods. The faithful churchgoer always finds the priest's statements convincing, and the singing of his fellow churchgoers wonderful, however he might criticize them from the point of view of form. So it is with advertising. It would have no hold on a person if he were not an orgiastic fanatic for consumer goods. It is deeply rooted in religious compost.[19]

Is it indispensable? Indeed it is, less for economic reasons than as a celebration of the mystery of modern times, as the liturgy of a new eucharist. That is why advertising untiringly repeats its litanies. It confirms man in what is no longer mere material and social action, but a path of fulfillment and transcendence. Propaganda, likewise, can succeed only when grafted onto the religious, onto a charismatic man, an absolute political truth, an ultimate sacrifice, a communal achievement, a scapegoat, a final meaning for life. We shall come back to that.

At this stage in our discussion, the important thing has been simply to point out that our world is so religious that objects and actions of the most materialistic kind, those seemingly most devoid of depth, are transformed into religious phenomena. [20] The whole person is now committed at *that* level. That is what makes the dispute on this ground so fundamental. It is very bad that some people should be undernourished while others succumb from overconsumption, that there should be misery and injustice. It is obvious that we should struggle against hunger, misery, and unequal distribution.

But that *reasonable* proposition is rejected by the judges. According to them, what I have just written is the statement of a heartless man, who moreover is a rightist. Those things should be talked about at the height of excitement, of indignation, with sacred fury, with voice trembling and eyes flashing despair and fire. That people should go hungry is the absolute in suffering. That

---

[19] Baudrillard *(op. cit.)* rightly stresses the dominating quality of consumption as identical with religious exclusiveness: "At the experience level, consumption produces the maximum exclusion of the real social world. That is the historic sign of maximum security." One also finds in it all the religious characteristics: the tendency to passiveness on the part of the believer, who falls back on outside forces, and also on the elaboration of a morality of action, of efficacy, etc. This internal inconsistency produces an intense feeling of guilt, and consequently an obvious desire to clear the passiveness of guilt. In reading this appraisal of consumption, one has the impression that he is reading an appraisal of religion.

[20] Moreover, it is possible that this attribution of the religious to consumption may have deep roots, and may be connected with the most primitive attitudes of man, as would appear in the works of Lévi-Strauss: *The Raw and the Cooked; From Honey to Ashes; L'Origine des Manières de Table*, etc.

there should be inequality of consumption is an absolute evil. This fury, this urgency, the quality of the ultimate in the arguments in this domain, the totalitarian nature attributed to these things, which excludes everything else and treats other problems as secondary, which makes it possible to decide exactly what is good and what is to be condemned, which involves the whole of humanity in the application—all this attests, more than anything else, to the religious character of consumption. The debate over "have/have not" has become a war of religion (I said "over," not "between").

All facets of the modern religious bring into prominence the deeply irrational character of modern man. He is not scientific, reasonable, rational, involved in tangible and demythicized matter, devoid of illusions—indeed not! "The dislocation of forms, of words, of sounds, of the person; the revolutionary erostratisms, which evoke Sade, Marx, Nietzsche and Freud all at the same time, are so many expressions of a devotion to intellectual ethylisms, which improvise a gigantic, anomic festival, in order to turn everything into play and into an intoxication of risks" (J. Brun).

What is here an intellectual attitude is only a reflection of the common feeling. It is the verbalized sublimation of that which every person in the western world experiences, expressed at a different level. It seems that the more technology and organization are rationalized, so that, logically, they should rationalize man and his behavior, the more, to the contrary, irrationalities increase. Everything is happening as though man could not stand this logic (even a living logic) and had reacted violently against everything which normalizes him. In the presence of technical rationality, we are seeing a ground swell of basic irrationalism. The more the technical universe becomes organized, the more man blows apart in disorder.[21]

Our irrationality is in no way a testimonial of freedom. It is a refusal to move into rationality. Man, swept along by science, is certainly not stripped of his illusions, his childish beliefs, dreams, reveries, uncontrolled passions and myth-making—quite the contrary.[22] In the midst of the stammering and questioning, the

---

[21] I study this at some length in Le Système technicien.
[22] One example among thousands is the childish attitude, purely religious and mythical, of men of science when they go political! Nearly all of them show a remarkable capacity for impassioned irrationality.

irrational is the great refuge against the horrors of systematization. In our era of mathematics, of science, of rigorous discipline, of exact knowledge and abundant factual information, to "know" something is the abomination of desolation. One must be nondirective, without knowledge, without experience (that crushes the poor other fellow). A professor must not give a course. An actor must not know his part. A writer must not know what he is writing (one writes in order to know who one is). The film producer must not know the film he is about to produce (as Jeanne Moreau said so well). One must not know how to resolve a social or economic problem (the thing is to leap into the revolutionary furnace without knowing what is going to result from it). One must give oneself over to the creative uncertainty of the happening. (It is not for nothing that I have employed the word "must" throughout, for it is a genuine moral imperative. This attitude is a shot in the dark. It wells up from the irrational as an emotional reaction. It is experienced as a religious certainty.)

One must act out the comedy of the not knowing, for otherwise one is a terrorist. One must take his stand at the zero point of scripture, of faith, of knowledge, and of art. One must not give a lecture or preach a sermon in which one knows what he is saying. Knowledge must give way to questions, to stuttering and stammering (that, at least, is a living experience, and the television announcers set a good example). One stays in the realm of "perhaps," of suggestions, of puerile and meaningless discussion.

Today's discourse par exellence is that of Bouvard and Pécuchet.* Everything must be left to the free choice of those who actually know nothing. Such is the profound "true-life adventure" of modern man, who no longer wants to say anything or hear anything. Swamped with news, crushed with technological rationality, he flees through this papier-mâché labyrinth, thinking to rediscover an origin and to find some fresh air. The great cry is, "Imagination to the fore," instead of reason. Man is at home only in the chiaroscuro of an imaginative, rationalized religious. He absolutely cannot stand either the merciless sun of the Sahara or the blinding uncertainties of the snows of the Great North. Each produces mirages in its excess of light. That is exactly what we are experiencing. The excess of rigor, of precision, of scientific explanation and of technical rationality produces the mirage of a

---

* Translator's note: *Bouvard and Pécuchet* is an unfinished novel by Flaubert, in which the chief theme is the ridiculous meaninglessness of life.

madness which destroys the self. It is at the moment of rationality that the intellectual rises up to say that the insane person is normal, that instinct is freedom, that there is no meaning, that imagination is the only authenticity, that questions and a blank page are all that remain.

This is not a matter of "attitude" or of "originality." It is a throwback to the deepest in man, who remains basically mytho-manic and sacralizing, who cannot live without a substructure which is thick, spread out in all directions, vague, inconsistent, but which is as crucial as the central sima. It is the irrational on the basis of which all the rest is constructed. The moment one tries to eliminate it, it reappears in some other form. When one curbs it on one side, it breaks out on the other.

Two small examples illustrate this irrepressible. Take the perti-nent analysis done by Escarpit of the re-creation of spontaneous and unintended theologies. It has to do with structuralism. "It is hard to see how structuralism can escape the dilemma of that shameful theology which is positivism, and which it thinks to negate. Behind the structure thus conceived, there is the Great Architect of the universe. . . . M. R. Bastide proposes defining structure as a bound system, latent in objects, susceptible of universal generalization and free of all diachrony. What we have here, obviously, are attributes of divinity. . . . Unable to structure itself into a universal church, the structuralizing revelation is reduced to private chapels." [23]

This analysis of Escarpit, of which we have given a mere indication here, is confirmed in an article by Foucault,[24] in which is seen a sort of delirious glorification of structure playing the role of a creating divinity. In the beginning was the structure. It was inscribed beforehand in that which did not yet exist. The chicken didn't exist, nor the egg either; only the genetic code, in and of itself, was in the absolute. There was no subject. There was no reader. There was no meaning, but there was a program and a production. What we really have here, under the pretext of an interpretation of scientific results, is a mystical interpretation of a meaning which rejects meaning.[25]

---

[23] *Le Discours social*, No. 1, 1970.

[24] "La Logique du Vivant," *Le Monde*, November 1970.

[25] It is also possible to list as a sign of this "religious renewal" the multiplication of sects. Cf. Bryan Wilson, *Religious Sects* (1968), and the rather disgraceful and partisan book of R. Delorme, *Jesus H. Christ* (on American religious sects) (1971).

It may be of interest to conclude these observations with a look at the man who is taken for a prophet by the most avant-garde among the youth: Wilhelm Reich. Reich is a strict materialist, and even a bit simplistic. His biologism was criticized by the psychoanalysts, and there is no doubt that this biological materialism would have been rejected by Marx, who did not take kindly to that form of materialism. In any case, Reich is that kind of materialist. But, being both Freudian and Marxist, he finds, on the one hand, that Marxism is in fact a blind alley when it comes to resolving personal problems, and that Freud is of no use in resolving the socio-political problem. Therefore he is going to try to combine the two. He is honored as the pioneer of Freudo-Marxism.

But what he comes up with in the end is not a happy synthesis, a glorious apotheosis, but a failure. Through this mixture of the elements (for it is a mixing operation and not a synthesis, which I think impossible of achievement) of the thinking of Freud and of Marx, he arrives finally at the conclusion that all this amounts to nothing, nothing reasonably construed nor concretely applicable. The combination of the two factors is completely negative.

Finally, I know very well that for certain critics there is a true Reich (before 1933), the rational author of two or three works, and then a Reich gone crazy (author of nearly all the works) who is not worth paying attention to. I believe, to the contrary, that there is a perfect consistency throughout the whole of his work, and throughout its development. The conclusion is truly implied in the premise. *The Function of the Orgasm* implies the entire sequence. The impossibility of finding a satisfactory answer to the tragedies of every kind which he encountered leads him to fall back on the need for a total liberation of the individual, a liberation brought about only through liberation of the total energy, which is sexual. Orgasm is both the expression and the source of all energies which make possible all human and socio-political transformations.

From that, he is led immediately to the realization that orgasm cannot fulfill that role if it is merely a biological act of a few seconds' duration. In order to have its full measure, it has to be associated with (or emanate from) a universal force, from which it draws its full dimension and efficacy. That leads necessarily to a cosmic conception of the energy, the orgone, in which the entire

---

For a good demonstration of the fact that atheism is itself a faith, and plays the part of a religion of nature, etc., see Claude Tresmontant, *Les Problèmes de l'Athéisme* (1972).

world is immersed, from which the world receives its vitalizing energy, by which it was originated (not to say created), an orgone which, in Reich's thinking, plays exactly the part of God. So aware is he of the fact that his cosmic materialism links up, once again, with religion, that in one of his last books, *The Murder of Christ*, there is an astonishing mixture of the mystical with the biological. God reappears as the orgone, or the creator of the orgone. Truth is an emanation from this. He constantly refers to the revelation of a new religion in Christ (which, to be sure, is not Christianity).

I refer to Reich because his development seems to me typical (it would not be surprising if Herbert Marcuse were, one day, to rediscover God, it is inherent in the logic of "the sexual liberation revolution"). But it is also because we are seeing him rediscovered today, which is characteristic of the contemporary religious. Reich is in very fact the prophet of a new religion, sprung from the materialism in which one cannot remain.

This religious exuberance of our times, which multiplies its forms and finds new incarnations out of the religious drives and needs of man, also, to be sure, affects Christianity.[26] Gabriel Vahanian is the only contemporary theologian to have seen the reality of the situation, in his unrelenting assessment of "the Christian renewal" in the United States as, in fact, a religious renewal which is not at all Christian. It is, rather, a manifestation of the religious spirit of modern society. For, to be sure, this religious spirit can *also* revivify old forms and cover itself with the mantle of old religions. This religious orientation of new Christian beliefs was evident, of course, in the vogue of Teilhard de Chardin. It is not a question, here, of casting aspersions on the faith and person of Teilhard, but simply of noting that the movement which caused so many to follow him is religious, and not specifically Christian. What embarrasses him the most, in his theosophy, is the Christ. He doesn't know what to do with his incarnation, or with his crucifixion, or with his resurrection. He meets up with him again only at the end, as the cosmic Christ, which was also true of all gnosticisms and religions.

---

[26] The current religious explosion is being received with joy by many Christians, displaying always the same confusion between religion and Christianity. The bishops at Lourdes rejoice in this way. There is an identification between prayer and all forms of meditation, a return to nature, a rediscovery of the body, community liberation of creativity, the dance, etc. A good example of the confusion is an article on prayer by R. Solé, in *Le Monde*, December 1971.

Contemporary theologians are repeating the typical operation of "religionizing" Christianity when they pretend to formulate an areligious Christianity. They try to eliminate the religious from Christianity by treating as religious the old traditional manifestations which are outmoded (for example, the traditional designation of God). But they fail to take into account that the work of transforming Christianity into a religion is always the combination of the revelation of Christ with the basic beliefs of a given society. From then on, whenever they try, for example, to prove that the secular city, mobility, anonymity and the traditional festival conform to the biblical revelation, they are carrying out just the same procedure as did all those who tried to prove that a given factor in their society, of their beliefs, of their philosophy, was Christian. That was the point of departure for the transformation of revelation into religion. The combination is different only to the extent that the factors are different.

These theologians are totally blind to the present situation when they take the contemporary society for secularized, and modern man as grown up and rational. Under cover of that error, they reintegrate into their theology precisely what is religious in our age, in our society, without realizing that they are once again mixing the religious with "the Christian domain." [27]

It is not only the theological movement which is giving expression to the religious. The same thing is obviously occurring in practice. Thus in France we can take Taizé as exemplary of the religious, with its liturgy, which is both open and symbolic, its exceeding of ecclesiastical bounds, its commonplace ecumenism, its gatherings of great numbers of young people, with their contribution of adolescent uncertainty mingled with a certain authenticity of aspiration, the divergence between the inward and the outward, its exoterism and esoterism. Those are all fairly sure signs of religion. Of course, it is so closely entwined with Christianity that it becomes a most obvious expression of it, without exactly being taken for religion. Many similar examples could be found in the religious communities.

At the nonintellectual level, and in accord with the needs of the common man, we can uncover the same phenomenon. One

---

[27] It is obvious that, whenever one presents as the leading point of Christianity the statement we must unite with all men "who would contemplate existence as a mystery" (P. van Kilsdonk)—and I could cite hundreds of formulas of the same kind—one actually is in full religious regression!

example is the prodigious success of illustrated Bibles in fascicles, put on the market by large publishing houses. That such an illustrated Bible should sell a hundred thousand copies, generally in non-Christian circles, is quite impressive. Again, the success of the Bible in comic strips equals that of all the westerns.

Similarly, there are the attempts at renovating the mass through the introduction of popular religious elements. There is the pop mass, the celebration of midnight mass at the Olympia in Paris, the mass presided over by Duke Ellington and his orchestra, the music hall presentation at Saint-Sulpice, and Mireille Mathieu singing a mass in a personal style. All that took place at Christmas, 1969. Of course, under those circumstances the public comes, but surely also that has nothing to do with Christian authenticity.

It is the religious phenomenon of modern music which is being expressed in this confusion. One commentator, a non-Christian in fact, sensed the problem better than did certain Christians when he said, "Perhaps the moment has come to remind the public that you don't make mayonnaise with holy oil, and that you shouldn't confuse the ostensorium with ostentation." But Christians, only too glad to have an audience by methods of that kind, are ready to make manyonnaise, and ready to think they are communicating the gospel whereas, in the absence of any control over the situation, Christianity is being submerged under the enormous religious wave of our times.

Our learned exegetes also need to be reminded that "Christianity" is still very successful in quite a number of popular circles, and is producing a great many conversions. But it is Billy Graham on the one hand, and the Pentecostals and Jehovah's Witnesses on the other, who are having the success. What is taking place in modern man's belief is in no way a Christianity purged by science of all contagion of religion, and suited to the person who has become grown up, adult, sentient, capable of accepting a genuine Christianity—a person simply disgusted with the religious twaddle of traditional Christianity. To the contrary, it is the most mythical, the most imaginary, the most limited, the most religious in the Christian tradition, warmed over by a visionary mystique and by the technique of propaganda. That is the Christianity which is finding an audience among the public.

Developments in the United States at the present time simply serve to confirm Vahanian's assessment. What is now called "the Jesus revolution" is a gigantic religious expediency, in which Jesus and the revelation are served up to suit everybody's taste. Cox's harlequin Christ is nothing alongside it. The Way Word of Greenwich Village, the catacombs of Seattle, the transformation of a striptease joint into a Christian nightclub, the revolutionary Jesus, the black Jesus, the mixture of drugs and mystic exaltation— all that is in no way new. It never does more than reproduce all the religious conglomerations brought about in Christianity through the course of the centuries. They could be identified almost completely with the beginnings of the confraternities of the eighth to the eleventh centuries.

The interesting thing is that this is taking place at the very time when we are pompously being told that a religious Christianity no longer reaches modern man! It is factual proof that a religious Christianity is the only thing that does reach modern man—and religious in the most classic, the most traditional sense, the most tried and tested of all!

Very curiously, Cox notes this, and is happy about it (*The Feast of Fools*). He sees a return to religion in the United States, and he undertakes a condemnation of the separation between revelation and religion, between Christian faith and various religious beliefs. He restores value to religion as such. In his care to conform to the existing social condition and to adopt an optimistic view, he rejoices at the strides being made by religion, and bends his energies toward a reinstatement of Christianity within this trend. He thinks that Christianity will be carried along by the religious wave (in which he is right, except that it will be Christianity and not faith in the Lord Jesus Christ).

How wonderful to witness this pure syncretism of voodoo, Tantrism, Zen, and the gospel! Thus he comes back to the most traditional, the most down-at-the-heel position, which gave birth to the most questionable party in Catholicism. He goes back to the time of "the quarrel over rites and images," and adopts the position dear to the Jesuits (moreover, the latter had a clear, not a sentimental, comprehension of what they were doing). He would be prepared to accept the Madagascan "return of the dead" as a Christian festival, etc.

It is an old, old story, of which we know the outcome through two thousand years of experience. But Cox's blind confidence ignores that, lost as it is in the implied certainty that, since Christianity is the best religion, all religious revival must necessarily end in a Christian revival. That is a specifically medieval heresy, which makes a connection between sentiment, human religious aspiration, and faith, between the institutions of religion and

Christianity. Better have a religious man than an irrelegious man, because his religious need prepares the way for faith in Christ—whereas, throughout the entire Bible, it would appear, rather, that there is a radical break.

What is more, one of the most remarkable channels for this current transformation of the Christian faith into a religion is the broadcasting of love. There we can all come together (no play on words intended), if Christians confine their preaching to love, all love, nothing but love. In that case, not only is physical, even carnal, love easily equated with the other love (and in fact many Christian intellectuals now reject the distinction between eros and agape), but again one finds a common ground of religious understanding with a great many people. It is not for nothing that a great many hippies wear a crucifix around the neck. That has no reference to the Bible. It represents Jesus as a guru, as a master of love, as the first hippie, etc.

Revelation goes up in the religious smoke of universal love, linked to a generalized orgasm and expressed in flower power, or in revolutionary commitment. Christians are quite happy to find so many people who agree with them. Love, provided nothing is specified, offers a common platform for all religious spirits. A relationship with love—everybody knows there is a little something of authentic Christianity in that. Thus Christianity, in all its aspects, recovers its religious frame.

Quite simply (at two different levels, which strengthens the analysis), there is an accommodation to the religious needs of our society on the one hand, and a propagandist accommodation on the other. One may very well wonder whether what we have here is not simply a survival of older beliefs, the stale odor of traditions not yet eliminated. It is nothing of the kind. What we have is indeed a renewal, a powerful outburst of the religious, a growth corresponding to the situation of man in our society. Religiosity is, at this very moment, fulfilling exactly the same function it has always fulfilled, and of which Marx saw half. He saw only half, for the thought of Marx is, even on its authentic side, now phagocytized by the religious spirit of the world.

The Jesus phenomenon, the Jesus revolution, the Jesus parade: "Jesus comes to Paris, Jesus on the posters," is a headline in *Le Monde.* "Jesus the idol of our times," is a title in *Paris-Match;* "Jesus is coming," in *Charlie Hebdo;* "Jesus against drugs," in *Lectures pour Tous;* "Jesus and the Tradesmen," on the first page of *Nouvel Observateur.* Then there is the huge broadcast by Mauge, on

Radio-Luxembourg, and the plays *Godspell* and *Jesus Christ Superstar*, and a number of secondary plays (e.g., *Come Back Jesus*). Together with these demonstrations, theatricals, and musicals mixed with pop and hippieism, there are badges containing slogans, "Jesus is alive," "Jesus loves you," "After Jesus, all the rest (drugs) is toothpaste," and the wonderful "Jesus watch." On the dial is the face of Jesus (of whatever race you like! there is a white Jesus, a black Jesus, a yellow Jesus, an Arab Jesus, etc.). At the center, the heart of Jesus carries the hands and shows the time—Jesus everywhere.

Moreover, there are odd divergences in terms of appraisals. While it is often acknowledged that *Godspell* is indeed more serious (limited to the retelling of the Gospel of Matthew in a more communicating manner), and that *Jesus Christ Superstar* is simply a spectacular, theatrical review, we find the opposite opinion expressed by Claude Sarraute, for whom *Jesus Christ Superstar* is in the Saint-Sulpice category, while *Godspell* is a form of clowning ("the Sermon on the Mount reminds one of a circus or an asylum"). For Fabre-Luce, *Godspell* is nothing but "hippie conformism," while *Superstar* is a great and authentic Christian play, presenting profound theological insight.

But enough of those divergences. The phenomenon as a whole is a phenomenon of fashion. A need was felt for the religious. Jesus is always a best seller, and that made it worth the investment of nearly a million dollars to put on *Superstar*. The investment was covered from the time of the first performance. In France, the production cost two million francs, and it would appear that the return was fifty times that amount (in new francs). Is that "a new reading" of the gospel? Certainly not! The discovery of the hippie Jesus, and the Jesus who was Mary Magdalene's lover, etc., is as old as Herod (exactly). It is a question of making Jesus over into the religious personage who suits us. That, put simply, is what "the Jesus revolution" amounts to. In the world of today's theater and spectators, it's nice to have Jesus a hippie, just as for a socialist newspaper it's nice to have Jesus against the trades people. In place of his being a sign of variance, he is once again assimilated to our desires and needs, and to our favorite models.

Roger Mauge's broadcasts and book are a sure guarantee that there is nothing new in all this. All the commonplaces, all the platitudes, all the modern banalities about Jesus are to be found there, and they are the commonplaces and banalities which are pleasing to man. Nothing whatsoever has been said that is new or true, just because, with Mauge, God has become the giant computer, or Jesus "God's clutch-disk on the world." Once again, those are false images. They are false because reassuring and explanatory. The process of "religionizing" Jesus Christ is always the same. It amounts to finding a Jesus who answers precisely to what I expect of him. It is not a matter of "modernizing the gospel message," which has been covered with dust in the churches. It is, rather, an accommodation to the demands of the modern conscience and vocabulary. *Paris-Match* is quite right in using the title "Jesus Idol." It is exactly that, the contrary, in other words, to what the Bible proclaims.

And *Paris-Match* continues: "People's anguish today makes of his person and message the great topic of the day." Here we find ourselves caught up in the non-Christian religious attitude. For, if we link the person and message of Jesus with such formulas as "the two great J's, *Jésus/Jeunesse* [youth]" and "Jesus the true drug," we see that we have simply gone along with the fashion of the times, nothing more. It belongs to the purely religious, usually combined with the sexual and with commercialization. At last the young people have a permissive Jesus, who validates sexuality and eroticism. Those who live by a scientific ideology feed on the new catechism published by *Paris-Match* (Teilhard de Chardin in comic strips), and above all, one makes lots of money in "the Jesus business," which is "the Jesus revolution" in reverse, yet inseparable from it.

The same people who, four years ago, were broadcasting sex, are broadcasting Jesus now. If one wonders where this fashion comes from, the answer is simply that it is a special case of the general phenomenon of the religious need of modern man. In the last analysis, the capacity for sexual satisfaction is limited, and the religious desire is not completely met.

Political enthusiasm is dying out. It is observed in the United States that many of the young people who are exalted and exulting around Jesus, the freaks, were formerly political activists, militants for civil rights, agitators against the struggle in Vietnam, and revolutionaries. They are disappointed. Having failed to find the total answer in politics, they are looking elsewhere for a glory theme, an engrossing cause. It is a known fact that to give oneself to a political cause does not satisfy man's needs unless it is powerfully orchestrated, as in Hitlerism, or communism, or the cultural revolution. One quickly finds out that the ultimate question (that of death, for example) finds no answer, and dear me!

Jesus isn't so bad, with his close connection with love, with death, with sacrifice, and with high philosophy, which can be mingled with Hinduism, and finally the Jesus-drug business. It's all quite satisfying.

In addition, the world is very disagreeable, brutal, full of hate. We need some "human warmth," some "communion," some "love," and right away that brings up lovely pictures of the baby Jesus in the manger. Moreover, this was proclaimed from afar. Why not hand over some "flower power," and some "hippie love" to this Jesus who talked only of love? Why not hand over some of the communal ritual (distribution of bread) of the "Bread and Puppet Theater" to him who instituted that communion? We are in such need of the person who will reestablish love, peace, etc.

With that beginning, it cannot truly be said that publicity was what created the movement. Publicity used and exploited something which was latent. This brings us face to face with a typically religious phenomenon, that is to say, the existence of the latent need to satisfy the esthetic-communal sensibilities, together with the need for a final answer to questions of life and death. It is the formulation of a collective and spectacular response to this expectation which is being satisfied in this way (and there is where publicity enters the picture, as in all religions, rituals, shows, etc.). It is an objectification of the means made available through multiplicity, to satisfy a need made genuine by the mass adherence of those who find their answer there. Publicity only exploits and puts in shape. It does not create the exaltation, the fervor, the semierotic dances on the part of the freaks. It does furnish them with the chance to crystallize their scattered beliefs.

Hence it is probable that this religious movement will not be as extensive in France as in the United States. In the United States there has always been a tendency toward revival meetings. Also, the forms of religious expression of the freaks are greatly influenced by black piety, dances, hymns, etc. In addition, it is frequently remarked that French skepticism and rationalism are hostile to these phenomena. Finally, French youth are more politically minded than American youth. All that is partially true, but it makes the obvious success of the "Jesus parade" all the more impressive.

May it not be that (as usual) the French youth are coming to it later, are beginning now to tire of politics, are beginning to increase their use of drugs? One can always hope. If the "Jesus trip" hasn't completely arrived, at least the rudiments are on the way.

Moreover, the effects of publicity are already being felt. There is an obvious change of religious opinion in France. It is amazing that, according to the I.F.O.P. poll,* early in 1972, 75 percent of the French believe in God at the present time. Fifty percent believe in the resurrection, and 32 percent in the fact that Jesus is still alive. That is more than double the figures obtained in 1960. It is obvious that we are not here dealing with a conversion of the French to the truth of the revelation, but with a religious response to religious publicity. The Jesus phenomenon is a remarkable indication of religiosity in the midst of atheists and secularists.

3. Added Note

At this point I cannot help putting the question whether, in all that I have just written, it is indeed really a question of religion, or whether that is an abuse of language, a "manner of speaking," a similitude which is imprecise and therefore without significance. First of all, I would call attention to the fact that, in this analysis, I did not give myself any leeway at the start. I did not choose an arbitrary definition of religion, nor formulate a personal idea of my own, selected to make the argument easier. If I have rejected crude definitions of religion, that is because there is no definition on which sociologists and historians can agree.

However, I have carefully held to the generally accepted forms and functions. I did not start with observations of facts which I would like to have called religious, in order, on that basis, to make choice of the convenient definition of religion. To the contrary, I started with those observations with which everyone is in agreement, while obviously refusing to equate religion with the four "great" religions. Also, I have maintained a specific characteristic of the religious phenomenon which, for me, is not to be confused with any other manifestation of a "superstructure," of "ideologies," of "cultural images." So it is from the starting point of a particularized religious reality that I have been able to consider that the current attitude of modern man is essentially religious.

But here one encounters another obstacle. Do not these secular religions lack an essential element, namely, a God, or a Transcendent? To that, I say that the truly essential thing is precisely to

---

* Translator's Note: I.F.O.P., Institut Français de l'Opinion Publique, similar to the Gallup Poll.

dissociate religion from God. We have already seen, above, that God is not indispensable to religion. "It is not the God who makes the religion. It is the religion which makes the God who makes the religion. It is the religion which makes the God, even when it refuses to call him by that name" (G. Crespy). In religions, God is a convenience for concretizing, concentrating, and specifying the ensemble of religious orientations. He serves to orient, and as a way of explanation; but this God is never the central item of the religious phenomenon.[28] Again, the concept of his centrality is a view taken from the standpoint of Judaism, Christianity, and Islam. Since there the presence of God preceded religion, and the latter finally derives from him, we are led to suppose that this is a specific characteristic of religion, whereas, to the contrary, those examples are exceptions in the world of religion.

Again, that is why, in the history of religions, we frequently see a religion change its object, i.e., God, while itself remaining the same. The permutation of the gods is a well-known phenomenon, but it would not be conceivable if God were the central item, inherent in the system and characteristic of it.

The same is true of the Transcendent. There again, it must not be forgotten that it is man, that is, the social body which designates and specifies the Transcendent. The latter is not a reality existing in itself, but a specification on man's part. Such a designation is not universally necessary for there to be a religion.

That brings up another objection: "Every society involves a culture, an ensemble . . . of ways of living and thinking, which impose themselves, sometimes as matters of fact, sometimes as obligations or prohibitions. Salvation religions, which were merely one element among others in the culture, decline in reality. . . . Yet the secularization of an industrial civilization does not, on that

---

[28] In this connection, Granel's important article on the situation of unbelief needs to be stressed (*Esprit*, 1971), in which he shows that there is, to be sure, the "problem of the church," but that, currently in France, there is not a "problem of God." That is to say, the possibility of faith in God remains completely open, provided we do not pose God as a problem. "Contemporary thought, with all its atheism and all its intrepidity in the realm of sexuality, political criticism, and the refinement of humanist mythology, in no way keeps one apart from God. In fact, it doesn't concern him. . . ." If there is a belief with respect to God, it derives from the religious version of Christianity and the umbrella of the church. Thus he tends radically to dissociate the possibility of believing in God from Jesus Christ and from belief with respect to the Christian religion. But in that case the converse has to be admitted, namely, that it is quite normal for a religion to be set up without any reference to a transcendent God.

account, create the need for a replacement religion. The social imperatives, of which the religious imperatives were only one category, continue to order the collective life." [29] In other words, the imperatives and prohibitions are not necessarily a sign of religion. It is a question of social imperatives only, with religion as one of them, and outmoded.

To that, Aron replies by showing that the secular religions constitute "the extreme form, adapted to periods of crisis, of a phenomenon manifestly tied to the industrial society," namely, "the dialectic of universality." The latter can come into play only when there is a religious problematic.

I shall not repeat his argument here, but I would add this: at bottom, that objection amounts to saying, "What good does it do to talk about religion in this connection? The concept of a social imperative is sufficient by itself." Indeed not! That concept is much too vague, and one can read anything into it. Moreover, as we have tried to show, the religious phenomenon is not characterized merely by the existence of an imperative. It is a complex ensemble.

Finally, it seemed to us essential to show that the opinions and attitudes of contemporary western man are specifically religious. That is to say, among the possible forms of the social imperative, the religious form has triumphed once again. Thus these objections appear to me without foundation.

But here we encounter another question: is there really a renaissance of the religious, or is it a disclosure of something always there? I shall not repeat what I have already said about "the religious nature of man." On that point I maintain a complete agnosticism. I note merely, from the point of view of history, that in the nineteenth century there was indeed a desire radically to do away with the religious. Everything converged toward that end— the politico-social experiments, everyday experience, the betrayal of the church, the triumph of science, the rationalist propaganda. There was an explicit will to rationality, and the unmistakable, shattering defeat of Christianity. The nineteenth century and the beginning of the twentieth century witness an overwhelming advance of rationalism, scientism, and secularization.

But all that came into play only in connection with Christianity. There was a no less obvious retreat of Christianity. What gave the impression that this was a fulfillment of the prophecy of Saint-

[29] R. Aron, *Les Désillusions du Progrès* (1969).

Simon was not only the fact, to which we have already alluded, of the ideological equating of Christianity with religion, but also the fact that the religious had been identified with Christianity for so long that it was unable to free itself from it. There was a retreat of the religious during that period for the reason that it could not find a new form, in spite of the tentative efforts in that direction exhibited by romanticism and rationalism.

Then, the moment the defeat of Christianity became obvious, when, also, enough time had elapsed to allow the religious to free itself, to invest in new objects and develop new forms, religion reappeared. That is what we have been witnessing for the past half century or more. Hence there was a temporary hiatus, but basically such interruptions are observed whenever a religious system goes down and another takes its place. The succession is never immediate. The replacement is not automatic, and those who live during that period always lament the irreligion of their times and the loss of sacred traditions. We have many proofs of that in the West as well as in China.

But we are not impressed, because those intervals seem very short to us (what is a "gap" of a half century, or even a century, at a distance of two thousand years?), whereas our own seems long. It is merely a matter of historical perspective. As a result, we treat as a mere passing attitude the lamentations of the ancients over the growth of irreligion, and their looking upon it as a value lost, while we ourselves are starting a hymn of praise for the victory and liberation of man. Thus our age seems new to us, but the experience of history shows that those excellent and virtuous people were wrong to be so regretful, and sociological analysis shows that those who glory in the irreligion and rationality of man come of age succumb to the same mistake.

Finally, a last question arises: Harvey Cox, in *The Secular City*, recognized that there are elements of religion in our time, in certain political ideologies, in magic approaches, and in ceremonies (as in the selection of Miss America), but for him all that is a *vestige* of social beliefs. Those are survivals of a magico-social residue, dogged remainders from a tribal and pagan past. That is already doomed and outmoded. The true movement is not to be found there. Whenever that sort of thing shows some vitality (as in nazism), it is a throwback doomed by history. To Cox it is obvious that nothing of this religious can subsist in the face of the advance of science in general, and of psychoanalysis in particular.

This argument by Cox seems to me remarkably superficial. That is so, first of all, because he has in no way gone to the trouble to analyze the religious phenomena, which he treats very summarily. Also, he nowhere demonstrates that it is a question of vestigial remains. The assumption is a way of avoiding the problem. "There are, of course, religious phenomena, but they are vestiges"—and that's that. He would have to prove that it is a question of doomed survivals, and not a resurgence. Yet there isn't a shadow of proof, nor even of serious study. It is not even clear just what Cox means by religion. We are confronted with an appraisal, a choice. "As between the scientific-rational-irreligious movement and the religious phenomena, we conclude that the former has the future ahead of it, while the latter are tribal vestiges."

But conclusion is not reason. Cox should at least respond to the following questions: why, after a period of religious retreat toward rationality, are we witnessing a resurgence?—for it is a matter of revivification and not of a mere survival, which has a quite different significance. How does it happen that such a fundamentally irreligious movement as Marxism should have given birth to one of the principal religions of the modern world? How does it happen that a people in process of laicization, and very advanced scientifically, like the Germans, find themselves suddenly crystallized into a neo-religious unanimity with nazism? How does it happen that a veritable transfer of the sacred onto the desacralizing object should have taken place? Is there any hope of escape through technology, when the latter becomes the sacred?—or through science lived in the mythical manner? Finally, can we treat as a doomed survival a set of phenomena involving more than three quarters of secular, adult, western humanity?

But none of these questions disturbs Cox, who prefers to sleep secure in his dogmatic affirmations. It is true that he seems also to have discovered a certain religious dimension in modern man, to which he alludes in his book, *The Feast of Fools*, but the problem then arises how to reconcile this *Feast of Fools* with *The Secular City*.[30]

---

[30] The case of Cox is strange. These two principal books appear exactly contradictory. In *The Secular City*, he explains that the modern world is secular, that nature is disenchanted, politics and values desacralized, that man is rational and mature, that urbanization produces phenomena such as anonymity, mobility, pragmatism, the profane, and that this is all to the good, that this new situation conforms perfectly to God's will for man. He justifies the situation absolutely from the Christian point of

view. Work should be emancipated from religion. The culture should be exorcized of all traces of the religious. The church should adapt to the secular world. Theology should treat God as a sociological or political problem.

Yet in *The Feast of Fools*, the same Cox explains, with the same conviction, that man cannot live without festival and fantasy, that in the modern world he is frightfully lonely, poor, and naked, because there is no longer the dimension of festival (which is strictly the religious dimension); that festival corresponds to a typically Christian orientation, that people (hippies, for example) are in the process of rediscovering fantasy, of getting away from dreary, technical rationality, of breaking out of set ways, of resuming myths in their fresh beginnings; that drugs are a blessing, because thanks to them one can recover the mystical experience; that the role of Christianity and the church is to reintroduce rites, festivals, and dance into worship, and to live the faith as a game (a typically religious dimension). After having said how wonderful it was finally to be rid of religion, he declares that it is a great blessing that, in spite of secularization, mysticism has come back again.

So he fights for the rehabilitation of religion from a Christian point of view. He discovers, as we have said, the continuity between religion and Christianity. He finds the current tendency to separate the religious from the Christian quite suspect. The Christian task now is to take part in this "spiritual renaissance," and to join in with it. . . .

I shall not present here the critique of Cox's monumental ignorances from the point of view of history, of his basic lack of comprehension of the sociology of the modern world, of the uncertainty of his concepts, of the lack of any scientific method, of the unbelievable weakness of his constructs. I would merely call attention to Cox's explanation on the subject of the fundamental contradiction between the two books (preface to the French edition).

He acknowledges that one could be disconcerted by what some readers feel is a complete change. For one thing, he does not look upon it as a complete change. (However, either the society is really secular, or else it is giving in to a religious renaissance. The two are not entirely reconcilable!) For another thing, and most particularly, he gives the following wonderful explanation: "What remains is my basic attitude, full of hope toward the modern world . . ." Here, in fact, is the entire thought (if it can be called that) of Cox. Whatever modern man is, whatever he does, whatever may be the orientation of our society, it is *good*, it is *full of hope*, it conforms to the will of God. A simplistic analysis leads to the conclusion that, given the city and technology, this is a world which is rational and secular, etc. How wonderful and Christian! Another analysis, no less simplistic, given drugs, hippies, and utopianism, leads to the conclusion that we are rediscovering festival, myth, etc. That's even more wonderful and Christian!

In this way Cox is recovering the great traditional function of the church, when she blessed cannon, hound packs, and dance orchestras. Man can do anything at all. The church should be on hand to assure him that it is according to God's will and that the future is his. Cox is a medieval theologian, in the sense of integrating Christianity into the culture (any culture) of the times. He is our most important witness today for theological nothingness.

VI

SECULAR RELIGIONS:
Political Religion

1. The Appearance of Political Religions

When Raymond Aron coined the expression "secular religion," he
was thinking essentially of political religion. We have seen that he
needs a much more extensive field of view. Still, political religion
remains a central, decisive, and typical form of the religious life of
modern man. What we have been describing up to this point has
reference to a general religious experience, more or less permanent,
and in line with the course of history. It comes through in terms of
all-embracing attitudes.

What we are now about to examine, to the contrary, arises
specifically in the modern West, is erected on the Christian
infrastructure, and can be denoted by traits derived from Christianity. It is also an aspect of post-Christendom. The *religious* legacy
of Christianity is taken over by the great political currents and by
politics. We actually encounter this, not only as expressed at
different levels, from the most obvious to the most subtle, in the
form of hidden religious tendencies, of a fixation of the religious on
objects not intended for that, of unexpected religious burgeoning,
all unintentional and unconscious, but also in the form of

organized religions, clearly instituted as religion, with dogma, myth, rites, and churchlike establishments, communal gatherings and sacraments, complete irrationality, the dialectic of anguish and consolation, mystical expression and prayer, a global interpretation of man, of the world and of history, and the singling out of heretics. It is a question of political religions.

Politics, after having been dominated as a subordinate sphere by the religious phenomenon, gained its independence from organized religion, and has been making a triumphal entry into the religious for half a century. It is the supreme religion of this age. This development was brought about by the growth of the state, with its need for psychological and spiritual influence, on the one hand, and with the appearance of a new kind of ideology, on the other.

Ideology can be defined as "a more or less systematic interpretation of society and history, considered by the militants as the supreme truth." Ideologies have multiplied with the growth of nations, modern states, and the democratic system. However, there appeared in due course a special type of ideology, with "Marxism-Leninism-Stalinism" and with Hitlerism. These entered into direct and explicit competition with Christianity. They claimed to be superior to the transcendent religions and to be replacements for them. This is correlative to the crisis and retreat of Christianity.

These ideologies, therefore, actually took on the functions and qualities of the religions, and of Christianity particularly. They became a sort of substitute for them. Marxism-Leninism-Stalinism has had an astonishing history. In the course of the nineteenth century, the philosophic and economic theories of Marx represented a complete system of explanation and interpretation of the world, coupled with a global view of the meaning of history and its trends, which assured man of a meaning for his life. But, although it bore an unconscious imprint of Judeo-Christianity from the outset, the thinking was accepted only by declared Marxists under its scientific aspect as a general analysis of the realities of the times, extending into the future by means of hypotheses and projecting actions to be carried out on the basis of the probable and the rational.

Nevertheless, as M. Garder has so well pointed out ("Une Théocratie matérialiste," *Le Monde*, April 1970), Engels had "endowed the system with a kind of divinity, by enunciating a veritable metaphysical postulate, according to which matter is uncreated. It evolves." He ended by deifying, if not matter, at least the *élan vital*, that is, the mechanism of the dialectical evolution of matter. Moreover, this idea fitted perfectly with that of Marx, which, however, had never gone that far.

The dialectic of history also could strictly be considered as a sort of *deus ex machina.* Moreover, it should be emphasized that the entire work of Marx is steeped in a sort of religious atmosphere, a religious environment or climate, manifestly derived from the strong Judeo-Christian impregnation it had received from its youth and infancy, and which he himself recognized. He never managed to free himself fully from the prophetism of Israel. In fact, that is less easy to achieve than the overturning of a system of thought like Hegel's.

But the religious quality suddenly appears when this thinking is associated with Russia. I do not say the Russian soul. The category of soul is at present rejected. There was produced a phenomenon identical with that of the transformation of Christianity from a nonreligion to a religion through its adoption by the Roman imperial circles. The power of the czar was religious. It implied a religious orientation and religious attitudes on the part of the people, and that is not as easily destroyed as a regime. Just as the rites and panegyrics directed toward the pagan emperor remained the same when directed toward the Christian emperor, so the religious faith toward the czar remained the same when directed toward the Marxist emperor. There was established a popular religion of the political power, which was all the more indispensable since that power had killed the czar, an inexpiable sacrilege which causes the sacred to redound to the murderer.

That transfer was to be the turning point in the creation of a materialistic religion, endowing with faith a system which was waiting to become religious. The outward works of Lenin, his establishment of a party on the model of the Jesuit Order and in the image of the Order of the Knights of the Sword (he said so himself), the accentuation of the role of the proletariat and the elevation of the writings of Marx; the outward works of Stalin, establishing a liturgy, dogmatics, an inquisition of heretics—all those things went to confirm this religion very rapidly. It was organized by the exact procedures followed by Christianity itself. It ended in the "materialistic replica, a striking morphological similitude, of Roman Catholicism."

This phenomenon of the transformation of Marxism into a religion has been studied in a systematic way by Jules Monnerot, in the admirable *Sociologie du Communisme*, and by Raymond Aron. It has been the subject of numerous statements, from Nicolas

Berdyaev to Alexander Solzhenitsyn. However, the most impressive statement on it has been given us by A. Robin, in *Fausse Parole*. His work required him to listen every day to all broadcasts in the Russian language from 1945 to 1955. He, though basically antireligious, was led to show the specifically religious mechanisms of relations with Stalin.

It is important to emphasize that in Robin's works, as in others, we are in no sense dealing with a vague notion of religion, with a superficial use of the adjective "religious" (to pretend that Hitlerism, Leninism, and Stalinism were religions is too easy and journalistic). Nothing of the kind. We are dealing with extremely precise and rigorous analyses of those regimes, showing just about a complete identification of the political phenomenon thus incarnated with everything known as religion over the course of three thousand years of history.

The young fascists, like the young Stalinists, represented, from the phenomenological point of view, an indisputable religious prototype. Psychologically and intellectually they were the same as the young Catholic ultramontanists of 1900. The phenomenon of religion was accelerated in the communist world in proportion as it came into competition with Hitlerism. It is needless to repeat the demonstration of what is, *above all,* the mystical and religious character of this movement. That is to say that, before it was the expression of a phase of the class struggle, before it was a response to an economic situation, before it was an incarnation of the basic German mind, nazism was a gigantic religious drive, in its inspiration as well as in its forms. People of that period who were not Germans were not deceived. The most current saying from 1930 to 1936 was: "In the face of the nazi mystique, we have only one hope, namely, to have a mystique of our own for the young."

That was felt especially in communist circles. They found themselves confronted by an explosive and onrushing mystique, and obliged to fight fire with fire. Democracy was unable to operate at that level. It could not set itself up as a religion. In Leninist-Stalinist communism, on the other hand, the path had already been entered upon, and the nazi competition only hastened and hardened the transformation. Once that character was acquired, it was irreversible. After nazism had been conquered, the religion remained. It was a global communist religion which affected all the communist regimes.

The Chinese regime, in its turn, took exactly the same course. The new incarnation of political religion is currently Maoism.

There we see the same traits as in the predecessors: a mystique, irrationality, a party of the clergy, identification of the god, attributes of divinity, etc., together with a dogmatic closure on all discussion, a global interpretation of everything, a totalitarian control over all actions and feelings, to the exclusion of all other values (cultural values, for example; we are struck by the systematic destruction of works of art from the past during the cultural revolution), the appraisal of all modes of conduct (the accusation against the wife of Liu Shao Chi for her elegance, her politeness, her manner of eating), the setting up of a moral and spiritual hierarchy of values and, above all, the celebrated determination to create a new man of virtue. We shall come back to that.

During the time when certain regimes were becoming religious, the process of the sacralizing of the state was everywhere being carried out. It is the coming together of the two phenomena which leads to the present situation. Politics has become a religion, not only because the political religions of nazism and Marxism have little by little won over all the political forms, but also because the latter were capable of that development only to the extent to which the object of politics, the power of the state, had itself become sacred. Such is the ensemble of actions and reactions which result in secular religion.

2. Extreme Forms

To analyze political religion in its structures, comparable in all points to those of Christianity, it is necessary to observe it in its extreme forms, which it takes on in Stalinism, Hitlerism, and Maoism. It must be stressed, of course, that these are not deviant forms. To the contrary, they are typical. It is a mistake to suppose that Stalin was a neurotic imbecile, suffering from a mania for persecution and tyranny. It is a mistake to suppose that Hitler was an uncultured and ridiculous paranoid suffering from delusions of grandeur. They were the exact incarnation of what could be done at a given moment of time in the political life. These are not accidents, which one hopes are over and done with. We continue to live exactly in their impetus. Mutually, Stalin is the exact continuator of Lenin, and Mao substantiates the line.

The first religious fact which strikes us in that regime is the cult of personality. To start with, it is interesting to note the use of the

word "cult," which in this instance was not applied by Christians
but by Marxists. This cult of personality was already powerful with
Lenin, not that he sought it for himself, but he laid the groundwork
for it by affirming the validity of the personal dictator. It must not
be forgotten that it was he who sterilized the soviets, and who
pressed the case against collegiate rule, as well as against self-rule.
At the Ninth Congress of the Communist Party of Russia, in 1920,
he declared: "Socialist soviet democracy is in no way incompatible
with the personal power of the dictatorship. . . . The will of a class
is occasionally carried forward by a dictator, who sometimes does a
better job by himself, and often is more necessary. . . ." He never
ceased to repeat that theme, asserting that collegiate control is by
no means an expression of the dictatorship of the proletariat.

From that point on, the drift toward the cult of the person was
inevitable. With the twofold factor of public spontaneity (*all* hopes
concentrated on one, fervently adored man) and the dictator's
determination to be effective (a psychological factor indispensable
for making the authority acceptable), one could list, trait for trait,
what happened with respect to Lenin as corresponding to what
happened with Octavian Augustus, which ended in the imperial
political religion. In fact, the cult of the person results in the
deification of the dictator. He is the supreme person, corresponding
to the personal God of Christianity. God is much more than a
charismatic chief, and so is the dictator. It is not a question of
casting doubt on the analysis of R. Caillois, but once in power, the
leader is deified through the collective worship, for he has not only
the gifts but also the totality of the power.

Mao, like Stalin, is the universal procreator, the source of
fertility, Providence itself. The person of Hitler, like that of Mao, is
held by the faithful to be transcendent. It is important not to take
the passages about them as being of no importance. To the
contrary, they mean what they say. No one laughed when Hitler
stated that he had been sent by the Almighty, and that he was
establishing his reign for a thousand years. The young Hitlerites
who died invoking aloud the name of the Führer took him for a
saving and transcendent divinity, for whom one must die, and who
would help one to die well.

Neither did anyone laugh upon hearing that "Josef Vissariono-
vich Stalin was the most genial, the most beloved, the wisest man
the world had ever known," and again, "Thou art the only one to
care for the poor and to protect the oppressed" (exact quotations).

No one laughed, not even his opponents. All that is now forgotten, yet it was a matter of declarations of love and faith, which were unshakable because religious.

Nor does one laugh when singing that Mao *is* the red sun that illumines all the earth, that he assures and makes possible a good harvest, that by applying the thought of Mao scientific research advances, or a difficult surgical operation can be carried out. "I bandaged him. Mao is healing him," was literally stated by a great Chinese surgeon in May of 1970.

These gods are indeed gods, with all the attributes of divinity. That is why Lenin was embalmed and worshiped in the mausoleum. Napoleon would have been the object of similar adoration and veneration had Christianity not still been so dominant at that time as to forbid such deification. But with the void created by the retreat of Christianity, and now with the death of God, which was experienced before the theologians found out about it, there arises a substitutionary phenomenon as a replacement. Whatever has the right to ultimate power, really to the absolute power of life and death, is pictured as a god, because that is the image which asserts itself in the Christian West.[1]

We have the extreme case of Kwame Nkrumah of Ghana. If he had not occurred in the general climate of secular religions, it could be said that he was simply a case of paranoid insanity, a "happenstance," hence without interest. To the contrary, he is remarkably representative of the general trend, having merely carried political religion to its ultimate. He is the Messiah, the Redeemer (*Osagyefo* is his official title). He is normally put on a par with Buddha, Muhammad, and Jesus. He is *Kasapeko* (he who speaks once and for all), *Oyeadieye* (the restorer of all things)—a striking reproduction of soteriological titles. In school, one learns that Nkrumah is "the equal of God and God himself," and it also goes without saying that he is immortal.

That was all combined with the most absolute, the most arbitrary, the most insolently personal, the most tyrannical power, from 1953 to 1966, that our times have ever known. When anything goes wrong, as it does in all the deified monarchies, it is not the god who made the mistake. It is his clergy. At the time of Nkrumah's death, an opponent could say: "The *Osagyefo* was never guilty of

---

[1] To avoid any misunderstanding, I repeat that in my view Maoism was oriented in this direction following upon, and in imitation of, Stalinism, with the former attitudes toward the emperors mixed in.

any excess, but certain members of his entourage," a classically religious statement. No control by anyone is ever tolerated in the completely autocratic decisions of the Messiah. All his death sentences are his own, and completely arbitrary.

Yet Nkrumah was entirely respected by Europeans, and by the World Council of Churches. His formula (blasphemous for a Christian), "Seek first the political kingdom, and all these things shall be yours as well," was enthusiastically applauded at the "Church and Society" conference of the World Council (1966). He is God incarnate, a perfect example of a political religion blessed by the religious authorities.

But the god does not reign alone. Political religion creates a pantheon of heroes, just as Christianity, contrary to its initial teaching, peopled the heavens with a host of personages close to God, who also were objects of veneration and served as examples of the life approved by God, the saints. This is undoubtedly linked to patriotism, but there is also unquestionably the need for moral examples to which to refer. Furthermore, revolutionary movements are always incarnated in heroes.

Yet it seems to me that our modern heroes, in spite of differences in theme, content, and motivation, closely approximate the legendary heroes, those of the pagan legend with its demigods, as well as those of the Christian legend, which tended, in fact, to equate hero and saint. How close the heroes of the Middle Ages are to saints. In the nineteenth century it looked as though the heroes were laicized, but now we are seeing the sacred hero emerge once again. The fact is that no culture, no society, can survive without a life model which is absolutized, unimpeachable, beyond criticism. There has to be a man who can be shown as such, and set forth as an unquestionable example. In this laicized age, attempts have been made to find such a model.

It has been necessary to find someone to worship. Movie stars and champions arouse a certain enthusiasm, but their lives are too empty, too meaningless. Most especially, they lack a relationship with a god. The modern hero, on the other hand, the hero of work, of revolution, of devotion to the god, is a complete model, because he is consecrated by the god. He is the life set forth by the god, and given over to him. The similarity of these heroes of all the secular religions is absolutely astonishing. They are all admired for the same qualities and the same inspiration. Nothing is more like Horst Wessel than Min Ho.

On this score Maoism, as is the case with all the others, has carried the Stalino-Hitlerite heritage to its ultimate. The Maoist heroes are typical of all the others. By reason of their origins, they are popular heroes on everybody's level, but they are carried to life's heights through their relations with the god. That is something exclusive with them (in spite of the official condemnation of the individual in Maoism, and the assertion that the masses are the only heroes). The hero is, above all, nurtured on the thought of Mao. He endures all in the name of the god. "Suffering is nothing. The really terrible thing is not to have the thought of Mao in one's mind." The life of the hero is scrupulously laid out in detail, so that he can serve as model and as intercessor. "The hero is the living application of Mao's thought. It is that thought incarnate." Most heroes die pronouncing his name and recalling his precepts.

Countless are the stories of healing, in which the first words, pronounced with difficulty, are "President Mao," in which the first characters, written with difficulty, are the characters which go to make up his name, in which a paralyzed arm is extended toward his picture. Better yet, when someone is asked about his family, he says, "I have President Mao."

How can we fail to liken to the saint of every religion the hero who is miraculously healed, who is entirely devoted, his personality given over to that of the god, yet who is an exemplary type, a model of the Chinese of tomorrow, perfect at all levels—at work, in the family, in patriotism, in honesty, in the struggle against egoism and selfishness—who is freed of all external preoccupations to concentrate on his revolutionary task, putting aside all problems of person and sentiment? "I think we should live in such a way that others can have a better life." Who said that, Saint Vincent de Paul or Lei Feng? In the end, he is himself the object of a cult of worship, organized and directed by the god himself, and which serves exactly as a mediating worship.

As far as France is concerned, surely Gaullism is not, in itself, a religious phenomenon. It lacks the depth, and it is not global. It exhibits none of the characteristics of the religious, which implies a lasting quality, among other things.

On the other hand, the relationship with de Gaulle shows a certain religious attitude. He was the Father, as has often been said. But the fact of the religious element is even more true now than during his lifetime. Yet at that time, too, the effect of one of his speeches was astonishing, and is only to be explained by a religious attachment. That he should have succeeded in ending the riot of

1968 by a speech is surely significant, for there was nothing special about the speech itself. Someone else could have said the same things without any effect. The opposition were so taken by surprise that they tried to explain their deflation by circumstantial causes, which is inaccurate. The truth is that the god was speaking through the Father. That was the sole motive for the restoration of order, and it implies, in fact, a deep loyalty.

This is being confirmed today. It is not the visits to the tomb which strike me, nor the books about de Gaulle, nor the multiplicity of portraits. What impresses me, rather, is the dedication of votive offerings to him at the cemetery (a crutch, necklaces), and then the purchase of little packets of earth from his tomb, and even more, because spontaneous and not commercialized, the kissing of the tombstone and the collecting of pebbles from around it, which happens often.

Here we are exactly at the level of the veneration of relics, of the saint, of the sacred tomb. It is not a matter of the hero, of the "Great Man," nor of mementos, nor of expressions of gratitude, but precisely of religious acts directed toward the man who incarnated the religion of the nation. It is not a result of propaganda (that means nothing without a respondent among the propagandized). It is, rather, an expression of the religious need of modern man, which focuses on all available objects.

But a place has to be made also for the less important hero-saints. We noted above that movie stars did not play a satisfactory role in filling the void of piety left by rationalism. Now however, thanks to political religion, the stars are finding their place. They are at last having a part in serious worship. The moment an artist is "committed," he becomes a hero. Joan Baez, Melina Mercouri, Yves Montand are beginning to acquire a dignity superior to Hollywood stars. They are having a part in man's struggle for man. They are not yet model heroes, but they have already entered the religious sphere.

In the presence of the god and the saints, the only attitude possible is that of faith. That, in fact, is how we are obliged to describe the attitude of the militants. Jules Monnerot has studied the characteristics of this faith at some length *(Psychologie des Religions séculières)*. He says, "We are dealing with a concept which is zealous, capable of uniting, of unifying into a communal whole great numbers of people over and above their personal differences. These zealots constitute a society, a unity." They live in a state of mutual influence. The faith takes possession of each person and of all his intellectual faculties. It sets the exact boundaries within which thought can develop and grow. It automatically rejects everything outside that scheme of things. It draws the line between what one can listen to and what one literally does not listen to. Within that defined area the individual enjoys great leeway. Since he cannot depart from the area, which is protected by the criteria of the faith, he considers himself perfectly free. The faith radically eliminates all spirit of criticism. The presuppositions are so imposed as matters of obvious fact that there is no way to question them by argument, either of fact or of reason. The "real motives" are sheltered from argument.

However, at this point we have to introduce a nuance. There is a complete absence of criticism for everything which concerns the object of faith, and, conversely, a hypercriticism of everything outside the select domain. Whatever is outside the faith is Evil. With that established, an excess of criticism of the *latter* makes up for an absence of criticism of the *former*. Psychoanalysts know the problem well. "Pathological blindness" is combined with "pathological clairvoyance."

Religious faith is the same as political faith. We have lived that in our own experience. The faith is expressed, of course, in an interaction between exclusiveness and monomania. "The subject's activity is concentrated and unified while combining with a great number of activities of the same nature and directed in the same sense." That obviously leads to a denial of reality. It is the object of faith which is true.

We have seen this with Hitler and Stalin. The case of the communists was particularly flagrant. The Moscow trials, the German-Soviet pact, the concentration camps, the purges, the betrayals, the repression of the Berlin revolts and the Hungarian revolt—all that was either denied, with accusations against the other side, or explained and embraced within the world of the faith. Judgment was completely obscured in the name of a faith which had to be kept intact if *everything* was not to collapse. It was obviously a case of all or nothing.

This is characteristic of religion. Communism, directed by the god, the genial chief, the little father of the people, must resolve *all* the problems of man, and bring us to a higher stage of humanity. It involves *nothing* subject to criticism. If it were merely relative, the whole would collapse. If it were subject to any alteration, any stain, one could not devote oneself to it. Faith makes possible a unity with the god and with the heroes, in complete innocence, in devotion *perinde ac cadaver,* with a system explanatory of all things. That is not a mere attitude of belief, for beliefs are numerous and often uncertain. It is indeed a question of faith, in the Christian sense of the word, with all the totalitarianism and absolutism which that represents. Political faith has exactly taken the place of, and assumed all the characteristics of, the Christian faith in the West. People, conditioned by centuries of Christianity, have found it impossible to live without this totalitarian organization of the person.

The fact that the object of faith can change is explained by the indestructible character. The very best Hitlerites, in a difficult crisis, can become Stalinists, and now the best Stalinists are becoming Maoists, for the faith phenomenon today is found chiefly among the leftists. In its psychic structure and expression, it is the same as with the Hitlerites and the Stalinists.

Faith's special privilege, intransigence, has been transferred from the Christian faith, now become soft, tolerant, and pluralistic, to political faith. Nothing is more formidable than these political believers. Like all believers, they have a monopoly on truth, but with the difference that the truth can never be dissociated from the political power. Here is where political faith seems to me incomparably more dangerous than any other. Buddhism in no way implies an association with the political power. The contrary is the case. Neither does Christianity. If Christianity remains faithful to its inspiration and object, the God of Love, it is incompatible with the exercise of political power. The combination of the two came about by accident.

On the other hand, political faith can be incarnate only in the political power, the modern state. In that respect it is the most atrocious of all the religions humanity has ever known. It is the religion of abstract power incarnated in the police, the army, and the administration, that is, in the only powers that are concrete and tangible. The sole defense against this had been the liberalism and laicity of the state. Those weak and reasonable dikes have given way. A spokesman for the left wrote me recently (when I was defending the laicity of the state, and the need to avoid disseminating a formal ideology through public instruction, and to fight against ideologies) that when a person knows the truth he cannot let it remain hidden. His truth was obviously leftist, and he explained to me that the mind of youth should be oriented toward the commune, etc. But the fact is that Stalin and Hitler had each placed the state in the service of the truth. There is no difference between a leftist believer and a Stalinist or Hitlerite believer. Their attitude toward the schools and the power are the same.

However, one also has to determine the object of faith, apart from and in addition to the faith in the god from whom all the rest flows. The content of the faith is given in a Holy Scripture, which is itself an object of faith. Indeed, it is worth noting that the secular religions are religions of a Book, like the three books which they follow: *Das Kapital, Mein Kampf,* and *The Little Red Book.*[2] We are indeed dealing with sacred books,[3] coming from the god and containing the revelation. They are holy because special, different from all other books, the point of departure for all thought, all of which must be holy, understood, and weighed. They are sacred because beyond criticism. There can be no argument concerning them. One can only enter that world and try better and better to understand. Every sentence in these sacred books is studied, analyzed, interpreted, and reinterpreted. No book since the Bible and the Koran has been the object of such knowledge, respect, and submissive obedience on the part of the reader. Holy Scripture should be known by all the faithful. The obligation rests on the people as a whole, and it constitutes the shared collective thinking.

There can be no error in it. The worst banalities and platitudes which it contains are piously treasured. It cannot be nonsense, because such a thing does not come from the god. Hence a profound meaning must be discovered. One digs endlessly deeper and deeper, to the point finally of coming up with an astounding meaning: "Power emanates from the barrel of a gun."

This Holy Scripture has a revelatory power which illuminates, but in order to profit from it one must apply himself without letup.

---

[2] Moreover it needs to be emphasized that the quality of this sacred literature declines with its evolution. *Mein Kampf* is obviously much below the level of *Das Kapital,* and *The Little Red Book* is the lowest of all. That may result from familiarity. Sacred Scripture is accepted without any requirement as to content. In Marxism, as in Judaism and Christianity, the body of Scripture is made up of successive layers of revelation, from the young Marx to the older Marx, followed by a series of interpreters, only some of whom are admitted to the corpus. Lenin, for example, is included in the sacred text, while other commentators are not universally recognized. Thus these do not have the authority of the one and only book, or of a single effort like the Koran.

[3] This term is expressly employed, for example, by Solzhenitsyn with reference to *Das Kapital:* "He dreamed of reading that sacred book" (*L'inconnu de Kretchetovka*).

"We must study the works of President Mao each day. If we miss only one day the problems pile up. If we miss two days we fall back. If we miss three days we can no longer live," so says the Maoist hero Min Ho, and Lei Feng adds, "Whenever we do not understand, we should say so." Every difficulty can be resolved by this Holy Scripture, which contains the answer to all questions. Whenever one is brought up short by a difficulty, he should look for a solution in the works of Marx, or Lenin, or Mao. The mere reading of a passage produces an "illumination" (the word is employed constantly), and one understands how to surmount the obstacle. Mao's thought saves, even in quite physical accidents, such as fire or shipwreck.

From then on, this Holy Scripture, like all the others, is characterized by an authoritarian method implemented in a body of quotations. A saying from the sacred book is all it takes for knowing what is the truth. Hence, the thing to do is to find the appropriate text for each problem. Reflection, analysis, and the drawing up of a problematic are useless, as is the scientific approach. Science is the knowledge and the application of the sacred book. All of science is contained in it. One quotation and you have the truth.

The authority of the author is sufficient to assure the weightiness of the thought derived from it. Of course, the argument from authority is valid only for the believer, but for him its validity is absolute. For others, who have not got into Holy Scripture, the argument is worthless, but that makes no difference because they are entirely outside the truth. Thus, to be certain of the truth and also of the effective procedure, it suffices to place the appropriate quotations physically alongside one another, together with the indispensable commentary. "Thought turns into the shortest path from one quotation to another," as is seen beautifully with Lenin and Stalin. It is a renewal of scholasticism at its worst.

Holy Scripture designates a Messiah, he who will completely fulfill the will or the foreknowledge of the god. At the same time, he makes and fulfills history by opening a meaningful possibility. This figure of the Messiah, however, appears foreign to Maoism, unless it be the youth who are called upon to play that role. In truth, it seems to be such a profoundly Judeo-Christian concept, and so completely foreign to the spiritual past of the Chinese, that its absence is understandable.

The Messiah is quite specific. He is the one who plunges into the

s, who enters the depths of despair, suffering, and death, to
erge luminous, glorious, and victorious. He carries all humanity
with him on the journey to hell, which opens a path for history and
humanity. Unless there is a total debasement and humiliation of
the bearer of God's will, there is no Messiah.

Now this picture is given exactly by Marx, in terms of the
proletariat, and by Hitler, in terms of the race. Marx's great
passage on the proletariat is well known:

> . . . a sphere of society having a universal character
> because of its universal suffering and claiming no
> *particular* right because no *particular wrong* but *unqual-*
> *ified wrong* is perpetrated on it; a sphere that can invoke
> no *traditional* title but only a *human* title . . . , a
> sphere, finally, that cannot emancipate itself without
> emancipating itself from all the other spheres of society,
> thereby emancipating them; a sphere, in short, that is
> the *complete loss* of humanity and can only redeem itself
> through the *total redemption* of humanity. . . . Her-
> alding the *dissolution of the existing order of things*, the
> proletariat merely announces the *secret of its own*
> *existence* because it *is* the *real* dissolution of this order.[4]

We have the same description with Hitler, of an Aryan race
which is noble and holy. It has been debased and used by the
business world, by money, by corruption, by democracy. It has
been plunged into corruption by the Jews, by an infamous treaty
which has emasculated it. It is surrounded by an entirely inimical
world, its spiritual depths denied by science and rationalism. It is
scattered among the exploiting nations, and is being undermined
by an ongoing plot. The Aryan race is profoundly victimized and
alienated. This aspect of Hitler's thought has too often been
forgotten.

Likewise, he never ceased to speak of the *resurrection* of the race
and of the *Volk*. This race is to be both the instrument for fulfilling
destiny and an opening for history. Trait for trait, it is exactly the
same model as Marx's view of the proletariat.

But it is obvious, as with the Christ, that the "time" when the

---

[4] *Writings of the Young Marx on Philosophy and Society*, trans. and ed. Loyd D.
Easton and Kurt H. Guddat (New York: Doubleday, 1967), pp. 262–263.

proletariat or the race assumes history and undertakes its ascent is a cut-off time for history. The entire past is absolute evil (except for a very distant past, the primitive commune of Engels, or the legendary, Wagnerian pre-Middle Ages). History can now, thanks to the Messiah, emerge into the stage of the future characterized by absolute good. The transition into the millennium, or into communism's higher phase, is precisely the fulfillment of the work of the Messiah, and it entails a last judgment.

The Messiah is the bearer of the hope of salvation and of the fulfillment of history. The person loyal to Marxism, or nazism, or Maoism is both a saved person and a new person. He is purified from all former evil, either by belonging to the body of the Messiah or by accepting its law. Such is the member of the proletariat, or those after him who enter into this movement of history, and who will be similar to him—the Aryan, and the "Aryans by reason of service."

The believer is totally placated. He knows no more doubt, division, or dilemma. He is assured of being on the right side, which is guaranteed him by the loyalty of those who are with him. He has the feeling of being finally in possession of a total truth which is indestructible (and one knows that to have the truth is a guarantee of salvation). He is pardoned from all his past faults, for this system tends precisely to efface all social faults. He is guaranteed against all the faults to come, since from now on everything he does in the interest of the cause corresponds to the good. It is a situation eminently characteristic of the believer. The cathartic function of universal religions has been emphasized for some time. When the religions disappear, it is essential that the functions of catharsis continue to take place, for man cannot live without purification. Psychoanalysis proved inadequate for the role. It was substituted for, and surpassed by, the secular religions, which conveyed catharsis through testing and sacrifice. The purified person becomes truly a new person. L. Aragon has attempted to show this in his great passage on *The Communists*.

It is noteworthy that when one gets down to actualities one perceives that the new man doesn't have much that is new. It is a question of industrious working habits, of devotion to the collectivity, of sacrifices for the Führer, and of being hard on the enemy. All that is quite ordinary, but it doesn't prevent the general assertion that the communists, or the nazis, are truly superior people. One absolutizes, and describes a black-and-white world. All the evil is on one side and all the good on the other, which is extraordinarily liberating.

There again is a similarity with religions, a similarity all the more extreme when one considers that this new person is only a person waiting for something. He is already new, yet not entirely, because all will be fulfilled only at the end of the revolution. Then one shall be in the completely developed (the higher phase) communist society, or in the millennium (a perfect likeness of the Christian tension between realized eschatology and subsequent eschatology). One awaits the time when not only the faithful will be new, but the whole world as well, the fulfillment of Marx's celebrated prophecy, when man is reconciled with nature, with his fellow man, and with himself—or that of Hitler, in which man will carry to the heights every potentiality of man, and will finally bring in the superman who will reign over all things. In both, it is a case of society without the state and without bureaucracy. That will be the fullness of historic time.

This apocalyptic expectation is expressed either in utopianism or in millennialism,[5] according to circumstance and moment. There is the Hitlerite millennialism, and that of the Chinese cultural revolution; or the soviet utopianism, and that of the dependent communist parties. In every case it is a matter of picturing a perfect state of affairs and of beings. One finds the same themes as in traditional apocalyptic: judgment, the passage through fire, the new stature achieved by man, the restoration of unity through the elimination of differences. Along with this is a return to the perfection of the first age, by integrating and assimilating into it the perfection resulting from historical development (the return to the primitive commune, but with all the achievements of science and technology; the return to the Germanic of the high Middle Ages, but, there also, with the inclusion of the most advanced technology)—in other words, the exact replica of the Judeo-Christian images, and in correlation with the oldest religious archetypes.

This faith is expressed and formulated in a theology. One cannot give any other name to the intellectual systematizing and the continued commentary on the sacred texts, for the purpose of answering objections, of enlightening the faithful in an absolute manner, and of establishing a body of untouchable verities, a

[5] For an analysis of these two phenomena, I refer the reader to Servier, *Histoire de l'Utopie* (1966).

dogma. The consideration of it as dogma and theology is not the act of a violently anticommunist or perverse mind. Here is a marvelous passage from Antonio Gramsci:

> The determinist, fatalist element has been an immediate ideological "aroma" of the philosophy of praxis, a form of religion and a stimulant. . . . When one does not have the initiative in the struggle and the struggle itself is ultimately identified with a series of defeats, a mechanical determinism becomes a formidable power of moral resistance. . . . I am defeated for the moment but the nature of things is on my side in the long run, etc. Real will is disguised as an act of faith, a sure rationality of history, a primitive and empirical form of impassioned finalism which appears as a substitute for the predestination, providence, etc., of the confessional religions.[6]

That is indeed a work of theology.

We can note three elements. First is the passage to the absolute. To be sure, neither Marx nor Mao ever claimed to introduce an absolute truth. The systematizing of the worship is what effects the transition. Such systematizing is precisely the work of theology, beginning with the recorded experience of Israel, Jesus and Muhammad, from which one passes on to an absolute ideology. By radically defining the true and the false, this quickly puts a stop to the very question of true and false.

But the absolute also has a bearing on ends (an absolute good), and on the means to those ends (the party), on the effect of historical conflicts, and on the conflicts themselves. The sum total of this work, which can only be seen as the elaboration of a theology through a reference to the absolute, ends in establishing a dogmatics. This is a set of truths stated coherently so that they mutually prove one another. They cover the entire field of knowledge *and* of the revelation (for dogmatics is nothing if it is not a complete system). The mechanism for absolutizing the ideology is the same as that for creating the dogmatics. In either case, it consists in objectifying "ideas, which would not have been

---

[6] In Louis Althusser, *For Marx*, trans. B. R. Brewster (New York: Pantheon, 1970).

produced without the faith, and which, when they become dogma, acquire a sort of autonomous power" to exist of themselves.

In the vocabulary of the various modern Marxisms, this is known as theory. The theory is to the Marxist religion what dogmatics is to the Christian religion. In each case there is, in fact, a claim of being strictly scientific, but it is a science which can be developed only from the standpoint of the presuppositions, which constitute an untouchable given, that one must be content simply to lay out in detail on the basis of faith. On the other hand, this systematization makes possible the interpretation of all facts. It accounts for them, makes them logically consistent with one another, and transforms them into so many proofs of the system. But this interpretation, which in both cases is rational, can be accepted only in faith.

Finally, both the theory and the dogmatics claim to be guides to action. How act on the world and on man so as to transform them? And for that both theory and dogmatics have an answer. The crux common to both is revolution, or conversion. These amount to the same thing. Once the dogma is established, it is presented as a judgment implying a certain line of action. The believer, entrusted with a dogma, has the duty to apply it and carry it out. This necessarily comes through in terms of assignments, commands, and watchwords. From that point on intransigence occurs, and the formation of heretics. The moment the dogma is fixed, there can be only one truth and one way to explain things. It is a truth which not only distinguishes the true from the false but, in addition, equates that distinction with the one between good and evil.

It is an incredible error of the Marxists to treat the religions of the past as instruments of conservatism, in view of the fact that no religion has ever pretended to put solutions off until paradise, but has always claimed to transform the world and man right now. By an unbelievably blind vanity, Marxists claim (on the basis of Marx's famous quip) to be the first to want to transform the world. Having made that claim, they resume the way of all religions, with its dichotomy between partial actualization and the eschatological solution.

The latter can take place only through the elimination of obstacles and enemies (especially heretics). Perfect unity of thought is the condition for perfect unity of action. The enemies, the heretics, are not people who have made a mistake. They are absolute evil. According to Monnerot's excellent observation, "One doesn't dispute dogma. One can dispute only from dogma." He rightly contrasts the scientific proposition, which protects itself from itself by its rationality, and dogma, which has to be armed, defended, and attested by a material victory over those who deny it. The existence of dogma prohibits research from zero. The current Marxist dogma (It surely is still current, despite Stalinism's pretense of abandoning it, and the apparent revisionisms. Its continued currency is attested by the arguments to the death among the diverse leftist trends!) would have forbidden Marx to do what he did. One could repeat in connection with Marx the exact saying of the Grand Inquisitor in connection with Jesus.

So an inward inconsistency is a genuine characteristic of dogma and of the religious phenomenon. Set up as dogma, it forbids people to do the very thing done by the founder, and without which the dogma would not exist. The adversary, the heretic, must simply be eliminated. The irrefutable proof of the veracity of the dogma is that it guarantees the consummation of history, or the approximation of the kingdom of God. Since these dogmatic propositions are certain only for the believer, are established only in his eyes, they can become incontestable only through the elimination of the unbeliever. "Science knows only error. Dogma knows only crimes," Monnerot rightly says.

Hence it is no accident that there are heretics in the secular religions. It is not Stalin's fault that there were trials and purges. It is impossible that there not be heretics. They constitute part of the system. It does not represent a deviation from the norm (Stalinist or any other), nor a special concept of Marxism. The moment there is the combination of a theory claiming to be explanatory and scientific, and a faith implying absolute loyalty—the moment, that is, that there is that kind of religion, there are of necessity heretics. Whether the latter are put to death, or committed to insane asylums (you have to be crazy not to accept the truth of Marxism), or handed over to the people's courts or to the vengeful fury of the Red Guard, it all amounts to the same thing. The heretic turns up for the same reasons, and with the same consequences, in Mao's China, or in Czechoslovakia, or in Cuba. There is no difference fundamentally.

To be sure, freedom is everywhere proclaimed, but it is only "freedom *to tell the truth*," as Hervé reminds us. In other words, it is "freedom to tell the established and consecrated truth." Historically, the inquisition never pretended otherwise.

Every religion implies a clergy, an intermediary with God, an expression of the messiah, an implementer of decisions, a staff for the masses of the faithful, an agency for organizing perseverance in the religion. In the secular religions, it is the party which is the actual clergy, fulfilling exactly, from every point of view, the role and function of the clergy of the traditional religions. This has to be stressed. It is not a facile, superficial comparison. All the functions of a traditional clergy are found again in the party. Conversely, all the functions of the party were found already in the clergy. The identity is perfect.

In charge of the clergy there is always an infallible chief, the head of a veritable materialistic theocracy, of which he is at the same time the living god, pope, and emperor. Reference is frequently made to the bureaucracy of the party. The fact is that the clergy play the twofold priestly (mediating or sacred) and administrative role, and what, to the contrary, becomes the real bureaucracy is the apparatus of the state. This is confirmed in the U.S.S.R., as well as in China and nazi Germany. It is especially interesting to emphasize that this duality exactly corresponds, along with the same problems and dilemmas, to the church/state duality of the Middle Ages. The church, like the party, possesses the truth which the state is to implement. It controls, directs, and verifies the ideology. It inspires and judges, but it does not lower itself to the carrying out, to the putting into operation of the politics. The secular arm is always needed.

The party cannot administer anything except the faithful. As far as the total body of the nation is concerned, that must be managed by another organization which, nevertheless, cannot escape the public dictating of the truth by a tribunal which is superior, not materially but spiritually (ideologically). The Hitlerite, Stalinist, and Maoist nations exactly reproduce the pattern of relationships of the authorities in Christendom. What is more, the party, like the church, must be considered a real organism, because the communal relations among all members produce a real psychological collective energy. This energy does not belong to any of the members composing the party. It is the result of the unified energies of all. The party derives from all the faithful the psychic energy which gives it reality and transforms it into an outwardly active power. That is an exact description of what also happens in the church.

This party/church concept, or rather, this inescapable similarity between the party and the former church (I am not the first, far from it, to point this out) almost completely explains the difficulties that Jean-Paul Sartre, for example, can have in dealing with the oddness of communist party life. He is involved in an imbroglio over spontaneity and democracy within the party, etc., an imbroglio which he cannot escape because he refuses to accept the communal quality and this church setup. By contrast, in going ahead with that comparison, one accounts for almost the totality of the characteristics of the parties and their problems.[7] One will never arrive at a clarification of the *question* itself by rejecting the comparison.

Surely one of the functions of the clergy is to conduct worship according to precise liturgies. As in every religion, we find a hierarchy of worship ceremonies, from the most grandiose, involving thousands of people in a solemn liturgy, down to intimate family gatherings, which are no less serious and persuasive. Thus the nazi assemblies have often been likened to a religious ceremony. There were the great festivals of Munich and Nuremberg, with a program expertly organized to produce a gradual increase in religious fervor, culminating in a fervor which can only be satisfied by the very presence of the god. Elements in this were the length of the celebration, the precision of the liturgy, the hymns, the mutual pledges, the readings from the sacred texts, the succession of talented speakers, leading up to the final moment when the Führer himself appeared. This was a crowning moment, an answer to prayer. Then there is the intensity of the message, and the length of the discourse falling on the ears of an ecstatic crowd. There follows, very briefly, the break after the peak (reproducing what has been called for the mass, to explain its psychological effect, its truncated tympanum structure). In its organization, that all reconstitutes for us the equivalent of a cult of worship.

Somewhat different, but retaining the same quality, are the Chinese assemblies of Tien Am Mem. Here the details are worked out differently. Occasionally, as in the case of the Red Guard, there was simply an appearance before a crowd worked up in advance, hence in no need of psychological preparation *hic et nunc,* and anticipating the presentation of the god. There are many passages to prove that the one thing a Chinese person wants is to behold the idol from afar. On other occasions there are festivals which are extremely well regulated, but in a way quite different from those of nazism. There would seem, in fact, to have been a very lengthy

---

[7] I do not, of course, pretend that the comparison is an explanation, or that the being of the church is so clear and obvious that the comparison can serve as an explanation!

preparation of the participants, who worked hard to learn their roles precisely (for example, in the extraordinary living tableaux, and the human mosaics), and who perform their service of glorifying the god with mechanical precision.

Somewhere between these two falls the cultist phenomenon under Stalin: "glorifying the living god, commenting on the sacred scriptures, exhorting the faithful to new sacrifices, exalting the soviet *paradise* in contrast to the capitalist *hell*. All this was in a new liturgical language, composed basically of commonplaces set up as magic incantations. In practice, ritual had taken precedence over technology in the U.S.S.R." (M. Garder).

In all these cases, hymns play a great part. They are most numerous in Maoist China. "The Red Orient," "Sailing the High Seas Depends upon the Helmsman," and even "The Warriors of President Mao are Those Who Best Grasp the Party Instructions" are the best known, but hymns and litanies are found in all the basic ceremonies.

Quite different from the great public acts of worship are those practiced in private, in small groups of fellow workers or friends, religious meetings which seem even more marked in Mao's China than they ever were under Hitler or Stalin. I can do no better than to cite an actual experience, that of Maurice Ciantur. Although at the time of his departure for a three-year stay in China (from 1965 to 1968), Ciantur was wholly in favor of Mao's regime and set out full of enthusiasm, he was most put off precisely by the religion of Mao. Like Robin, he is against all religion. His journal reads: "February 21st, 1968. It was interesting to be present at the ceremony of worship and allegiance to Confucius II [Mao], as it has been practiced for about two months in Peking, and more or less elsewhere. Lao-Che [the professor] read the proclamation of the Great Covenant while turned toward the portrait of Mao Tse-tung. After that, he asked the audience to rise and salute the living god, which each one did, bending the head very low toward the ground. Then the half-mulatto idolater intoned the song of the pilot [Mao] before resuming his seat. This ritual takes place twice a day in the factories." [8]

Elsewhere Ciantur cites ceremonies of prayers addressed to Mao, prayers for rain or for the rice crop, and also occasionally the burning of sticks of incense before the portrait of Mao. It is indeed

---

[8] *Mille Jours à Pékin* (1969). This journal of a sojourn of three years is straightforwardly honest. It defies all generalization and all suspect interpretation.

a case of the living god. The most striking aspect of this phenomenon is that it has to do with the Chinese people, of whom it has been said that they were the least religious people on earth, that they had "secularized" every religion with which they had come in contact. Now they have been transformed into a religious people. This time it is politics turned into a religion.

We have just been describing a series of phenomena. However, it is their combination which makes it possible to say that secular religion is a genuine religion, without any abuse of language or facile indulgence on my part. If there were ceremonies alone, or sacred books alone, or an organization alone, even if that one element could be likened to a religious factor, certainly no general conclusion could be drawn. It is the combination of these indices which is decisive. For what we find in the end is that, on the one hand *everything* which goes to make up the outward appearance of Christianity, for example, is reproduced in nazism or communism, with nothing left out, and conversely, *everything* which goes to make up the outward appearance of nazism or communism has existed already in Christianity. It is this perfect correspondence which obliges us to say we are dealing here with religions.

Gramsci, again, emphasizes: "In the current period, the communist party is the only institution that can seriously be compared with the religious communities of primitive Christianity. Within the limits in which the party already exists on an international scale, one can undertake the comparison, and can establish an order of relation between the militants of the City of God and the militants of the City of Man."

Another favorite comparison is in the area of the messages: Christian providentialism and revolutionary prophetism, the journey from original sin to salvation and the journey from the exploitation of man to the classless society. Then there is the harsh necessity shared by both, the burnings at the stake by the inquisition and the concentration camps, the high-handedness of the spiritualist God and the rude necessity of historical materialism. Everything leads us to this comparison. In our situation, political man has become the perfect equivalent, the unalterable substitute for traditional, religious man.

3. And Now?

Yet there is one question which is bound to be raised. We have spoken mostly of Stalinism and Hitlerism. After all, those forms have retreated. Germany is democratic, and Stalinism is a bad memory (even though we are still faced with a totalitarian state). Doubtless there is Maoism, but can we still speak of a secular religion? Isn't that a phase, an attack of fever, whereas now we are returning to normal?

Before replying to that question, I would point out that these religions were not set up by chance or caprice. They answer to the convergence of two needs. The first is the need of the political power, which is only able (as always historically) to attain the limits of absolutism, of exigence, of totality, of effectiveness, to the degree in which it is loved and worshiped. The second is the need of the ordinary person, who feels a religious need to receive an absolute command and to give himself completely. Thus these religions are instituted because they are indispensable to the strength of the political power, to its completeness, to the comprehensiveness of its requirements, to the transcending of human strength for the grandiose task proposed by politics, to absolute consecration in order to overcome all difficulties. However, they succeed because they respond to a fundamental need of man, who cannot manage to live in the cold and rare atmosphere of reason, of reality. He can tolerate his life only on condition of having a direction in which to go, of receiving light from above, of sharing in a superhuman work.

Hence it is not a fundamental wickedness on the part of the dictators which brings them along a religious path. It is the need for an increase of power and for an answer to the need of man. Man is lost in an anomic society, and he finds his way again thanks to the public religion.

Therefore it can be said that these religions are both spontaneous and fabricated. They are spontaneous because man, of his own accord, will contribute his worship of the supreme head, the father, the saviour, the director. He has need of grandeur, of truth, of justice, of good, of pardon. He will find these there, and only there.[9] They are fabricated because the power, in its role as technician, is

---

[9] This is the same phenomenon which I studied in *Propaganda*. Propaganda succeeds only to the extent to which man is prepared to receive it, and where there is a sort of previous connivance between propagandist and propagandized.

precisely in need of love and adoration. The state no longer is willing to be "the coldest of all the cold monsters." It needs to be warm, friendly, neighborly, hence the paternal and benign visage of Stalin, and the joyous, open, and understanding visage of Mao. One can say that the more a power is organized, rationalized, and strict, the more it needs the irrational and mystical behavior of the people with respect to it. It has to be given a love and a warmth by man.

It is a genuine law of sociological interpretation that "the more rational a system is, the more it secretes the religious." If it were otherwise, the love and the religious sentiment of the individual would issue in nothing visible or tangible. Conversely, we must always remember one does not qualify religion artifically, nor by a series of tricks. No matter how clever the political power might be, it would be incapable of fabricating a new religion if the latter did not answer a deep desire, a passion, and an expectation on the part of all.

So back to our question of fact: are the secular religions over and done with? Michel Garder (*L'Agonie du Régime en Russie soviétique*, 1965) gives an elaborate analysis of such a decline for the U.S.S.R. There is no more god, no pope, no emperor. The holy inquisition has been dismantled. Concessions have been made to the capitalist adversary, who is no longer treated as an absolute enemy. The pontifical function has been desacralized (Stalin's infallibility called in question). We are witnessing the liberation of science and technology from the religious iron collar. The role of scientists and engineers is being expanded. Khrushchev called in question some of the elements of dogma. Resumption of contact with the heretics (Yugoslavia) is acknowledged, and one is getting around to tolerating a plurality of doctrinal interpretations, as well as a variety of possible paths for revolution and for entering communism's higher phase. Hence there is some freedom of choice. In addition, information is becoming fairly free, and there is a new possibility of circulating critical texts, which are supposed to be secret.

The one thing still untouchable is the party, but that alone does not make a religion. Garder concludes that "what is now bankrupt in the U.S.S.R. is the Leninist-Marxist idolatry and the horrible system of oppression which incarnates it, but not socialism."

I quite agree, in fact, that in the U.S.S.R. and the satellite countries there has been a recession of the religious phenomenon, but does that imply doubt concerning secular political religions? It must not be forgotten that throughout the entire history of any religion there are geographical displacements. Buddhism did not remain anchored to its birthplace. The explosive Christianity in Asia Minor and North Africa has totally disappeared, only to take root in an altogether different soil, that of western Europe. Now that it is declining here, lo and behold, it is sending up astonishing shoots in Indonesia and Latin America. In other words, even if it is true that the Marxist-Leninist secular religion is receding in the U.S.S.R. (of which I am not completely convinced; I see there rather a cooling off, an adjustment), that is in no way a mass action. It first moved to China. That is where we again find the phenomenon, with its excess, its grandeur, its absoluteness. Moreover, China makes no bones about its sympathy for the Stalinist regime.

But over to one side, how can we fail to notice the leftists, who exhibit, exactly, all the traits of the religious politicians? Their present hatred and rancor toward the U.S.S.R. bears precisely on this point. The soviet regime is no longer religious. It has betrayed the cause by becoming bogged down in rationality, and by abandoning revolutionary radicalism. It no longer is carrying out the theory, but is going bureaucratic and compromising with heretics and antisocialists. It is no longer at the point of mystical incandescence.

What the leftists are recreating is not so much "a further shift to the left" as a mystique. That is what has made them so attractive (and so seductive to Christians, who are back again in their good religious atmosphere). They are the die-hard prophets of a religion which is being phased out. Like all prophets, they are scattered and disorganized. For there to be a true secular religion, what is missing is the intervention of a directing and unifying power which gathers all the spiritual energies together into the combination analyzed above, of a basic zeal and a religious structure. Leftism lacks the latter. Hence it exhausts itself in disorganized effusiveness, in a mystique without result.

Having magnificently replaced the adoration of Stalin with that of Mao, here is China, in its turn, supposedly abandoning the religious attitude. A certain number of journalists and China specialists now tell us that the phase of the liquidation of the cult of personality has set in. It is a phase of rejection of the religious, of criticism of attitudes of servile obedience. It is almost a "de-

Maoization." "The cult of the personality of Mao is about to disappear. Still more remarkable is the fact that it is Mao himself who put an end to it. He denounced the cult as excessive and obtrusive. Today one can see factory halls without the portrait of Mao. The red and gold insignia bearing his effigy and pinned to blouses are disappearing. As far as *The Little Red Book* is concerned, which millions of Chinese were still leafing through last year, we saw only one Chinese getting ready to read it, and he was on a visit from overseas. *The Little Red Book* has come under criticism. There is no more Marxism in a nutshell . . ." (Guillain, *Le Monde*, August 1972).

Already in December of 1971, A. Bouc noted the criticism expressed in *Chine Nouvelle* of heroes and personalities. "It is not the heroes, emperors and saints who make history. Individuals can play an active role in history only when they reflect the will of the mass of the people." "Even the sun has its black spots." "It is a question," says Bouc, "of depersonalizing the power. The portraits of the President are withdrawn from public places, and he is less frequently quoted."

The religious period is presumably over, and it is Mao who criticized it in his famous declarations to "his" journalist Edgar Snow (December 1970). The wicked person who wrongly oriented China in the direction of the cult of personality was Lin Piao. The fabricator of the horrible *Little Red Book* was Lin Piao. Religion is not a product of Maoism, which follows the straight Marxist line.

Even so, one is forced to ask the question raised by Etiemble: did Mao not know about all that tremendous religious promotion? "Was it at the cinema, or on television, that we saw those frightening pictures, in which the great helmsman applauded those who, by the hundreds of thousands, brandished the talisman under his nose?" The entire huge religious wave obviously was known to Mao, who lent himself to it perfectly. Moreover, he brought off the cultural revolution thanks only to the religious adoration of those zealots. That revolution, in sum, was a religious action, and Mao was in no way ignorant of that fact. He even willed it. From 1965 to 1970, all the specialists were stressing the fact that Mao was always in complete control of the machinery of propaganda. But now, at last, that's all over, and one is returning to a lay and rational state.

In spite of these certainly sincere witnesses, I reserve the right to remain skeptical. In the first place, man cannot be treated as a lump of dough. You cannot cancel by a stroke of the pen something that you have built up and let loose. The Chinese have lived for years in the religious fervor of Mao. They cannot be told, "Now it's all over. We no longer believe that." This has been done several times in history (under Octavian Augustus, for example), but it has never worked. The god remained god, even when he didn't want to. This argument amounts to very little.

We have some quite different witnesses on the other side. Claude Julien (*Le Monde*, February 1972), with his customary guilelessness, mirrors for us a China in which the Mao religion (which, of course, is not a religion in his eyes) is very much alive. He tells us of his visit to the workyards, where the workmen in their blue jeans keep *The Little Red Book* close to the heart. He tells a remarkable story of workmen working on high-tension lines without shutting off the current, "thanks to the thought of Mao." "Thanks to the thought of Mao, the electric line has become a paper tiger." During this dangerous operation, the chorus of workmen chants two of Mao's thoughts, stressing every word. The "engineer" explains how Mao's thought changes the nature of the electricity.

In rural work areas, M. Julien saw slogans in ideograms twenty meters high which reproduced thoughts of Mao. The foreman explains that one draws inspiration from this thought for reforestation, etc. Likewise, M. Margueritte (July 1971) still sees banners, slogans, and portraits everywhere. "More than one statue of Mao reminds one of the images of Buddha." He encountered "miracles." The blind, and deaf-mutes, had been healed in the course of the cultural revolution simply by the thought of Mao. Little children three years of age, too young to read, learn Mao's thoughts by heart.

I would be happy to think that this all took place in July of 1971, and that everything had changed by July of 1972. Unfortunately, that is not so clear. In June of 1972, Mao's thought is still taken by the army newspaper as the absolute and indisputable criterion of truth. If Lin Piao was wrong, this is seen by a comparison with the thoughts of Mao. That's all there is at that level of Magianism, but there is just as much dogmatism based on a religious kind of faith. The writings of Mao still are holy books containing the absolute truth.

Another point needs to be emphasized, which is of no little importance, namely, that Mao is everything, all by himself. Since the year 1965, there have been in China neither parliament, nor constitution, nor president of the Republic, nor any clear and announced economic plan, nor organized government. Mao is everything, and that is an eminently religious situation. So the fact that the portraits have been removed, and that there are no more grandiloquent "ceremonies" for *The Little Red Book*, does not, in my view, allow us to speak of a religious decline.

Therefore I would like to present a hypothesis. Everyone points to the fact that it was from the time of his interview with Edgar Snow that Mao entered upon the struggle against the religious aspect of Maoism. Mao's beautiful saying is quoted: "What would I have been?—nothing but a solitary monk going around on foot, under an umbrella full of holes." He is the equivalent, we are told, of "the mendicant pilgrim of classical Chinese painting, the sage," and editorials picture for us a human, hence a mortal, Mao. How beautiful!

But after all, Mao, and he alone, is still in power, and what power—what absolute power! When Charles V was overcome by the vision of his own life, he abandoned everything and retired to a convent. Not so Mao. He reminds one of the millionaire contemplating the vanity of riches, and the saying, "You can't take it with you," but still, of course, hanging onto his millions. Mao is becoming human, which is the normal evolution of the religious hero.

We have witnessed the same transmutation of movie stars. After having been "stars" in the strict sense (and they had to be inhumanly beautiful, the women in nickel and the men in bronze), they were transformed into the homely, the ungainly, the ordinary person, you and I, intimate, close, but still just as much the star, making just as much money and having just as many passionate admirers and fans. The same thing happens in advertising. It has to be human, goodnatured, with friendly smile and outstretched hand, close and intimate, etc. Yet it is still the liturgy of the cult of consumer goods. There is a similar metamorphosis of the mass. The pomp and exaltation are gone. Everything turns horizontal, direct and human, but no less religious.

The process is the same in China. After the grandiose, the monumental, the hyperbolic, after the exalting and the mystical, there comes a period in which the god draws near to people, declares himself a person like ourselves (while retaining his almightiness), and gets himself even more adored in his condescension, his nearness, his humility, than he was in the days of his thunder and lightning. The gigantesque smiling face, so genial, so human in its weaknesses, its wrinkles, its defects (the famous warts), inevitably makes me think of that other gigantesque face, just as fatherly, just as meek and smiling (but with big whiskers), the typical grandpa to whom little children can entrust their fate. It is a trait-for-trait replica. Only after his death is it discovered that he was an ogre, and that his humility was an instrument of more cult of personality. Mao is still the red sun, and religion is not dead in the Orient!

Raymond Aron, in his turn (*Les Désillusions du Progrès*, 1969), faces the same problem. Doctrines of collective salvation, of a class or a race, would seem to be declining in recent years. "We find it hard to understand how dogmatic ideologies of such poor intellectual quality, and of even poorer spiritual quality, could have had, or could sometimes still have, such a hold on superior minds." He offers a lengthy analysis of the causes and signs of this decline. He finds it due in part to the growth of a national spirit, the wear and tear of prolonged daily application, the spread of industrial civilization (an experience of the communist regime which cannot be entirely covered up by propaganda), advances in applied science, in political economy and in sociology, which imply a violation of the dogmas, the deterioration of the Marxist ideology, in accordance with the experience of all religious ideologies which are "honor-bound to be spiritual, universal and egalitarian, yet with a hierarchical and national order." All becomes tinged with a certain skepticism and entails a renunciation of religious universalism. The great secular religions of the years 1925–1955 take on the tameness of the habitual, and become routine and lukewarm.

Nevertheless, Raymond Aron reminds us that "we would be wrong to judge the present situation too hastily. Twenty years ago, Westerners tended to overestimate the historical significance of the secular religions. It could be that, today, we are inclined to underestimate it." He outlines some aspects of the persistence of these religions. Especially does he stress the fact of transformation. After all, Christianity lost its fervor and absolutism after the first century, only to establish itself as a religion claiming to change the world, and to recover a new fervor in its syncretisms. Is that not what is tending to take place with the secular religions?

On the one hand, Marxism imposes a view of the world and of history. It sacralizes a mode of ownership and management. It changes what is never more than a problem of social organization and administration into a struggle to the death between good and evil. On the other hand, it cannot avoid the collision with reality. At that point, in the established regimes it can be said that communism loses its religious character. The triumphal goal recedes with every step of tangible progress. The doctrine serves to justify the established order. The exaltation and the dogmatic strictness begin to sag. The mystical unity obtained through the common belief is broken, and it can look as though secular religion is in retreat. The nazi regime was too short-lived to have known this recoil, and the latter is what Mao is desperately struggling to avoid, through undertakings like the the cultural revolution.

What is really happening, however, is a new phase of religion. The doctrine, the practice, and the church are becoming guarantors of the established order. "Respect for order does not necessarily require the expectation of a radiant future." The religion produces a morality which then becomes the major factor. At the same time this belief becomes the implicit but indispensable foundation of the regime, the legitimacy of power, the basis for social cohesion.

That is, indeed, another function of religion. Everyone becomes a believer in Marxism-Leninism without even trying, just as in the Middle Ages everyone was a baptized, believing Christian-without-a-problem. Hence there is no decline of the secular political religions in our time. There is merely a stasis, a passing through the classic period in the history of all religions.

This persistence of political secular religion, which is not accidental but basic to modernity, calls for an expansion of our observations. The mutation we are now witnessing is not a retreat of the religions thus far studied (Marxism, Leninism, nazism, Maoism), but the extension of the religious character into all forms of political activity. In other words, while there is a lowering of religious tension in socialism and communism (with the nuances indicated above), there is a sacralizing of all political activity elsewhere, in the liberal democratic, bourgeois, and capitalist countries, which, by that very fact, are ceasing to be liberal.

The bitter dispute which has so transformed the United States over the past ten years is the convulsed visage of this "religionizing." A state which is less and less able to tolerate opposition, which employs increasingly totalitarian methods, cannot justify itself except on the basis of a political religion. The opposition is no longer willing to play the democratic game, but expresses itself in violence, turning political decision into an ultimate, and political action into the criterion of good and evil. Youth dedicates itself and execrates others, expressing extreme judgments in connection with every political action.

What we have here is not the rise of fascism, but the transformation of political relativity into a religious absolute. The same thing is happening in the new countries, especially in Africa. In other words, Leninism-Stalinism and nazism were precursors which have shown us the way. Widespread political religion is an expression of the sacralizing of the state.

The political behavior of the modern citizen makes manifest the sacred of the state, and the fact that the participating citizen is endowed with an exciting grandeur. Politics has become the place of final truth, of absolute seriousness, of radical divisions among men, of the separation of good from evil. The classic theological religious conflicts are being minimized (which facilitates our blithe ecumenical agreements), but this is part and parcel of the fact that the true ruptures are in the political domain. In the end, it is there, and there alone, that people experience the deepest conviction that everything is at stake. Political action demands all; finally, life itself at the national level and also at the party level (if the latter is ever to be serious).

If that is the way things are, it is because politics commits one more than does life. It is worth the sacrifice of everything. What better evidence could there be that it has entered the domain of the sacred? The death of a soldier in war, like the death of the militant, is not an accident. It is a sacrifice. It is the entrance into sacredness of the "dedicated." If these "dedicated" ones finally accept the burden, that is because their belief is more basic than an opinion, or than their personal lives. The absolute gives meaning to their lives, color to their thinking, and communion to their being. It is the final play of all-or-nothing. If my cause triumphs, *all* is won; if not, *all* is lost.

However, this seriousness, this absolutizing, this implacable decision, is not a matter of reason, nor even of politics. It is not merely emotional, nor is it an agonizing search for truth. It is a matter of possession. On that foundation, then, everything makes its appearance which also, in fact, appears out of the sacred.

On the one hand are values, which are vague and unnamed, yet are deeply experienced and felt. There are commands and prohibitions leading to judgments which could be called ethical, except that they are not, in truth, "moral." They are a more profound distribution of beings, actions, and things, which are to be found either in a positive sacred or in a negative sacred.

So what we are witnessing here is the strange, transitional stage, characteristic of all religions, of a total faith which implies a total nihilism—an active nihilism of the elite and a passive nihilism of the masses. The key word of this nihilism is "commitment," which is the equivalent of conversion in traditional religious language. Individual commitment is the counterpart, the visible face, of the nihilism of the intellectuals. Since nothing is any longer worthwhile, since the most unbearable uncertainty reigns, one takes the leap into the truth by clinging to something which exists, a victory in actual operation, an effective action, "something strong which avoids the implied negative judgment the newly committed apply to themselves." National Socialism was proclaimed, we recall, by waves of commitments in all directions, but essentially the political directions. It was a religious substitute.

Whenever one talks with these politically committed, on some burning problem of the hour, one notices immediately both the impossibility of communicating anything else one might want to talk about, and also that one is, himself, drawn into an all-powerful, irrational sphere through imperious necessity.

After the elimination of the king, political importance was transferred, we said, to the institutions. But that didn't last. Man, who felt his politics keenly, very quickly found it necessary to have proposed to him an incarnation mediating between this world and the other world. What was characteristic of the regimes known as totalitarian is now becoming characteristic of almost all political regimes. There is no more relativity. There are no more "good-natured" elections and reasonable discussions. The whole person is at stake every time.

Everything is political. Politics is the only serious activity. The fate of humanity depends on politics, and classic philosophical or religious truth takes on meaning only as it is incarnated in political action. Christians are typical in this connection. They rush to the defense of political religion, and assert that Christianity is meaningful only in terms of political commitment. In truth, it is their religious mentality which plays this trick on them. As Christianity collapses as a religion, they look about them in bewilderment, unconsciously of course, hoping to discover where the religious is to be incarnated in their time. Since they are religious, they are drawn automatically into the political sphere like iron filings to a magnet.

Of course they do not believe in the crude, explicit dogmas. Like Helmut Gollwitzer (*Christian Faith and the Marxist Criticism of Religion,* 1970), they can be clairvoyant about the religious nature of communism, but they think they are cleared of the religious simply because they have denounced the cult of personality or the mystique of its practice. The fact is, however, that all they have criticized is the *now defunct* (except in China) religious phase of communism. They fail to see that we are now in a new phase of political religion *extended into political action itself.* Gollwitzer, an active partisan of political involvement, is a good example of this Christian attachment to the neoreligious. Politics has become the principal justification. Christianity no longer means much, but it is restored like new, and reinvigorated if Christians get into politics. Now it is Christianity which is justified by being legitimized in this way. Everything which carries the political message, everything expressed in terms of political commitment, is now justified and legitimized.

That is the new soteriology. Think of the books, the works of art, the thought. No matter how inconsistent, redundant, banal, and infantile the "thought," it makes its mark whenever it carries a political "message." Any work of art, stage play, or painting is legitimized thanks to the political message. It is obvious that twenty years hence one will burst out laughing at plays and films which are our daily fare today. We take nothing seriously unless it contains some political exaltation, such as an appeal to resist the war in Vietnam, or a revolutionary exhortation in the name of Che.

All this rubbish is on the level of the most grotesque pieces of the epoch of the French revolution (1793–1797), of the sculpture of Arno Breker and the poetry of Déroulède. But the absurdity doesn't touch us, because these films and plays are in *our* context of the politically religious. The moment there is a political message, the work is automatically given consideration.[10]

Faced with this new qualification of politics as religious, one can search for a fundamental explanation, over and above the descriptions of phenomena and the historical explanations, which I have attempted. That of Simondon seems to me perhaps the most enlightening, and I gladly subscribe to it.[11] He considers that man had at first a global (not to say communal) relationship with the world of nature. He calls this the period of the primitive, magical world, in which man operated through a network of magic. But this primitive unity was broken by the discovery and application of techniques for the elaboration of the natural world.

---

[10] Thus one can cite, among a number of others, the film *Le Conformiste*, which is practically nil as far as thought is concerned, infantile as political reflection, but it has the political conformity required for great success. One simply fails to reflect that, here, the conformist is the producer.

[11] Simondon, *Du mode d'existence des objets techniques* (1958).

Man could not bring himself down to this role as a mere operator of techniques. He had to retain a global view of the world. That is the moment at which religions are formed, giving meaning to the world and supplying a thinking about man's destiny. Consequently, a pairing of two elements is set up, which takes the place of the prior magical unity, the pair being religion and technique.

These two activities, these two thoughts, cannot be separated. They are indispensable to man, the one as much as the other, and each in its own sector. It is a question of sectioning off, and is a result of "the ability to diverge contained in the autonomous development of the techniques and of the religions." By reason of that fact, "religion is no more magic than is technique. It is the subjective phase of the result of the sectioning, while technique is the objective phase of that same sectioning. Technique and religion are contemporaries of one another." Neither the one nor the other is a degraded form, nor a survival, of magic.

Then there is a second stage in this evolution. Techniques had acted only on the material, concrete world. Now, however, technical thinking is turned to the world of the human as well, to man and his social organization. It proceeds toward him as it had toward the natural environment, that is, by analysis and by a breakdown into data or elemental processes. As Simondon says, "It reconstructs him afterward according to working diagrams, preserving the structural configurations and leaving to one side the basic qualities and forces" (just like the material techniques). An excellent example of this procedure is economic technique, and this, as a matter of fact, marks the point of departure for these techniques of the world of the human.

But then one is faced with the same situation as at the time of the splitting apart of the unitary world. Man cannot be satisfied with this fragmented situation, so he also develops types of thinking as well, to bear upon the human world, this time taken in its wholeness. This is political thinking. But the latter is in the same relationship with the new techniques that religion had been in with the original techniques. Such is the real and inevitable synonymy between politics and religion for the modern period. Politics fulfills the same role in relation to techniques that religion had fulfilled formerly.

"The moment the techniques about man broke that network of connections (concerning the human world) and treated man as a technical object, there was a new rupture of the configuration-base

202 · THE NEW DEMONS

relationship. From this there arose, in correlation with one another, one thought which grasped human beings below the level of unity (techniques for human manipulation, for example) and another thought which grasped them above the level of unity (political and social thought)." In this breakdown, politics acts toward man as religion formerly had acted toward the natural world. It classifies and judges man by placing him in categories comparable to the earlier ones, of pure and impure, etc.

To be sure, this thought is not known by the name of religion, simply because tradition reserves that name for "contemporary modes of thinking of the techniques for expounding the world. Nevertheless, modes of thought which assume the function of totality, which are the great political movements, are indeed the functional analogues of religion, in contrast to techniques applied to the human world."

On the basis of this remarkable analysis, Simondon shows how national socialism, Marxist communism, and the American democratic system, in fact play the same roles, exhibit the same characteristics and, as politics-religion, are mutually alike, granted there are forms of application and points of entry specific to each.

I cannot claim that this interpretation of Simondon is the only one possible. It does seem to me to correspond both to the state of politics in this age and to the technical identification of this category of phenomena. Therefore, in my judgment, it is the best working hypothesis.

EPILOGUE

So we are in the most religious of all worlds, at the sacred heart of a technical universe. How could it be otherwise? Consider man, or rather, his situation. Here we are, torn between three experiences, in a situation which is conflicting and penultimate.

Our first and obvious experience is that of the most remarkable, glorifying adventure ever known to man—*known*—for the primitive undertaking to utilize fire, to domesticate animals, or to set out over the waters was perhaps not a conscious one. It perhaps was not something which man reflected on, and so he may not have been able to think about himself and admire himself. Now we are entering the sphere of the superhuman, are reflecting on the fact that we are about to do so, and we cannot help being filled with pride.

Our mastery over things, over the universe, and over others is almost limitless. We are breaking open the cosmos and plumbing the ultimate of matter. We are reducing the unknowable to a formula. We are expanding our brain possibilities ad infinitum. We are daily increasing our consumption of energy. We are reaching into the sources of life, and are pushing back the frontiers of death. What could be more glorious, more admirable, more astonishing! —and I am using those adjectives in their strong, etymological sense. Frightened at what we are doing, fascinated by the greatness which is seen and recognized, elevated above ourselves—that is the feeling which overwhelms us with joy and hope, and sends us onward eager to know the brimming future.

Yet, at the same time and in the same place, we, the same we, are having another experience, that of atrocity carried to its limit. What upsets us, fills us with anxiety, and sends us into deep trauma is not merely "future shock." It is the unending vision of the most bloody of all worlds. Massacres are a daily occurrence, after we thought we had put an end to that horror in 1945, that we would never again see Hitlerian concentration camps and the holocaust of Hiroshima, that perhaps we were putting an end to *war*. We have discovered the Soviet concentration camps. We have witnessed massacres in India, then those of the Congo, of Biafra, of the Kurds and of the Bengalis. We are living in a world of widespread warfare, sitting on a powder keg, and knowing that one mistake can blow everything up. We are also surrounded by a world of famine.

We *know* and are seeing all that, in contrast to our ancestors, whose surroundings were probably no brighter or reassuring, but who were not aware of it, or at least who learned of it after the horror had passed.

The third factor in our overall experience is the growing conviction that we are faced with seemingly insoluble problems and insurmountable difficulties, and the good apostles of progress fail to console us. There are enormous problems which concern us all, and we are well aware that we cannot put the solutions off onto others: from the problem of famine, to that of overpopulation, to that of pollution.[1]

The situation is made the more difficult by the fact that everything is changing with incredible rapidity. We are swamped by a flood of news which leaves us no time to breathe, nor any chance to reflect and to put things in perspective. It is also made more difficult by the fact that we are being uprooted from our traditional soil, are turned aside from our known paths, and are going, without any signposts, into an unknown country, which literally is being remade every day before our eyes. We cannot send scouts ahead to explore the road or hire native guides, because the place where we are going does not yet exist.

Under such conditions, how can modern man not fall back on

---

[1] All the elements of the situation which I am here sketchily indicating, I have studied in detail in my other works. I am not, of course, saying that the problems are insoluble, but that they seem so in the eyes of modern man.

the sacred, on myth, and on the religious? It is not "the religious nature" of man which drives him to that. It is the situation itself in which he finds himself today. What recourse is available to man in an unknown country, except to transform into myths and religions whatever is admirable in his experience? The moon of history and the sun of science are our only points of reference. The enigma of the state and the mystery of money endow us with superhuman power. With the coming together of these three dominant factors, how could man not be religious once again?

But why religious? Why that reaction, and not some other? I suppose that is a consequence of man's former habits, of a custom which has come down from the beginning of time, of an ancient reaction of defense and flight, a refusal to know and to will, a search for a refuge and an explanation. At least, in re-creating the religious and the sacred, man is recapturing an ancient experience. He is in gear, once again, with a known movement.

All is new, but it is still possible, even so, to pick up one end of Ariadne's thread. One can still hope to resolve the unsolvable by the worship of a supreme power according to the original formulas, and to alleviate the horror by sacrificing to a divinity which stands ready to help.

The initial mistake of those who believed in a world grown up and reasonable, inhabited by people who controlled their own destiny, was essentially to have a purely intellectual view of man, or indeed of a man who is purely intellectual. Just as *Homo oeconomicus* was thought to be a mechanism perfectly obedient to his own interests, so adult man is an organism perfectly obedient to his conscience and his reason.

However, being nonreligious involves more than intelligence, knowledge, practicality, and method. It calls for virtue, heroism, and greatness of soul. It takes an exceptional personal asceticism to be nonreligious. All of us have known great atheists, genuinely strict ones, who didn't deceive themselves about a god. For them, atheism was an honor, the highest form of human courage. They maintained those heights only by a constantly renewed act of the will, stretched to the limit against every suffering, and finally death. This is no easier today.

So where do we get the idea that modern man, the average man, he whom we adjudge to be atheistic, indifferent, and irreligious, has achieved those heights? In the routines of a society of comfort, of moral flabbiness, of an absence of willpower, of debasement, what is there to prepare a person for lifting himself to the heights of atheism's rigorous virtue? What readies him for that merciless clarity about himself and about the world, which irreligion always involves? Where do we see the spiritual greatness, the morale, the quality of exactitude, the rigor on which criticism of myth and the rejection of the sacred are always based? The scientific method and a smug materialism are not enough! It takes men who are hardheaded with their feet on the ground.

I do not see them. Everything points to the opposite. We see people on a bed of ease, and wishing no other happiness for others. They whimper at the slightest danger, the slightest suffering (look at the leftists!). Flabby skepticism and exuberant disdain are not enough to produce an adult man and an irreligious society. We can rest assured, to the contrary, that in the current psychological tendencies, in the absence of any character-preparation for facing up to great progress and great tests, in the transfer of human energies to the exclusively cerebral, in the collapse of the will in favor of the imagination, in the rejection of all self-discipline, the only way of escape is into the social and the religious. Everybody since Bergson has proclaimed the need for a soul-supplement. All right, we have it in the new religions.

But in taking that course, in making his world bearable and in giving himself the impression that he is able to live in it, man closes the trap on himself. He provides the most complete confirmation ever of the Marxist analysis of the religious phenomenon, without, of course, meaning to. What Marx so admirably described is not historical but prophetic. He was not really assessing the first religions, but the last, not the religion of Islam, of Judaism, or of Christianity, but modern religion in the developed capitalist countries, in the socialist countries, and in the underdeveloped world.

Now, more than ever before, man is enslaving himself to things and to other men through the religious process. It is not technology itself which enslaves us, but the transfer of the sacred into technology.[2] That is what keeps us from exercising the critical faculty, and from making technology serve human development. It

---

[2] We must avoid a misunderstanding. Technology being what it is, the sacred is *inevitable* and impossible to reject. Man is absolutely not free to sacralize or not to sacralize technology. He cannot keep from reconstructing a meaning for life on that as a basis.

is not the state which enslaves us, not even a centralized police state. It is its sacral transfiguration (as inevitable as that of technology), which makes us direct our worship to this conglomerate of offices. It is not sex which is wicked and which perverts us. It is the ideology of repression, and at the same time equally the ideology of the liberation of man through sex. That is when man enters a mystique still just as infertile.

So the religious, which man in our situation is bound to produce, is the surest agent of his alienation, of his acceptance of the powers which enslave him, of his adulation of that which deprives him of himself by promising, like all religions everywhere, that this self-deprivation will allow him finally to be more than himself. That is how it works with drugs. As always, this process of alienation combines with dreams and the imaginary, with a transference into the world of imagery.

It would be helpful to have a detailed analysis of the similarities and contrasts between the "primitive" world of myth and the world of news and productions broadcast by the mass media, between the society of spectacle and the world of illusory pictures such as ours. The world of pictures from the technological apparatus overruns man. It engrosses him and satisfies him, while preventing him from acting effectively. The world of myth, perhaps, was created from within, and as a transposition having coherence as its aim, together with an explanation of the natural environment. However, those two elements are not foreign to the myths of our day either. We indeed have to act, but in the place where it is possible, and in the delusion that we are changing the world and life. Everything denied us must indeed be projected onto the utopian sky, everything which, perhaps, we shall never lay hold of.

Alienation and illusion—that is the modern religious. Should it be destroyed then?

Ah! How simple that would be if it did not involve man! How can we forget that that is the very thing which keeps him alive, which enables him to accept his difficult situation in this society. We must indeed be prudent! It was not through perversion that man fabricated anew this mythical matrix and this sacred topography. It was not at all through stupidity, but because of the impossibility of living in this tension and with these conflicts. It is easy to accuse man of cowardice. That solves nothing, for it all happens outside the limits of the intentional and the conscious. As in the primitive religions, man is feeling this threat to himself, this sense of being cornered, this need to have to change everything. He feels his lack of means at the same time, so he looks for a way around the problem, for a protection, for a solution, and all unknowingly.

To destroy those shelters, to close those escape routes, would be precisely to drive the great majority of people to insanity or suicide. Only the most energetic, the most intelligent, and the most clearheaded would be able to survive, only those who, when they are cornered, have the temperament to fight back, to break impasses and settle questions. They are few in number. Could one, by desacralization, cause almost the totality of the people to go under?

Desacralizing could be done only if, along with it, one supplied a reason for living adequate really to sustain life, and an answer really satisfying and clear. The answer and the reason for living must go together. May the person who cannot supply this enlightenment allow the rest of civilized, modern, and scientific humanity, be it Chinese or western, to sleep peacefully in its religious dream.

CODA FOR CHRISTIANS

The punishment reserved for unreason and the
abandonment of the self is precisely unreason.
—Spinoza

Surely the confrontation at the present time between Christianity
and our western technological society is very valuable and instructive. It is true that Christianity, mongrelized since the seventeenth
century, has been in need of a sort of cultural revolution, but the
true cultural revolution came from the theology of Karl Barth and
not from the current pitiful efforts. It is possible that Christianity
may be passing through fire from which it should emerge purified,
but that is not at all certain.

When people preach the transformation of Christianity into
politics, when they urge us to join with communists, for example,
just as Christians joined formerly with monarchists or capitalists,
when they affirm Christian pluralism as the only Christian possibility, without stating the strict counterbalance of unity and truth,
when they present atheism as one ingredient in faith, or even
Christian faith as an ingredient in atheism, and this as something to
be desired, as something excellent, not as a tragic necessity, a
testimony to our powerlessness to live the faith, then I think we are
in the full process of reintegrating secular religion into Christianity,
or of the absorption of Christianity by secular religion. At the very

moment when one claims to be freeing Christianity from the religious hodgepodge which has burdened it for twenty centuries, and from such religious mistakes as the belief in miracles, or the unconditioned authority of Scripture, or the formulation of the name of God, one reintroduces religion. This is not done in the traditional idiom but, as always, in the contemporary idiom. Thus the theology of the death of God is, above all, a theology of the modern religionizing of Christianity.

That theology, in fact, is based on a certain number of beliefs, taken as uncriticized and unverified postulates and treated as genuine axioms. Thus the world is secularized, modern man is come of age, and everything is integrated into "the cultural." This primacy of the cultural over everything else, this subordination of Christianity to the cultural, past and present, is the ad hoc expression of the myth of history. Out of this comes an odd reversal: whereas it was Judaism which "invented" history, whereas faith in Christ is what gives meaning to history, we, completely enslaved by the myth of history, have come to think that everything is integrated, inserted into history, and that the truth of Christianity, the revelation, is in reality dependent upon history.

The second pillar of this theology is the myth of science. But, in addition, this entire theology of the death of God is based afterward on the popular beliefs and passions of modern man. To the extent that one takes these beliefs as criteria, one arrives at the conclusion that, since man no longer believes in the biblical God, this God was merely a human construct. It is a wonderful pretense in order to make room for the modern religion. We void what has been revealed on the ground (which is true) that it was mingled with the religious. Meanwhile we open wide the gate to all the current beliefs, and are quite prepared to welcome them. What we have voided is not only the religious, but also the absolute of the revelation.

Christian intellectuals are so imbued with all the modern myths, they live so much in today's sacred, they participate so much in all the rites, all the beliefs, especially those of political religion, that they fail to realize that, there too, it is a matter of religion. That is the fate of all those who live in a myth. They are incapable of assessing it as myth.

We have to come out of it. This can be through the passage of time, which wears down belief and enables us to step back from the object of myth. It can also be through a shock, which jars one into another orbit of thinking, of interpretation, and of belief. Such had been the shock of Christianity with regard to the ancient myths and religions. Today, however, it is, rather, the shock of science which is driving us out of the Christian orbit, and is opening up to criticism the myths and religions of Judeo-Christianity, as though we were emerging from the religious cosmos.

The fact of the matter is that the theology of the death of God, as a justification of the actual current situation and as a cover for the process of increasing worldliness, is the best way to reintegrate the religious into Christianity, for, in their critique, these theologians focus on the religious which is outmoded. Then they start to apply that critique to the contemporary religious. They are so dominated by this sacred and its beliefs that their one problem really is how to incorporate these into Christianity.

In order to accomplish this, they claim to continue the theological criticism of religion such as Barth had carried out, or also the sociological scouring which I had undertaken. We often heard it said that "Barth stopped half way," or in connection with me, "There are areas which have escaped Ellul's sociological critique." I am supposed to have stopped short through timidity. The valiant modern theologians want to go all the way. This going all the way does not consist in doing away with the "religious surplus" of Christianity, but rather, with the very center from which the critique of the religion is possible.

This is the heart of a revelation, the "extra" point, on the basis of which it is possible to view all the rest, since it is transcendent. It is the nonplace, the unlocated place which enables us to locate the rest. It is the never-achieved prospect in relation to which everything has its place. No serious critique of current religion can be made if there is no transcendent, for every religion necessarily is lived as the pure and simple truth by those who are within it.

Quite obviously, that is just what modern man is living; and the modern Christian as well, whenever he lowers himself to the condition of the average person by voiding the specific character of Christianity. To make Christ's self-emptying *the* central doctrine, on the basis of which, alone, everything is to be judged, including the remainder of the revelation, is to assert that the specific character of Christianity is precisely not to have any. It is to preach being steeped in the world, and, if this world is religious, it means adopting the religions of the world.

I must not, of course, be made to say what I am not saying. The great passage of Philippians chapter 2 is *one* of the central texts. It is the most complete expression of the Incarnation and the cross, but taken alone, and in isolation, it gives a view of the revelation which is just as false as the Decalogue taken alone and treated as the center and heart of the revelation. The theology of the death of God does not want to see the irreducibly different character of the biblical revelation about God (God as the Almighty Creator, etc., not just as humbled and crucified man, etc.), and everything that all the other religions have been able to say about God.

It is this irreducible which makes the transmission of the kerygma and witnessing about God difficult. It is not at all the outmoded quality of the God-notion in a different cultural context. Yet the modern theological trend does away with the irreducible, since it proceeds essentially by reduction. That is the great method and approach. There is the reduction of the multiplicity of textual levels to structures. There is the reduction of the complexity of the message to a single theme. There is a reduction of the multiplicity of facets of the revelation to a single aspect. There is a reduction of the revealed to the cultural, a reduction of the cultural to the political, and a reduction of the two dimensions to the one horizontal dimension, etc.

The reduction process is the antirevelation. It also consists in favoring whatever we find suitable about God, and eliminating the impractical. But by that very fact, one makes it impossible truly to desacralize and seriously to do away with religion. Every reduction goes along with the acceptance of the sacred and of the religious, for it is indeed true that the revelation of the living God is desacralizing.

When God enters the picture he destroys man's sacred. It is true that he secularizes (and, to be sure, that he opens the door to man's action on a secularized nature), but one forgets that it is the word of God which secularizes, and not philosophy, science, or technology—that this word of God is independent of our analyses, and that either it is given in the Bible and in the incarnation or it is just our imagination. It is forgotten that in this word of God there is attestation of man's sin, of the rupture between man and God, of man's situation within evil. To void that, to reduce it is, on the one hand, to render the remainder of the revelation completely meaningless, and on the other hand, it is to prevent oneself any longer from seeing modern man's sacralizing, for this man creates a sacred for himself and finds himself a religion only in order to counter the prior situation. To deny that situation is to accept, without seeing it, the religion created by man in an uncritical manner. Any critique could be applied only to outmoded and dead religions of the past, which man has abandoned because they no longer do him any good.

So we can say that the "secularization" stemming from the rejection, or reduction, of the revealed truth is the opposite of the desacralizing of things and of religions stemming from the revealed truth. It is the opposite because the first secularization is never anything but the enthroning of new religions.

Here once again we encounter Harvey Cox's childishness, when he sings the praises of scientific exorcism: "Exorcism is that process by which the stubborn deposits of town and tribal pasts are scraped from the social consciousness of man and he is freed to face his world matter of factly" (*The Secular City*, p. 134). And science, of course, is the great handmaid of exorcism—as though he had never heard of the house which was swept and garnished. Scientific exorcism, like psychoanalysis, is in fact the very remarkable operation whereby one sweeps the heart and mind of man, airs it out, and cleanses it. Then, when the house is empty and open, seven other demons come in to take the place of the one. Consequent upon this scientific operation, modern man is much more religious, much more dependent, much more sacralized than ever before, and more insidiously so.

What we have just said concerning secularization/desacralization can be repeated in connection with religion. Everything being said about the opposition between the revelation in Jesus Christ and religion is right enough, but it is the revelation, not science or reason or modern culture, which destroys religion. Furthermore, there is no overlapping of those two procedures. There is, rather, a strict antinomy. The elimination of the traditional religions by modern culture is a process which creates new religions, and that is all.

In other words, modern Christian intellectuals, theologians, journalists, and clergy have made a gigantic mistake in their interpretation of the contemporary world, and that, in turn, leads to a gigantic mistake in the orientation of Christian and church action.

It seems to me that throughout the history of the church there have finally been three phenomenal mistakes, on which all the rest hangs. I am referring to mistakes more fundamental than the heresies, which were differences in the manner of explicating and understanding what was revealed. What I am thinking of has to do with mistakes concerning the relations between the church and the world, concerning the church's situation in the world. The difference is as follows: in navigation, one must make an observation, calculate the declination and drift, plot the course, and read the compass. If the compass is off, everything else is off. Whether one prefers sails or motor power no longer matters. In either case, the course is not what had been intended. Such, in my view, is the difference between mistakes of orientation and heresies.

The first such mistake can be listed as Constantinism. This must not be taken merely as an acceptance of the state and an agreement with the political power. From the outset it is an orientation toward wanting to win over to Christianity the rich, the powerful, the control centers—which necessitated the creation of a neo-Christianity.

The second such mistake can be called the cultural mistake. It is the incorporation into Christianity of all the cultural values. By that action, Christianity becomes the receptacle for all the civilizations of the past, the establisher of culture and a synthesis of the philosophies—which necessitates the elaboration of another neo-Christianity.

The third such mistake is the one we are now making, that of believing that we have to locate ourselves in a world that is lay, secularized, scientific, and rational, and that we should build a neo-Christianity in those terms.[1]

---

[1] One example of the results of this mistake is given us by the uncertainty of judgment concerning the "Jesus phenomenon" and the "Jesus revolution." Among Christians of good will we frequently encounter two kinds of positive assessments. One says: "Once again it is 'the world,' the 'non-Christians,' who are bearing witness to what Jesus really is. Whereas the church has mummified Jesus and dogmatized the gospel, it is the non-Christians who are discovering, over and above all the Christian rubbish, what the word is. They will make it live again in their heartwarming experiences. The Christians should learn a lesson from the pagans. Christians should withhold all judgment on these undertakings, because their appraisals are dictated by their sclerotic ideological definitions and the narrowness of their dogmas. This rediscovery of authenticity should shake you up." The other says: "After all, if these revues, these excesses, seem to us a bit strange, and sometimes painful, still the gospel is being set forth and the name of Jesus is being proclaimed. It's good that it be done by those outside the Church. In *Godspell*, after all, it is simply the Gospel of Matthew which is being directly presented on the stage. How can we fail to see it as a 'witness'? God uses every means to have his word heard. The person listening to these plays is also hearing a word of God, so let's not criticize."

I have to say that those two arguments should be taken very seriously, for they both express a truth. However, they cannot be accepted unconditionally and as such. After all, we always find, throughout the course of the history of Christianity,

But the first question concerning this gross error in the assessment of our times concerns its origin. Surely the psycho-intellectual soil was prepared for it. Political, scientific, and technological pressures, the upheavals (of various kinds) in our society, and dechristianization, all prepared Christians to follow that path. But the trigger, the "reason," and at the same time the justification, for following this conformist trend was the dissemination of Bonhoeffer's *Letters and Papers from Prison*. Surely one has read into these passages more than they say explicitly, and has separated them from the corpus of Bonhoeffer's work, whereas what we should do is to interpret them on the basis of that work, in which case they lose part of their impact.

But, after all, the letters are there, and indeed they offer a diagnosis of our society and a Christian orientation which appear to me fundamentally false. If the demonstration has been produced that our western world is sacral, that the thinking of modern man is developing in terms of myth, and that the secular religions are triumphant, then we need to ask whence comes the great mistake of Bonhoeffer.

To begin with, how can he say that the modern world is not religious, that man is becoming adult and rational, when he himself lived in the midst of the most formidable mystical, religious, and irrational outburst that we have known for three centuries? It is a mysterious blindness. Whatever respect one might have for a man who put his life on the line in political action (which, to be sure, he had to carry out), whatever admiration one might have for a

---

queer movements undertaken in the name of Jesus and the gospel. For example, there were prostitution movements for the purpose of spreading the gospel among the customers of the prostitutes who were charged with "witnessing," and a lot of other things. It isn't enough that the name of Jesus be pronounced, and the Gospel story told, for the action to be in the slightest degree a witness to the truth. I am fully prepared to hear a new presentation and a new language. I am prepared to have my theology and the traditional church called into question, but I absolutely refuse to do so in the presence of just any extravaganza or just any declaration. The fact that they come from non-Christians is no guarantee of the validity of such undertakings.

There is the little problem of the tree and its fruits. When I see that the chief fruits are, on the one hand, the accompanying of this gospel with drugs and pansexualism and, on the other hand, the making of large sums of money and the building of commercial capitalistic enterprises, I am obliged to say that I reject the content of these statements because of their inward orientation and consequences. When I observe that everything is based on ultramodern publicity, on the exploitation of sensuality and suffering on the part of the people who make use of it, I say absolutely No to this pretense of a message.

When Christians were wondering about that prophet of the transformation of the

theological work of the first order, however cautious one ought to be in speaking of an authority considered indisputable by Christian intellectuals, one cannot help saying that he was mistaken, and wondering about that incredible blindness.

It seems to me that there can be only three explanatory hypotheses. One is that he was greatly troubled and traumatized by his arrest, imprisonment, and interrogations. That would be nothing against him. In spite of his spiritual greatness, he could very well have gone through a crisis of discouragement, uncertainty, and perhaps even panic. From then on, his famous "questioning," the calling into question, the new theological problematic, did not come from his faith or from any special lucidity, but from his troubles as a prisoner, from the fact that he was virtually condemned to death. Secondarily, that brought about a false view of the world.

A second explanation is that, with complete clarity, he may have felt that nazism, and the period in which he was living, was simply an accident. I can understand this on the level of purely political and sociological appraisals. This wave of fury was only one wave in a worldwide tidal movement in the opposite direction. Hitlerism was only an epiphenomenon without special significance. One had only to let this wave of fury go by, and his country would come back afterward to the modern world, the basic nature of which was nonreligious, adult, etc. After all, such mistakes can be excused. I

---

gospel into a religion, which is Billy Graham, I said No, because he was using the most modern methods of propaganda. His entire witness was falsified, vitiated, and changed by the very fact of the technical means of propaganda. Here we have the same problem. I readily grant that people may eventually be reached by these revues and posters. That doesn't prove a thing, for in fact God does make use of everything; but when Hitler in his speeches appealed (quite frequently) to the Almighty I often heard it said: "You see, he isn't as bad as all that. He is calling upon God, and it may well be that he is sent by God." It is possible that God may have made use of him. It is possible that people may have heard some word of God in Hitler's speeches. I have to say that that does not at all suffice for me! Hitler was demonic in spite of his invocations of God (even if he was sincere), and I say exactly the same thing here. We must firmly resist the "Jesus revolution" and the Jesus parade.

The virulent criticism expressed in the film *Tout le monde il est beau, tout le monde il est gentil* should be enough to show what is really behind this low prank about the gospel and the name of Jesus. Once again, what makes me reject some beneficial "novelty" is not a dogmatic image of Jesus Christ, nor rigid catechetical truths, but the alloy of money and pornography. That is what forces me to say that it cannot be genuine, and if it isn't genuine, then it is diabolical, for the devil is the perversion of

personally made a similar mistake when I believed with all my heart in the formula we came up with in 1944: "From Resistance to Revolution." It is nonetheless a terrible misunderstanding, and nothing is to be gained from passages based on such an error. The unpardonable people are those who, ten or twenty years later, use those thoughts as a basis for a new theology, a new way for Christians to be present to the world, a new ecclesiology.

Finally, a third explanation is that Bonhoeffer's attitude was prophetic. That is to say, it was an affirmation of the faith in the face of the reality, a proclamation of the message notwithstanding the events. A declaration is indeed prophetic when faith returns to its foundation despite the obvious. The negation of the religious character of Hitlerism, even the refusal quite simply to see it, could only be faith's surpassing of the circumstances. "You imagine that the situation is such and such? By no means. In truth it is quite other than that, and here's how . . . ."

To be sure, the ardent admirers of Bonhoeffer are tempted to adopt this interpretation. What bothers me, however, is first of all that the prophetic attitude is generally an affirmation of the unshakable revelation and the certainty of faith in the face of the obvious political situation, or of the questions raised by events. Bonhoeffer, on the other hand, would seem to be going in the opposite direction. What we have is a calling in question of the faith, of theology, of the church (which can perfectly well be prophetic) in the name of a certain new fact of society. I cannot see that the prophets would ever be oriented in that direction

---

the word of God in order to lead people astray. It is the utilization of the word of God so as to have man do or think the opposite to what God expects. It is the utilization of the revelation (and the imitation of that revelation) for something quite other than the glory of God (and in writing this I am, of course, supposing that the diabolical exists also in the churches).

Before phenomena of this nature, Christians must abandon their timidity and guilt feelings. They must once again be able to say that what is diabolical is diabolical. In so doing, to be sure, they must always be ready to listen as well to the criticism which the devil directs at the church and at Christians, for he is quite clear on that subject. But he is still the devil. This gigantic politico-commerical enterprise of the Jesus phenomenon has nothing to say to us except, in fact, that we have no right to make Jesus Christ the prisoner of the established church, that indeed the truths of the revelation are not hidden to us and can be revealed to the "simple" (but the producers of plays and the publishers of best sellers are not simpletons!), that finally every new presentation of the gospel differing from our tradition we should receive, examine, discern its spirit and, in the face of that, make our criticism and receive its criticism of us. But having done this, faced with the Jesus phenomenon, we can conclude in all serenity: let the dead rejoice with the dead.

(especially when they were harshly attacking the rituals and religions of their own times).

Another thing which bothers me is that the prophets generally received some confirmation of their political clearheadedness. They had seen through appearances, and more profoundly than other people. Ten or twenty years later, their interpretation was confirmed (which gives rise to the whole rationalistic explanation by historians of prophecy *post eventum*). In the present instance, however, nothing that Bonhoeffer says about our society is confirmed. That is why I still question the reasons for this attitude of Bonhoeffer, which may be accidental. It seems to me a mistake to build on such dubious foundations.

Without getting into the fundamental debate on the mistaken interpretation of the modern world by Christians, I would at least like to raise three questions. The first relates to the fuzziness and the conceptual uncertainty of the statements about the world's being grown up. What do you mean by world?—by being grown up? In connection with the secular city, we have already seen the emptiness of these terms, as well as their lack of precision. It is hard to believe that our society could be characterized by the few features listed by Cox. The "world," is that the society? Adult man, is that a reference to man in himself? In that case, I don't know what it is we could be talking about. If we are talking about really living people, then there should at least be some serious analytical study of their behavior, opinions, etc. But one is content with general statements. And then, what is an adult? It's a little too easy to reply, "He who has killed the Father," or, "He who takes his destiny in his own hands." A lunatic neither does nor claims to do anything different from that.

My second question has to do with the future of this declared secularization. It is too easily forgotten that throughout the course of history there have been other periods of secularization. China has known at least one long period of secularization, and Rome as well. That can seem odd, accustomed as we are to the reassuring vision of the Roman Pantheon. The fact is that in the fifth century B.C., during the transition from kingship to republic, there was a powerful laicizing trend in Rome. To be sure, it was not a laicization based on scientific knowledge, but it was nonetheless real. This secularization and laicization that we are reveling in are not the first. Only our ignorance of history allows us to think that.

A wave of that type is speedily absorbed every time. It

disappears into the sand, leaving only some foam to be scattered by the wind. The laicized societies have inevitably become religious once again, but religious with a difference. Only a telescoping of history, a conceited ignorance, and a sketchy survey would allow one to characterize the whole history of humanity as religious up to the eighteenth century. We need only ask ourselves what will be left of the period of laicization and secularization, from about 1880 to 1930, for man to consider in the year 3000 (if our society is genuinely committed to a neoreligious phase). Our experience is not unique. Secularization is always an intermediate stage between a religious society on the way out and the appearance of a new religious structuring.

My third question has to do, again, with the death of God. It may be perfectly all right, in the intellectual domain, to abandon the "God hypothesis." Scientific honesty and intellectual rigor would have it that we no longer speak of God today. (But is this really a scientific requirement, or is it, as for Galileo, a partisan extension of the scientific method? It isn't so simple as the disdainful eliminators of the "stopgap God" think, when they would exclude him, step by step, from his domain as fast as science develops!) So at least the question ought to be raised whether, with this change in intellectual premises and scientific presuppositions, there is necessarily involved a change in the relationship to the revealed God, a different way of explicating the faith, a need to adapt Christianity to a world supposedly grown up, and finally, a mode of Christian life and faith no longer commensurate with what had been known before. I see no inevitable link, no logical consequence, from the one domain to the other. The theologians of the various currents of "new theology," in the wake of Tillich, Bonhoeffer, Bultmann, etc., seem to me mostly to be giving way to panic.

This flagrant error and panic entail a no less flagrant consequence. If in fact we are faced with a secularized and desacralized society, with man grown up and demythologized, etc., then we need to change the biblical message, the expounding of the faith, the church's presence and Christian ethics in those terms. But what if that view of the world is false? In that case, this whole painful structure we see going up before our eyes rests on thin air, for the reinterpretation being attempted is not derived from the facts themselves, but from our interpretation of the facts. We must realize that social facts and historical events never act of themselves, but only through the interpretation placed upon them. If the latter is basically false, it entails reactions, statements, adjustments, and interventions which are also false, hence out of tune and inappropriate, which is always catastrophic, and often mortal for the group that has thus interpreted the events incorrectly. If perchance our world is not in fact secularized, laicized, and grown up, but rather, is sacral and religious, what will be the consequences of our Christian efforts at adjustment?

First of all, it is obvious that Christians are letting other religions grow and develop, and since the latter are nothing other than "fantasy interpretations" of what people are factually living, with technology, economic growth, the expansion of political power and of the institutions of the state, it is obvious that people will more and more fall away from Christianity and turn to the new sacred. The phenomenon of dechristianization goes on apace, but it is *no longer* a dechristianization resulting from science and secularization, but from the derivative growth of a religion of the world which occupies the former secularized universe.

When that happens, Christianity sustains a double loss of impact. First of all, it doesn't even imagine itself capable of entering into conflict with the new sacred. It fights nothing which seduces, captivates, wins away, fascinates, and hypnotizes modern man. To the contrary, it plays its part through its renunciation, since, on the one hand, it accepts, blesses, and legitimizes the facts (techniques, politics) on the basis of which the myths and religions are blossoming, and, on the other hand, it in no way contests the enticing power of those "ideologies." It is putting up an off-balance fight and mounting great battles against windmills. Modern Christianity is incapable of tackling the current false and seductive spiritual forces. It prefers to assail those of yesterday, which are already dead.

In the second place, Christianity is losing its impact through endless self-criticism, a self-criticism which is just as false as its attacks. There is, in fact, no end to criticism of the parish, of morality, of theology, of the language, etc. It is a criticism based on what one *imagines* to be the reality of modern society, but since one is mistaken about that reality, the enormous amount of work means exactly nothing. Even if the method were valid (to criticize Christianity and the church on the basis of a point of view of the world held to be true), it would still at least be necessary to have a correct view of this world and of this society. But now, if one were to become aware that this point of view of the world is one of a non-Christian myth, or of a non-Christian religion, it is obvious that Christians would be unwilling to make their *mea culpa*, their self-criticism, on the basis of that point of view. They would be unwilling to do so precisely because they have been assured that it is a nonreligious point of view, and that is the very reason why it seems valid to them.

In other words, Christian self-criticism on the basis of science, history, and sociology can be perfectly valid. But in making such self-criticism, Christians must not imagine that they are thereby penetrating the culture of our western society, or that they are in the slightest degree in tune with the average person living in that society. The latter understands nothing of scientific language, though he believes in the ideology of science. The consequence is a complete absence of interest on the part of non-Christians in all the braggadocio, swagger, and grandiloquence of Christians over their aggiornamento. Christians can vote for the pill, revolution, abortion, free sex, and the marriage of priests; and against imperialism, unequal opportunity, etc. They should be aware that that interests no one but other Christians, who are congratulating one another.

The man in the street chuckles a bit, and he definitely is not tempted to enter a church or believe the Christian word. The militant, of course, is happy to have an ally, but he isn't at all interested in whatever is Christian about him. From then on, this mistaken appraisal should normally lead to the disappearance of traditional Christians disheartened by the changes of which they have no understanding, and by the lack of any new Christians coming in. The more Christianity is modernized, the more it will lose its place, and the more the last Christians will be isolated. The proponents of the new hermeneutics and the neo-Christians will very shortly be the most lonely people in our society.

We mustn't delude ourselves about the "dialogue with non-Christians." Who are the non-Christians in question? If we look around us in France, we note that they are always *former Christians*, such as G. Mury and R. Garaudy. If they are prepared for dialogue, if they are interested in what is going on in the churches, that is because they have received a good, solid Christian training, and have, since their youth, been alerted and warned of these problems, but the others completely scoff at it.

Insofar as Christianity remains a religion, it is on a par with other religions. It talks with them as equals, and can attract people for religious motives. The same would be true today. For the people of the West at the present time—seized with anguish and fear, with the prestige of science, with the fascination of almighti-ness, with the frenzy over consumer goods—if Christianity is to make contact with them, is to find them where they are, it must be more religious than ever. It must *recover* its authentic festivals, its mystic ecstasies, its mystery, its sacramental rites (I am not saying it should keep the same rites and mysteries), its sacred priesthood, its supreme, undisputed authority, its miracles, its timeless way of life. It must banish discussion, theology, criticism, democracy, and the incognito. In so doing it will enter the lists and get into the race with the other current religions, and with no small chance of winning. It will gather many new converts into the fold once again. But be not deceived. It will be a case of a *religious* revival. I have tried to show above that certain bold moves of "the new theology" are unwittingly tending in that direction.

If one does not adopt this line, then it has to be understood that Christianity is a break with our society, as it has always been a break with the world, of which our society is but one aspect.

But the situation is complex. It is true that the church and Christianity live on a cultural past which needs to be criticized, not in accordance with the imperative of science and the maturity of modern man, but in accordance with its own inherent critique, in accordance with the power native to the revelation, and which periodically bursts out of the ecclesiastical and theological covering placed upon it.

Conversely, if one adopts the line indicated above, one is not likely to reach an agreement and a mutual understanding with our society and our contemporaries. To the contrary, this Christianity coming back to its own origins (not necessarily those attested by modern exegesis!) will be even less grasped and understood, for Christianity's self-criticism involves, by the act itself, the rediscovery within Christianity of what remains the most completely incomprehensible for man, and at once the critique and the rejection of man's religious paths, modern as well as ancient.

Apart from an unfortunate spirit of syncretism or of resignation, there is no reason to consider that our times are the dawn of the Lord's promises, promises now taken up and fulfilled by man himself. Faced with the religions which man sets up for himself, the only Christian attitude possible is one of struggle and elimination, not in order to substitute a Christian religion for the others, but to get man out of the religious trap from which he is far from emerging! In other words, it is a resumption of the struggle of the prophets and of the early Christians.

What? Desacralization? Demythicization? Demythologizing? Dereligionizing? Isn't that precisely what all the intellectual Christians are saying today? Isn't what I was writing on that subject thirty years ago now banal, a well-established opinion, an obvious commonplace? Everybody's doing it, and it is no longer especially interesting. To the contrary, I contend that that represents a great misunderstanding. When I was setting forth the need to desacralize and demythicize, I was viewing the realities of the world from the standpoint of the truth of the gospel, whereas the path now being taken is one of demythicizing Holy Scripture and of dereligionizing the church from the standpoint of the truths of the world. As far as political and social realities are concerned, that is easy. Let each day take care of itself. The world is desacralizing itself through its own drives.

The prophetic message now goes about like this: "Our Yahweh is a concentration of our dreams, desires and hopes as Jews. Happily, the chariots of the Chaldeans, the agricultural techniques of the Egyptians, and the commerce of Tyre will enable us to realize those dreams. Thanks to them, we can attest that our Yahweh is not so false as all that . . . ." The message of the first Christians now is: "Our experience of the resurrected Christ will be able to be attested thanks to the unification of the world (as by Rome), and his universal Lordship will be concretized thanks to the means of communication and the mass media. If he is the Son of God, that is because in this new universe we can easily unite all peoples, and his resurrection is merely the symbol of the Augustan identity which fulfills the designs of God . . . ."

That is the diametric opposite to what the entire biblical message cries out to us. The power to desacralize is solely and uniquely the power of the gospel, of the word of God contained in Holy Scripture, and of a word preserved in its text, of a word which we have no need to demythicize, to dissect, to come out with, because in its form, inseparable from its content, it conveys the only possible truth, through an actualized decision on the part of God (here I remain ultraclassical, since classicism is the only possible outcome in the face of the gods of this world). It is the word which demythicizes, provided we leave it in its integrity and do not pretend to demythicize it, in the name of what? It is the word which desacralizes the church as fast as the sacred keeps coming back. It is the word which destroys that religion which would smother the faith and the revelation among Christians.

But that is on condition that we leave it its freedom, and neither cover it with the wrappings of tradition and theology, of moralities and rites—making a mummy out of it—nor expurgate it, cut it to pieces and scatter it, like the *membra disjecta* of Orpheus—making an experimental corpse out of it. All that is necessary is to let the explosive power of the word act, just as it is. There soon takes place a self-cleansing of the church and of Christians, but provided we take that path.

This cannot help being accompanied by the work of desacralization and of secularization against the gods of the present world. That means seeing to it that technical objects are never anything but objects, reduced to utility, measured with a cold eye, and scorned for their always base usage—being sure that they in no way give meaning to life. It means seeing to it that technology is nothing more than an ensemble of means, which need to be put through the mill of truth, an ensemble of useful procedures, interesting of course, but which do not enrich life, do not open a door to spiritual progress, and in no way characterize man.

It means seeing to it that science is one possible representation among others of the world in which we live, and never is the key to truth. It means working to see that the state be strictly lay and secular, refusing, in consequence, to accept any political ideology put out by it, whether Gaullist, or communist or democratic. It means looking upon it as a useful manager, acceptable, of course, as administrator, but *ne sutor ultra crepidam* ["Let the cobbler stick to his last"]. We reject the nation-state structure, and the state-providence role, whether it be as an object of adoration, of confidence, or of hope. It means seeing history as an interesting novel of the human adventure, and nothing more. Nothing more—not the great goddess who enables us to live.

So we must be iconoclasts, but not of the statue of Jesus Christ nor of God. For the destruction of those statues, a conjunction of forces is at work. On the one hand, as we were saying, the word of God is taking the matter in hand, but the world is also on the attack. We can only applaud the destruction of the divine idol fabricated by Christian traitors, a destruction wrought by Nietzsche and Bakunin, but we don't have to resume their accusations or dance a scalp dance around the true God of Jesus Christ. That the God envisaged by Voltaire and that envisaged by Bakunin are dying is well and good, but we have to take into account that this in no way refers to the God-creator of the cosmos, the God working miracles in answer to prayer, the God of Sinai, God the Father, the Almighty God, transcendent and sovereign. To claim to do away with that God in the name of Nietzsche's critique is, on the one hand, to apply that critique where he did not apply it, and on the other hand, to confuse this God, who is the God of Jesus Christ, with the rationalized idol of Christian lukewarmness.

Iconoclasts, yes. That really means destroying the gods of the world which Christians see without observing them. It means standing up to them while taking them for prince charmings—gods of the stadium, of speed, of consumer goods, of utility, of money, of efficiency, of knowledge, of delirium, of sex, of folly, of revolution, of agnostic learning, of politics, of ideologies, of psychoanalysis, of class, of race, gods of the world calling for unheard-of holocausts. The person who attacks the biblical God in order to demythicize him and desacralize him, instead of attacking these divinities, is giving millions of people over to death, not only to spiritual death but also to physical death. That is where Christian responsibility rests.

Millions of people are suffering from hunger, but there are millions of people who are dying from the divine power of political ideology. The person who takes the political route in order to save people, so that people should no longer be exploited, should no longer be victims of war, that person is the surest guarantor of exploitation to come and of further wars, for he is given over to the worship of the political god. If he is not Christian, he cannot do otherwise, and is not responsible. If he is Christian, he is responsible. I am saying that it is the Christian cronies and companions of the communists in 1944 who are responsible for the millions of victims of Stalin, holocausts of the political god. The same is true today with Mao. It isn't a matter of political choice. It is a matter of the worship of a god and of a sacred calling.

Precisely as Jean Brun emphasizes, demythologizing "should be applied, not to the myths ordinarily attacked, but to the very attempts which pretend to deliver us from them." The former myths are known. They are recognized as such, and are no longer dangerous. Once recognized as a myth, the latter no longer means anything. It is childish for Christian intellectuals to sing their paeans to myths which no longer exist, and the biblical myths first of all, while the truly living myths are those not recognized as such. That is when prophetic lucidity, coming from the Holy Spirit, should enable Christians to designate them and earmark them. Again, to be sure, it is important not to reject the power of the Holy Spirit in advance, and then pretend to make Scripture contemporary and vital through hermeneutics. If Christians do not fulfill this role, no one will.

It will be said that the old revelation serves no good purpose in the newness of our times. Modernity has nothing in common with the biblical period, so, for the very purpose of fulfilling that role, why wouldn't the biblical message have need of refreshment, rejuvenation, and renovation in the direction of modernity? And that is indeed the problem. Should the message be remodeled, or is it meaningful as it is? I am surely fully cognizant of the novelty of this age, yet I am immediately struck by the modernity of the biblical proclamation. When Scripture tells us that man is dominated by the spirit of power and of conquest, by the spirit of independence and surfeit, that he wants to put together a world for himself, and himself alone, to the exclusion of God, that he wants to exploit the world for himself, and that he proclaims, "Where then is God? What can this inoperative, unseen and illogical God do?" is that indeed an old-fashioned speech in need of being demythologized?

Doubtless the Bible calls that attitude pride, sin, a break with God—and condemns it. The modern world, on the other hand, is convinced that finally, in this manner, man will realize his potential, fulfill himself, mature, become adult, and take charge of his own destiny. But has the Bible ever said anything other than that? It says, in fact, that man thinks to take his own destiny in hand when he makes his own law for himself, when he kills God, and fabricates for himself gods according to his own measure, "who walk before us." Christians, no doubt, instead of preserving the judgment of the Bible concerning this attempt on the part of man, have given their allegiance to the attempt itself. They approve the secular city and triumphal man, responsible in his own right and to himself, and attaining, finally, his majority.

Has the Bible ever said anything other than that the people of Israel were constantly brought to give their allegiance to that conquest of man by himself, that almost inevitably they gave approval to the political power, to the amassing of riches, to the advance of wisdom (science), and that that is where they put their success? They associate themselves with human conquests. I see nothing new, relative to the biblical elucidation, either in the amazing advance of science, technology, and contemporary politics, or in the attachment of Christians to those marvelous successes. The judgment which Scripture brings to bear on these efforts and accomplishments is in no way a product of a cultural atmosphere stemming from a sacral environment with a religious distrust of every conquest on the part of man. To the contrary, it is the product of a rejection of that cultural environment. It is a rejection of it, both as a sacral, religious milieu and as an expression of man's will to power.

The forms have changed. The problem remains the same. The proportion of human success is incommensurate with the minor successes of the Egyptians and the Chaldeans, but the meaning of the primary judgment is the same. The difficulty man is getting himself into is the same. There is no need for the response to go through demythologizing and the death of God. It is available immediately.

That is why I both agree and disagree with Rudolf Bultmann's famous formula: "If formerly the Word of God had to snatch the word 'God' from idolatry, today it has to snatch God from anonymity and pseudonymity" (*Foi et Parole*). I agree, because it is indeed true that the modern gods are no longer known explicitly by the name of God, and there is no need to snatch God from that confusion. To the contrary, it is a question of restoring the specificity of the name of God out of undifferentiated anonymity, and of reaffirming the uniqueness of the God of Jesus Christ in the midst of the idols. I disagree, however, because this can be implemented only by a clear and open fight against idolatry.

The latter has not disappeared; far from it. If there is no need to withdraw the word "God" from idolatrous confusion, there is a need to give it meaning, by denunciation, challenge, and accusation against the veiled, hidden, and secret gods, who besiege and seduce all the more effectively because they do not openly declare themselves as gods.

It is clear that the task facing Christians and the church differs entirely according to whether we think of ourselves as being in a secularized, social, lay, and grown-up world which is ready to hear a demythicized, rationalized, explicated, and humanized gospel— the world and the gospel being in full and spontaneous harmony because both want to be nonreligious—or whether we think of ourselves as being in a world inhabited by hidden gods, a world haunted by myths and dreams, throbbing with irrational impulses, swaying from mystique to mystique, a world in which the Christian revelation has once again to play its role as negator and destroyer of the sacred obsessions, of the religious phantasmagoria, in order to liberate man and bring him, not to the self his demons are making him want to be, but to the self his Father wills him to be.

At the mention of a struggle of faith against the modern idols, which are the real ones, I immediately hear indignant protests: "So here we are, being put back into the mind-set of the Middle Ages. Ellul is inviting us to take part in a crusade against the infidels and, at the very least, to adopt a completely superannuated apologetic."

That would be a total misconception, not only a misconception about my thinking, which is not serious, but a misconception with respect to the realities. Crusade and apologetic are, in fact, institutions specific to the age of Christendom. There cannot be a crusade unless there is a *Christian world* facing a non-Christian world. There cannot be an apologetic unless the non-Christian is included in the problematic of the obvious posed by the Christian. No longer are we in that situation. To suppose that it is still possible to have a crusade or an apologetic is to be out of your mind.

What I am talking about here can have no more to do with crusade than did the rejection of "Caesar" during the first century of Christianity. I can't imagine the few faithful in Corinth or Rome launching a crusade against the army of the *Princeps.* We have come back to that stage. The fight of faith lies ahead of us. It is necessary, if we believe that there is truth in the revelation of God in Jesus Christ, as set forth in Scripture.

Surely that implies that the modern religions and the modern sacred are errors or lies. Of course, if we feel it necessary to reject all distinction between error and truth, that is our privilege, but then, for goodness' sake, let's stop talking about Jesus Christ, who is designated as the Truth. If need be, we could recover "Christianity" as an "ism," and make it into a nice amalgam of anything we please, but that is not what the Bible is talking to us about.

The fight of faith to which we are committed is not a fight against man. It is not a question of destroying him, of convincing him that he is wrong. It is a fight for his freedom. Reinserted into a sacred, a prisoner of his myths, he is completely alienated in his neoreligions —this brave "modern man." Every religion is both necessary and alienating. To smash these idols, to desacralize these mysteries, to assert the falseness of these religions is to undertake the one, finally indispensable liberation of the person of our times.